C000151516

ISRAEL:
LAND AND PEOPLE OF DESTINY

Israel:
Land and People
of Destiny

JOHN V. COLLYER

THE CHRISTADELPHIAN
404 SHAFTMOOR LANE
BIRMINGHAM B28 8SZ
ENGLAND
1988

First published 1988

ISBN 0 85189 118 7

Reproduced from copy supplied.
Printed and bound in Great Britain
by Billing and Sons Limited
Worcester

Colour plates
by E. Hannibal & Company Limited
Leicester

PREFACE

ISRAEL!—the name evokes so many different things. Israel the *man* introduces us to the patriarch called to be a 'Prince with God'. Israel the *land* takes us to that place at the crossroads of the continents which has been at the heart of God's purpose with mankind. Israel the *nation* leads us into the story of a chosen people, "to whom pertaineth the adoption, and the glory, and the covenants, and the giving of the law, and the service of God, and the promises, whose are the fathers, and of whom as concerning the flesh Christ came" (Romans 9:4,5).

In this book John Collyer encompasses in a single narrative —inevitably with great brevity in parts—glimpses of the Israel of Bible days, Israel the newly founded State we see at present, and the Israel of the future. "The hope of Israel" has always been the cherished belief of Christadelphians: over a century ago they watched with excitement the movements which led to Zionism, to the 'Aliyah' of the past 100 years, and to the establishment of the State in 1948—a sure sign that the Coming of Christ is near. The excitement created by these events is tempered for the moment with the sadness that the returned exiles still for the most part lack faith in God and a true understanding of Messiah. Bible believers long for the day when that will change: like Paul, their "heart's desire and prayer to God for Israel is, that they might be saved" (Romans 10:1).

There is much to learn about this fascinating people and their "delightsome land". This book will answer countless questions about the Jews, their history and traditions; about the Israel of the Bible and the Israel of today. But in the end, the book is not intended to be just an encyclopaedia of facts; rather is it a source-book of material aimed to help the Bible reader understand more fully, and more sympathetically, the place of Israel in the purpose of God.

JOHN MORRIS

v

ACKNOWLEDGEMENTS

THIS work was designed to fill a gap previously occupied by Cyril Cooper's *Modern Israel*, to which warm acknowledgement is made. In preparing this new compilation, the help of a large number of friends is most gratefully acknowledged: in particular the expertise of Josef and Ruth Cofel, of Leen and Kathleen Ritmeyer and others with special knowledge of the Land. Considerable assistance has been given in the preparation of illustrations: most of the maps, charts and line drawings are the work of Paul Wasson. The colour photographs have been kindly loaned by those who have visited Israel. The Britain-Israel Public Affairs Committee has been particularly helpful in giving access to its photo archive. The assistance of all is very much appreciated.

Most quotations from the Bible are from the Revised Standard Version, copyrighted 1946, 1952, ©1971, 1973 by the Division of Christian Education, National Council of Churches of Christ in the U.S.A. and used by permission.

Permission to reproduce material from the specific sources listed below is gratefully acknowledged. If proper acknowledgements have not been made or any copyrights overlooked, the author and publisher offer apologies.

Black and White Illustrations:

B.I.P.A.C.—pages 49, 51, 72, 73, 75, 100, 105, 109, 116, 118, 119, 125, 126 (lower), 133, 140, 147, 148, 152, 163, 168, 176, 190, 191, 192, 205, 212, 221.

Deutsche Bundesarchiv, Koblenz (Germany)—page 229 (right).

Israeli Postal Authority—pages 7, 22, 61, 104, 150 (upper), 214, 233.

Jewish National Fund (London)—page 12 (Emblems of the Tribes: adapted from illustration in *The Journeys of the Children of Israel*, by Moshe Davis and Isaac Levy).

Mark Hale—page 223.

ACKNOWLEDGEMENTS

Photo Archive, Yad Vashem, Jerusalem—page 229 (left).

The Calendar in Ancient Israel (page 67) was adapted from an Australian Christadelphian source; the cartoon on page 217 was reprinted in *The Jerusalem Post* from an unnamed Jordanian newspaper. The originals of the illustrations on pages 248, 252 and 254 are held at the Christadelphian Office, Birmingham.

Colour Photographs:

David Ashley—Plates 28, 35.

Edna Bartlett—Plates 16, 36.

B.I.P.A.C.—Plate 7.

Gladys Blake—Plate 38.

Cyril Cooper—Plates 13, 23, 33.

Mark Hale—Plates 21, 24, 25, 26, 37.

Klaus-Otto Hundt—Plates 1, 3, 4, 5, 6, 8, 9, 10, 12, 14, 15, 17, 18, 20, 22, 29, 30, 31, 32, 34, 40.

Philip Tanner—Plates 2, 19, 27.

Sarah Tanner—Plate 39.

David Wagner—Plate 11.

Cover Illustrations:

David Ashley—Menorah Sculpture in Jerusalem.

Edna Bartlett—Synagogue Ruins at Capernaum.

B.I.P.A.C.—Immigrants Working in the Fields; Yemenite Scribe at Work on a Scroll

Klaus-Otto Hundt—Grapes on a Negev Farm; David's Tower, Jerusalem.

Useful Addresses

Israel Tourist Office, 18 Great Marlborough St., London.

BIPAC (Britain-Israel Public Affairs Committee), B.M. Box 391, London WC1B 6XX.

AIPAC (American-Israel Public Affairs Committee), Suite 300, 500 North Capitol Street N.W., Washington, DC 20001, U.S.A.

CONTENTS

LIST OF COLOUR PLATES

INTRODUCTION

THE story of Israel is at the centre of God's purpose with the world. It is for this reason that Israel is worthy of study in depth, as this work will seek to do. A right and full understanding of the relationship between the Creator and His creation can only be reached by digesting the revelation of Himself that God gave to His people and the world as recorded in Holy Scripture. God's written Word was penned by men of one nation, Israel. There was perhaps one exception to this, and he had adopted Israel's aspirations. If, at this point, it be argued that therefore the Holy Scriptures have a Jewish bias, in reply it must be pointed out that the Jewish Bible is so condemnatory of the Jewish people, that if there is actually any bias it would appear to be a bias against the Jews.

Hebrew Scroll

It is not the purpose of this work to go into the vast evidence for the authenticity of the Holy Scriptures. The writer accepts both the Hebrew Holy Scriptures (Old Testament) and the Greek New Testament as being the totally inspired Word of God as it was given to the writers in the original tongues. The student of the Bible must be ready to consult a concordance or a literal word-for-word rendering from time to time. Hidden gems can be unearthed this way.

HCENCHMEIONϪⲉ
ⲄⲞⲚ·ⲞⲨⲦⲞⲤⲈⲤⲦⲒⲚ
ⲀⲖⲎⲐⲰⲤⲞⲠⲢⲞⲫⲎ
ⲦⲎⲤⲞⲈⲒⲤⲦⲞⲚⲔⲟⲥⲙⲟ
ⲈⲢⲬⲞⲘⲈⲚⲞⲤ·
ⲒⲤⲞⲨⲚⲄⲚⲞⲨⲤⲞⲦⲒ
ⲘⲈⲖⲖⲞⲨⲤⲒⲚⲈⲢⲬⲉ
ⲤⲐⲀⲒⲔⲀⲒⲀⲢⲠⲀⲌⲈⲒⲚ

Codex Sinaiticus (4th Century): a fragment containing John 6:14

1

ISRAEL

Israel, in spite of themselves, are at the centre of God's revelation of Himself and His purpose in His Word. Israel have been the writers of it, the transmitters of it, the custodians of it, and the fulfillers of many of its prophecies and unwitting witnesses to its truth. For these reasons Israel is sometimes called "the people of the book". In no other part of the world has the story of a land and its people been intertwined for so long (4,000 years), yet, paradoxically, no other people have been separated for so long from their homeland, and yet have been able to return to it. The reason for this will be worth looking into. There are so many extraordinary features about both the land and the people that a study of both will prove to be a unique experience.

The Geographical Background

In whichever century we look at a map of the land of Israel, it can be divided conveniently into seven distinct geographical

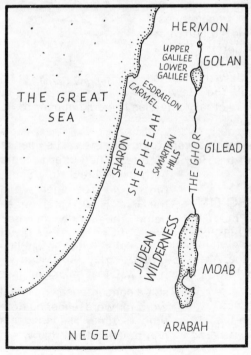

The
Geographical
Divisions
of the Land

areas that lie between the Mediterranean Sea and the Jordan valley (see map opposite):

1. Sharon (Hebrew for 'plain'). The low sandy coastal plain.
2. Shephelah (Hebrew for 'lowland'). An area of limestone hills less than 1,000 feet above sea level, inland from the Sharon.
3. The Judean and Samaritan Highlands. The 'backbone' of the land, which turns north-westwards to terminate at Carmel.
4. The Jordan Valley ('the descender'). A great trench, all below sea level, in which the river drops 580 feet in 65 miles. Also known as the Ghor.
5. Esdraelon, or plain of Jezreel. This cuts across the northern end of the Samaritan Highlands and is drained by the river Kishon ('winding') which runs into the sea at Haifa.
6. Galilee (meaning 'circle'). A country of hills that were well wooded at one time, and merging into the mountains of Lebanon.
7. The Negev (meaning 'south'). A huge area in the south, consisting of hilly dry land, but not desert.

The area east of Jordan was originally occupied by Israel, but is not as this is being written. It consists of three tablelands that are divided by the gorges of the rivers Yarmuk and Jabbok, which drain into the Jordan. Northernmost is the Hauran ('district of caves'); south of this is Gilead ('rocky'); south of this and east of the Dead Sea is Moab. At present this area is mainly occupied by the Kingdom of Jordan.

The Two Seas

Within the land are two unique bodies of water. Kinnereth ('the harp'), named for its harplike shape, more usually known as the Sea of Galilee, 700 feet below sea level, mainly fresh water; and the Dead Sea, known in Scripture as the Salt Sea (Genesis 14:3), the Sea of the Arabah (Deuteronomy 4:49) and the Eastern Sea (Ezekiel 47:18), which is 1280 feet below sea level and shrinking.

The Kinnereth is supplied mainly by the headwaters of the Jordan, flowing from the snow melt-waters of Mt. Hermon. It also has small hot water and salt water springs that flow into it. For centuries it has been a source of fresh-water fish and an attraction to holiday makers. Its overflow forms the lower portion of the river Jordan, which after a very tortuous journey down the valley of the Ghor reaches the Dead Sea.

The Dead Sea is not known by that name in Scripture. Its saltiness is mainly imparted by the solution of mineral salts from its surrounding rocks and includes sodium chloride, magnesium, bromine, potassium, calcium and sulphur. No fish is known to swim in its waters. However, the salty water has a good reputation for aiding the healing of various human ailments. During recent years an extensive industry has developed extracting some of the minerals for commercial use.

Contrasts in a Small Land

'From Dan to Beersheba' is about 140 miles, and from the sea coast to the Jordan about 50 miles. Yet in this limited area, within a distance of 15 miles, the elevation may vary from 3,300 feet high to 1,300 feet below sea level, from barren hills to lush tropical vegetation within 10 miles, and from snowy mountain tops to semi-tropical growth within sight of one another. Within the land is a wide range of natural resources, some of which have yet to be tapped.

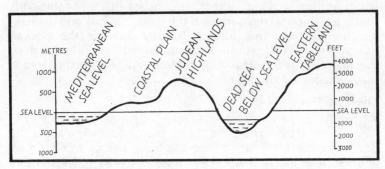

A Cross-section through the Land, from West to East

The land was described beautifully by Israel's God when they first entered the land:

"For the LORD your God is bringing you into a good land,
a land of brooks of water, of fountains and springs, flowing

4

forth in valleys and hills, a land of wheat and barley, of vines and fig trees and pomegranates, a land of olive trees and honey, a land in which you will eat bread without scarcity, in which you will lack nothing, a land whose stones are iron, and out of whose hills you can dig copper.''

(Deuteronomy 8:7-9)

Natural Resources

The natural resources at the time when Israel first took possession of the land under Joshua were doubtless greater than they are now. Centuries of devastation by enemies, neglect of forests and terraces, and God's curse on the land (Isaiah 24:6) have made much of that divine description to Moses no longer true. Besides the attractions offered in God's prospectus of the land, Israel was able to grow flax for making linen; sheep, goats and cattle were raised; pottery was made on a large scale, and asphalt was extracted from the Dead Sea. The Philistines had access to iron ore, but the location is not known for sure — probably Galilee.

By Ezekiel's time, Israel had become an international supplier of such items as wheat, honey, oil and balm (or rosin) (Ezekiel 27:17). The strange names that Ezekiel mentions, Minnith and Pannag, were place names on the wheat export routes. It is particularly obvious that Israel was the only exporter of oil mentioned in that list of the world's international trade. This, of course, was olive oil. While small amounts of this would be used for food or cosmetics, the bulk of the olive oil used at that time was for lighting. Thus Israel in those days literally lit the world, but lamentably failed to *enlighten* the world as God had wished them to. It is also probable that Israel supplied many of the little oil lamps that burned the oil. It is known that vast quantities were made by Israel's potters.

Wool from the sheep and flax from the fields were used to weave the cloth for clothing. It would be a mistake to think of the people of those days going about in skins and rags. When the men of Gibeon sent a deputation to Joshua (Joshua 9:4) they deliberately put on old clothes, which suggests that they did not normally dress like that. The divinely designed patterns for the priests' garments, even while Israel was in the wilderness, must surely mean that the materials for weaving and dyeing were available. Tents were made of coarse goat's hair, a trade that has continued for many centuries.

Trade Routes

The situation of the land is such that for centuries it was between the two great world power centres on the Nile and on the Euphrates. The land was therefore on the great trade routes running north-south. The first obvious route was along the coastal plain, a way known later as the 'Via Maris', or way of the sea. This road went inland to cross the Carmel ridge at Megiddo, thence either by Hazor or Bethshan to Damascus and the north. A hilly route that was used more for internal traffic was the high road from Beersheba through Hebron, Bethlehem, Jerusalem to Shechem and Bethshan. East of Jordan were two

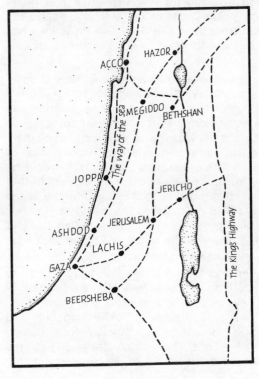

*Principal
Ancient
Highways*

north-south routes. The 'King's Highway', still used to this day, and a parallel route further east now used by a railway.

There was less traffic east-west. The main routes were for the export of grain and oil. One was from Petra in Edom to Gaza on the coast. Another was from Amman down the Jabbok, across Jordan to Shechem and the coast. The grain harvests of the Hauran went via Bethshan and Esdraelon for shipment. There were no good ports on the coast of the land. Large vessels stood offshore and trans-shipped their goods by small boats. This was done at such places as Gaza, Joppa, Dor, Akko and Ashkelon. In New Testament times the Romans sought to remedy this lack of a port by building an artificial harbour at great expense and with very sophisticated construction at Caesarea. The skill used in its design has amazed the archaeologists who have been exploring it in recent times with modern equipment.

A Good Land

Abram was not sent by God into a desert land. There was ample grazing for his vast flocks of sheep and goats. Even when he and Lot decided to separate, they were both still in the land. When the new nation of Israel entered the land again after 400 years, it was ample grazing that was the prime requirement. Trans-jordan offered an extensive area for the flocks of Manasseh, but doubtless flocks and herds crossed the Jordan into the hill country also.

Once in the land, the opportunity to cultivate a wide range of foods was open to them. Wheat and barley, vines, olives, figs and dates all grew profusely in their new homeland.

Postage Stamp illustrating Israeli produce: "Then your barns will be filled with plenty"

Of the other resources, perhaps the one required first of all was a good supply of building stone. Marble was there for special purposes. The hills were wooded by a wide range of trees. Water flowed from streams and springs, conserved by the trees on the hills. Exotic foods and products came to the land via the caravan routes that criss-crossed it.

Few, if any, other lands have such a variety of climate within so small an area. There can be heavy snow in Jerusalem while Engedi on the Dead Sea is sweltering. The Judean highlands can have very heavy rainfall, while 50 miles south the Negev usually has little. In normal years the 'former rains' fall from October to January. These loosen the soil for ploughing and cultivating. When the seed has been sown, the 'latter rains' from February to May nourish the seedlings. A vast tree-planting scheme has created forests of over 100 million trees, and the current programme envisages further planting of some 3 million trees each year. A number of Christadelphian ecclesias have taken part in this scheme. The forest tends to retain rainfall and release it slowly, thus avoiding flash floods.

Transport

For centuries, the usual mode of transport of goods across the hills of Israel and the Negev was on the backs of sure-footed asses, and, to a less extent, camels. Oxcarts were in use from early times. Jacob was carried to Egypt this way, and so were the heavy items of the Tabernacle in the wilderness. The Philistine action of sending the Ark back to Israel on a cart suggests that this was a normal method of transport on the coastal plain. Chariots came into use later, at first only in warfare, then by notable people as a means of regular transport.

The extensive passage of caravans through Israel gave rise to a supply industry providing food and shelter for the travellers. The men of the caravans also carried news from one country to another, so that information of great events soon got spread around. At first the caravan trade was a monopoly of the Ishmaelites and the Midianites, then it came into the control of the Ammonites, and much later the Nabataeans, from bases in Edom and the Negev. To some extent Israel benefited from the passage of the caravans by levying tolls.

In prosperous times Israel must have been an entrepôt of some importance. Solomon engaged in buying and selling spices and other goods brought in by caravan. But it is doubtful whether Israel ever really rivalled Phoenicia in international trade. It is noticeable that Israel in old time did not engage in trade by sea, with one notable exception, ending in disaster.

What's in a Name?

It is easy to overlook the fact that both the land and the people have been known by various names. The land was at first named Canaan, after its early settler, the grandson of Noah. Many place names still recall the names of Canaan's sons (Genesis 10:15-18).

The well known port of Sidon was named from his firstborn, the Arkites are remembered in the modern town of Tell'Arqa, the Sinites in the names of Nahr-as Suin and Sinn ad-darb, all in Lebanon. Sumra, north of Tripoli, may be the site of the Zemarites, while Hamath in the Orontes valley still bears its ancient name (meaning 'defenced'). Thus the very place names in use today bear witness to the accuracy of the Bible record in Genesis.

The name Canaan (Hebrew 'Kena'an') applied to both people and land. Early historians such as Sanchuniathon and Philo of Byblos used it, and it is used on some early Phoenician coins. A secondary meaning was in use by Mesopotamian people who used the name for purple cloth that was made by the coast people. In the famous Amarna letters, Egypt's territories in the general area were called Canaan.

The Promised Land

It only became the Promised Land as a result of the covenant that God made with Abraham (Hebrews 11:9). In Egypt, the people of Israel were reminded about the Land of Promise while they were in slavery. Moses instructed the elders concerning the Passover: ''When you come to the land which the LORD will give you, as he has promised, you shall keep this service'' (Exodus 12:25).

Just before Abram's time, the coastal plain had been invaded by the 'sea people', who had been repulsed from Egypt. These were the Philistines, whose ancestry is traced in Genesis 10:14. Both Abram and Isaac had friendly relations with them, and made a covenant with them. From them the land came to be known later as Palestine. The ancient historian Herodotus used the name of Palestine for the whole area of southern Syria. After the return of the Babylonian exiles, the land was called Judea, as it was in the time of Jesus. However, after

A.D. 70 the Romans tried to rid themselves of all memories of Judea, and re-named the land Palestina. From that time until 1948, the name of Palestine continued to be used on maps and official documents. This name still lingers on in the name used by the Palestine Liberation Organisation. Even this name is confirmation of the record of names in Genesis!

The term 'Land of Israel' was first used to contrast the hill country occupied by Israel with the coastal plain occupied by the Philistines (1 Samuel 13:19). But after the division of the united kingdom in Rehoboam's time, the southern kingdom was known as Judah and the northern as Israel.

ISRAEL TIME-TABLE

B.C.	
ca. 1900	Abraham received God's Covenant
ca. 1470	Israel's Exodus from Egypt
ca. 1430	Israel entered Promised Land
ca. 920	David king of Israel
ca. 720	Assyrian captivity of ten tribes
606	Babylonian first invasion
586	Babylonians took Jerusalem
536	Return of Judeans under Ezra
63	Roman conquest of Judea
37	Herod appointed king of Judea
A.D.	
30	Jewish Messiah crucified
70	Romans destroyed Jerusalem
135	Jerusalem ploughed as a field
637	Moslems captured Jerusalem
1099-1250	The eight crusades
1580	Spanish inquisition of Jews
1793	French revolution
1799	Napoleon invaded Palestine
1897	First Zionist Congress
1917	Palestine freed from Turks
1948	State of Israel proclaimed
1967	Jerusalem unified under Israel

The crusaders (A.D. 1099) called it the 'Holy Land', and religious writers have used this name ever since. It is appropriate, for 'holy' means 'separate', and this land was separated from all other lands by God in order to put His name there, and given to Abraham's descendants, the 'separate' people. It was on May 14, 1948 that David ben Gurion announced that the name of the newly formed state he was founding would be 'Israel', and its people would be 'Israelis'. For centuries these people have been known as 'Jews'. At first this was only used for the inhabitants of Judah (2 Kings 16:6), but it soon came to be applied to all Jacob's descendants, and is so used today by both Jew and non-Jew. There is a distinction between Jew and Israeli. Most Israelis are Jews, but only some Jews are to be known as Israelis, that is, when they become citizens of the state. Israelis born in the land are called 'sabras' (the name of a fruit that is hard outside and soft inside!); those who have returned to the land are the 'yishuv', and Jews who are still dispersed in the nations are the 'diaspora'.

Personal Names

It is not proposed to look at all the meanings of the many personal names recorded in the Bible. A concordance or specialist book will provide this fascinating study. But to whet the reader's appetite here is a brief look at the meaning of some of the names of early characters in the history of Israel.

We begin with Abram ('the father is exalted'), similar to the Semitic names Abiram and Abarama which have been found on cuneiform inscriptions of the time. This name was changed by God to a more significant one — Abraham ('father of a multitude') (Genesis 17:5), which was a prophetic name, since at that time Abram had no child. At the same time God changed the name of Sarai ('Yah is prince'), which suggests that her parents were worshippers of the Most High God, to Sarah ('Princess') and the promise that she should become the mother of nations. Their son, born of a divine miracle, was named appropriately Isaac ('laughter') because of the joy that was realised by his parents at his birth. Isaac married Rebekah whose name is variously said to mean 'tied fast' or 'flattering', depending on which root word it was taken from. Her twin sons were named Esau ('hairy'), obviously a description of the

11

child, and Jacob ('supplanter'), probably in the first place from the manner in which he was born, but which was to prove prophetic of his dealing with his twin brother. Jacob's name was changed by God, after his character had been well tested, to Israel ('prince with God', or 'ruling with God'), another prophetic name, for this was God's intention for Israel's family and nation. It is a sad fact that the nation bearing that divinely bestowed name should have preferred to go their own way. But that name was not given in vain, for ultimately the nation will acknowledge that God rules in the kingdom of men, and then they will live up to their name.

Reuben	Simeon	Dan	Judah
Naphtali	Gad	Issachar	Asher
Zebulun	Benjamin	Ephraim	Manasseh

The Emblems of Israel's Tribes

Of Jacob's twelve sons, his third son bears a name that is another example of great significance, Judah ('praise'), and from this name is derived the common appellation of the whole nation, Jew. How paradoxical it is that this name with such a meaning should have been the most accursed name in the history of mankind! Yet it is the divine intention that the Jews

12

will live to praise God, and will themselves be a praise in the earth. In the meantime a modern cult of 'Humanistic Judaism', a purely secular society, seeks to eliminate God from Jewish thought and offer all praise to the accomplishments of man.

May these few examples of Hebrew names with a significance that is both intriguing and enlightening lead the reader into a deeper study of this subject, and a fuller realisation that the God of Israel has had, and still has a concern for the affairs of the nation whom He chose as the vehicle of His written revelation, the Holy Scriptures.

ISRAEL

THE MAN
THE PEOPLE
THE LAND

Israel was a divinely bestowed name upon the man Ya'acov (Jacob), whose descendants became known as the People of Israel, and whose territory, also divinely bestowed, became known as the Land of Israel.

13

1

ISRAEL OF THE BIBLE

THE time of Abram seems very remote today. It was only a few centuries after the great Flood. The confusion of tongues that had scattered the unholy concentration of people at Babel had resulted in widespread activity in many parts of the world. But cities were arising again, some well designed such as Ur of the Chaldees, where Abram's family lived in comfort. The type of house to which he was probably accustomed has been excavated. It was most likely of two stories arranged around an inner courtyard with a substantial gate into the street. Towering over the city was the massive ziggurat, an artificial hill with a temple on top.

The
Ziggurat
of Ur

The World in Abram's Time

Archaeologists have evidence that there was extensive movement around the world in ships at this time. The city of Ur is known to have traded by sea with the cities of the Indus valley in India. Villages in Scandinavia are known to have traded by sea as far as the Great Sea (Mediterranean). The people of the Nile valley traded up the river as well as across the Great Sea. Caravans crossed the deserts with goods, and raiding bands of soldiers went hundreds of miles to wreak havoc on far-off settlements.

The people of Abram's time were not primitive, nor without skill, nor were they illiterate. Archaeological discoveries such as the great stele of Hammurabi (copy in British Museum) containing the codified laws of that great king, prove that life was organised to a surprising degree. Highly skilled craftsmen made finely wrought jewellery, as has been found in the ruins of Ur, and elsewhere. Great libraries of cuneiform writing on clay tablets have been found, which reveal something of the extent of knowledge at that time. The great monuments of Egypt were being erected, proving that the sophisticated principles of physics and engineering were not unknown.

The process of empire building was beginning in both the valleys of the Euphrates and the Nile, as also among the Hittites and the Minoans and others. The land of Canaan had been settled by the sons of the grandson of Noah, Canaan (Genesis 10:15-20). Their population was widely scattered in little walled 'cities', each one an independent city-state with its own king. Between these settlements there was still plenty of room in the wild countryside.

The Unique Man

The Most High God chose Abram, a man of unique character, to go to this heathen land and become the founding father of a unique people. He not only believed in the one God, whereas his neighbours believed in numerous idols, but he believed God's instructions and obeyed them. His life, as well as the road to his life's goal, was never to be a "bed of roses", but was to be full of mental suffering, trial and tribulation. From the time when he was directed to leave the comforts of Ur and go to a land

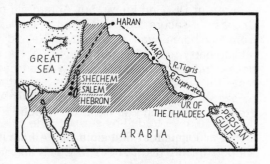

*Abraham's Journey from Ur:
the shaded area suggests the extent of the land promised—"From the river of Egypt to the great river Euphrates"*

15

that God would show him, to the time when his faith was tested to the utmost by the command to offer his only son to God in sacrifice—Abraham's faith was tested many times: the following table lists twelve occasions. It is likely that he was tested in many ways that are not recorded.

ABRAHAM'S TWELVE TESTS OF CHARACTER

1. Leaving Haran for unknown land (Genesis 12:4)
2. Denying Sarah was his wife (Genesis 12:13)
3. His generosity to Lot (Genesis 13:9)
4. His rescue of Lot from slavery (Genesis 14:14)
5. Unselfishness in dividing the spoil (Genesis 14:23)
6. Believed promise of a seed (Genesis 15:6)
7. Attempt to solve problem his way (Genesis 16:4)
8. Concern and responsibility for Ishmael (Genesis 17:18)
9. Compassion for any righteous in Sodom (Genesis 18:23)
10. Again denying Sarah was his wife (Genesis 20:2)
11. Sacrifice of Isaac (Genesis 22:2)
12. Concern for suitable wife for Isaac (Genesis 24:3)

Abram's first test was to be cut off from his past, from the security of Ur. God knew, but Abram did not, that the city of Ur was not secure, but was about to be destroyed. His exodus from his home was providential. He did not go out with a raiding party to conquer and to pillage. He went in peace, with flocks and herdsmen, with his wife and aged father. His last test, if it was his last, was to cut himself off from the future, by sacrificing his only son and heir. Thus Abram was made to stand alone, putting all his trust in God.

It would appear at first sight that Abram had no human moral support for his faithfulness to God's instructions. Perhaps we should not discount Sarah as a woman of faith, in spite of occasional failings. Nor should we eliminate Isaac. As a strong young man he could so easily have resisted his father's cords and the threat of death on the altar, but he must have known and understood the divine instructions and agreed to submit, even though he may not have understood their full significance.

Abram was very much alone in the world, even as his descendants would be a lonely people, separated to God. Yet, although he and his family were distinct from the people around them, they were to be a blessing to all people. Abram was doubtless tempted to be assimilated to those around him when the king of Sodom offered him a share of the booty, but he resisted the offer and testified to faith in the Lord God Most High (Genesis 14:22). Later, Israel would also be tempted to seek assimilation, but this would be as a way of escape from the fruits of their unfaithfulness.

After Abram's faith had been thoroughly tested, God changed his name to Abraham (Genesis 17:5). Abram meant 'father of height' or 'the father is exalted', while Abraham had the significant meaning 'father of multitudes'.

The faith of Abraham in God's promises, although it seemed unlikely that they could be fulfilled, earned for him the name of 'father of the faithful'. This is based on the reasoning of Paul in Romans:

"He received circumcision as a sign or seal of the righteousness which he had by faith while he was still uncircumcised. The purpose was to make him the father of all who believe without being circumcised and who thus have righteousness reckoned to them, and likewise the father of the circumcised who are not merely circumcised but also follow the example of the faith which our father Abraham had before he was circumcised"

(Romans 4:11,12)

The Land of Canaan

Abram came into the Land of Promise as a stranger, not as a conqueror. For the most part he avoided contact with the locals. There was one little city that he did visit. Only once is it on record that he visited Salem, but since Abram had a faith in God in common with the king-priest of that city, it would seem to be likely that he may have been a regular visitor. This king, named Melchi-zedek ('king of righteousness'), was acknowledged by Abram to be his superior, for he paid tithes

17

to him. Many students have wondered whether this king was indeed Shem, from whom Abram was descended, and who was still alive at this time, and who would be the oldest member of the family of Semites. But if this was so, to reveal such a relationship would spoil the profound symbolism that was to be used in later centuries by David (Psalm 110:4) and Paul (Hebrews 6:20). So we are not told of his identity, except that he was both king and priest and that he reigned in the city that was to be the centre of the worship of the Most High God in years to come, and that he officiated in the place where God said that He would put His name. Thus the land of Canaan was not entirely heathen in those days, nor without a representative of the one true God. The inhabitants of the land had a lightstand by which to see, if they cared to use it. Thus, their eventual condemnation to utter destruction was not unjustified.

The Covenant Land

The reader of the Bible is soon introduced to the land that God covenanted to Abram. "The LORD said to Abram 'Go . . . to the land that I will show you' " (Genesis 12:1). Eventually he did come into the land and arriving at Shechem, the LORD confirmed to him, "To your descendants I will give this land" (Genesis 12:7). First came the promise of the land, afterwards the promise of a people. Indeed, the land was promised to his descendants before it was promised to him.

After Abram and Lot had parted, Abram stayed in the hill country with his flocks. Again the Lord spoke to him, saying, "Lift up your eyes . . . for I will give it to you" (Genesis 13:14,17). Then, when Abram showed concern about who should inherit the land that the Lord had promised to him, the Lord said, "I am the LORD who brought you from Ur of the Chaldees, to give you this land to possess" (Genesis 15:7). "On that day the LORD made a covenant with Abram, saying, 'To your descendants I give this land, from the river of Egypt to the great river, the river Euphrates' " (Genesis 15:18). This promise was again confirmed when Abram was 99 years old, and his name had been changed to Abraham (Genesis 17:5). The Lord said, "I will give to you, and to your descendants after you, the land of your sojournings, all the land of Canaan, for an everlasting possession; and I will be their God" (Genesis 17:8).

18

CHART OF ABRAHAMIC COVENANT

	Abram/ Abraham	Isaac	Jacob/ Israel
1. The LAND promise: "All the land of Canaan"	Gen. 12: 1 13:17 17: 8	26: 3 26:24	28:13 35:12
2. The PERSONAL promise: "I will give it to you"	Gen. 12: 2 13:17 17: 8	26: 3	28:15 31: 3
3. The "SEED" promise: "to your descendant" (Galatians 3:16)	Gen. 12: 7	26: 4	28:14
4. The FAMILY promise: "a great nation"; "as the sand of the sea shore"	Gen. 12: 2 13:16 17: 6 22:17	26: 4 27:29	28:14 35:12 46: 3
5. The EXTENDED FAMILY promise: "as the stars of heaven"	Gen. 15: 5 22:17	26:3,4	
6. The INTERNATIONAL promise: "all families of the earth blessed"	Gen. 12: 3 18:18 22:18	26: 4	28:14
7. The EVERLASTING promise: "an everlasting covenant"	Gen. 13:15 17: 7		48: 4

None of these seven aspects of God's solemn covenant with Abraham was fulfilled in his day. His faith was such that nevertheless he implicitly believed that they would all be fulfilled. It is true that his descendants have occupied the land from time to time, but never has it been securely theirs. He did not live to see a great nation, nor to see all families of the earth being blessed. While Abraham lived a long life, he did not live for ever.

Abraham's faith foresaw the complete fulfilment of all aspects of the divine covenant, a confidence that was shared by Isaac and Jacob. This was later to become known as the 'Hope of Israel', the same hope that is the basis of the Christian faith, when it is rightly understood (Acts 28:20; Galatians 3:26-29).

The Land of Promise

Yet, when Abraham required a burial place for his wife Sarah, he did not possess even enough of that land for that sad purpose, but had to buy a field for 400 shekels of silver (Genesis 23:15,16). The writer of the letter to the Hebrews, nearly 2,000 years later, commented on this strange situation: "By faith (Abraham) sojourned in the land of promise, as in a foreign land . . . For he looked forward to the city which has foundations, whose builder and maker is God" (Hebrews 11:9-10). The 'city' for which Abraham looked was not one in the sky, although it would be a heavenly city, but a divinely provided political occupation of the very same land that the Lord had promised him and had covenanted to him and to his descendants.

Abraham is the prime example of a man of supreme faith. He fully believed the solemn promises that God had made to him of a land and a people, when the land was occupied by others, when he did not have a child, and his wife was barren. It is not given to many men to have a faith such as that. But his faith went even further, for he realised that neither he nor his descendants would have that land during his lifetime. His faith therefore was extended to believe that God could and would raise him from the dead, even as his son Isaac had been given back to him, as from the dead. These divine covenants with Abraham are the basis of the 'Hope of Israel' which is the theme that gradually unfolds in the Bible, which takes on deeper meaning with the advent of Jesus Christ, and which is about to reach its tremendous climax with the second advent of Messiah, the promised specific descendant of Abraham through whom the whole of the covenant will be completed.

The Unique Land

It is not surprising that the history of this land and its people are so carefully chronicled in the Bible as the centuries rolled by. This land had, and still has, a very special place in the purpose of the Creator, the Lord God of Abraham. Seven times in the messages that came through God's prophets, He calls it "My land" (Deuteronomy 11:12; Psalm 85:1; Isaiah 14:25; Jeremiah 2:7; Ezekiel 38:16; Hosea 9:3; Joel 2:18). The prophet Ezekiel calls it "the most glorious of all lands" (Ezekiel

20:6). The prophet Zechariah uses the term "holy land". Even more specifically the terms "holy city" and "holy mountain" are used of the capital city Jerusalem, where the centre for worship of the Almighty has been, and will be sited.

If this land is described in such glowing terms by the Lord who gave it to Abraham, what is so unique about it? Is it its location, its geography, its associations or its prospects? Its location at the meeting point of the earth's land masses is significant, being central to three continents. Its situation at the junction of Asia and Africa has been the cause of fierce disputes for centuries. It may be the most fought-over patch of land on earth for this reason. But for the same reason it could be the ideal site for radiating peace to the world around.

The location of the land is unique in other ways. The vegetation of three continents meets in Israel, it being the eastern limit of many Mediterranean plants, the southern limit of European plants, and the northernmost extreme for several African species. Although it is a small land, much of it inhospitable for wild life, yet it is the home of nearly as many varieties of birds as Britain, and a much greater variety of wild animals. The Siberian wolf, the Asian leopard and the African coney may all be found in this little land.

Its geography is unique. Within a few miles of one another are the deepest natural hollow on earth and high mountains of perpetual snow. A lush tropical valley and desert wastes rub shoulders. On the Mediterranean coast is a typical mild climate, while the hills 40 miles away may be bleak and bare. Within this small area are being found mineral resources that Abraham had no knowledge of, and which are only just beginning to be put to use in these last days.

The Holy Land

The Holy Land is in a general area that is named Eden in the Bible, more usually termed the Middle East today. It has been suggested by some students that perhaps the Garden in Eden (Genesis 2:8) was in this same land that was promised to Abraham. It seems to be significant that Abraham's sacrifice of his son Isaac (which he was prevented from completing), the altar of sacrifice for Solomon's Temple and the place of the sacrifice of Jesus were all on Moriah, one of the hills on which

Jerusalem is built. Hence it has been suggested that may be the very first sacrifice, when Adam and Eve witnessed a lamb being sacrificed to provide them with a covering for sin, was on the same site (Genesis 3:21). It would seem to be appropriate if this was so, and would make this location the very centre of the Lord's dealings with man from the beginning to the end. Prophecies of the future Temple to be built for world worship, as described by Ezekiel, locate it on the same site, albeit a revitalised mountain (see Isaiah 2:2-4; Ezekiel 40-48; Zechariah 14:16).

The Unique City

Not only is the Land uniquely special to the God of Israel, but so is the city of Jerusalem. Ezekiel wrote: ''Thus says the Lord GOD: This is Jerusalem; I have set her in the centre of the nations, with countries round about her'' (Ezekiel 5:5). Yet strangely, in the wilderness, as Israel approached the promised land, they were only told of ''a place which the LORD would choose to put his name there''. It was not named, nor did Moses set eyes upon it. At that time it was a heathen city, and at that time Israel were not ready for such a focal point for worship.

*Postage Stamp:
''Joshua''*

Joshua and his God-guided victorious forces overcame Adoni-zedek the king of Jerusalem and his confederates (Joshua 10). But the city remained in the hands of the Jebusites. Years later the little hill-top citadel was attacked by the tribe of Judah (Judges 1:8) but as a result the Benjaminites seemed to co-exist with the Jebusites (Judges 1:21). The city was not taken by Israel until David had been king in Hebron for seven years (2 Samuel 5:6-9). It would seem that the city of God's choice was not to be occupied by His people until they had a king of the divinely appointed line of Judah.

David was a member of the first generation in the line of Judah that was qualified to take this office. Thus God's chosen city and His chosen king were now united for the furtherance

1. Grapefruit: "The land will yield its fruit, and you will eat your fill, and dwell in it securely" (Leviticus 25:19)

2. Clusters of Dates: "You are stately as a palm tree"
(Song of Solomon 7:7)

3. Spring Flowers in the Negev: ''As for man, his days are like grass; he flourishes like a flower of the field'' (Psalm 103:15)

4. Watering the Sheep at a Desert Well: ''With joy you will draw water from the wells of salvation'' (Isaiah 12:3)

5. Bedouin Harvest Time: ''A good land . . . a land of wheat and barley . . . you will eat bread without scarcity'' (Deuteronomy 8:8,9)

of His purpose with the people. That Jerusalem had been the place chosen by God from the beginning is made clear in Psalm 132:13: "For the LORD has chosen Zion; he has desired it for his habitation: this is my resting place for ever; here I will dwell, for I have desired it . . .", and in Psalm 68:16: "Why look you with envy, O many-peaked mountain, at the mount which God desired for his abode, yea, where the LORD will dwell for ever?"

From the time of king David, Jerusalem has been the national and spiritual centre for the Jewish people. Even when no Jew was allowed to live in the city, it still remained the focus of their thoughts and their hopes. The national concern for the city was expressed in the sad words of Psalm 137:5,6: "If I forget you, O Jerusalem, let my right hand wither! Let my tongue cleave to the roof of my mouth, if I do not remember you, if I do not set Jerusalem above my highest joy!" For centuries the words of this Psalm have been recited before each meal by exiled Jews. That the aspirations of God's people will eventually be realised is assured by many divine prophecies such as, "At that time Jerusalem shall be called the throne of the LORD" (Jeremiah 3:17). For a preview of the future of this unique land and city see Chapter 12.

Milk and Honey

The people of Israel were encouraged to take possession of "a land flowing with milk and honey" (Exodus 3:8). What sort of a land does this picture offer? Not a highly cultivated land like the valley of the Nile, nor a wilderness like the land they had come across; but

Olive Press

23

a land with ample wild food for their flocks of sheep and goats that supplied milk, and with a richness of wild flowers for the honeybees that nested in the hollows of the rocks. It is true that Goshen, from which they had come, had been described as a land flowing with milk and honey (Numbers 16:13), but that had been soured by their slavery and oppression.

The land of Canaan, at that time, was well wooded with native oaks, pines, firs, cypress, junipers and brambles on the hills, and with palms, willows and acacias in the valleys. It is probable that olives, vines and figs were already being cultivated by the local people. It is evident that grain was being grown in Jacob's time, for the time of wheat harvest is mentioned in Genesis 30:14, and it was for lack of grain that Jacob's sons made the long journey to Egypt, and so came to meet Joseph.

As soon as Israel crossed the Jordan and entered the land, the daily supply of manna ceased and "they ate of the produce of the land, unleavened cakes and parched grain" (Joshua 5:11). As they had not had time to sow and reap this grain, it must have been obtained from local sources. It is not known whether the rainfall was greater at that time; God described it as being well-watered. The extensive tree cover on the hills would ensure that the rainfall would be released gradually in the springs and streams, and not cause flash floods as sometimes occur now on the barren hills. That much of the land was covered with forest is evident from the words of Joshua, when he was apportioning the land: "The hill country shall be yours, for though it is a forest, you shall clear it and possess it to its farthest borders" (Joshua 17:18).

The Unique People

"I will make of you a great nation" (Genesis 12:2) and "I will make your descendants as the dust of the earth" (Genesis 13:16), and then the people and the land are united in the divine promise: "To your descendants I give this land" (Genesis 15:18).

Eventually, after his faith had been tested for many years, Abraham did have the son of promise by his aged wife Sarah. Isaac was born miraculously in the couple's old age. Apart from divine intervention the child could not have been born, for

Sarah was past bearing. In course of time Isaac married and had twin sons. The inheritance of the divine promises was now complicated by the rivalry of the twins. By right Esau was the heir, because his birth was just before that of his brother. But as a young man, Esau scorned the value of his birthright, not being a man of faith, and sold his inheritance to his brother for a savoury meal. Jacob did have an understanding of the value of the birthright that he had acquired so craftily, and thus to be seen as a man of faith. As Jacob experienced increasing difficulties in his life, so his faith increased. Just as God had confirmed the promises to Abraham repeatedly, so He did to Isaac and now to Jacob. All three were left in no doubt as to the reality of God's purpose with the land and with their descendants (Genesis 26:4; 35:11).

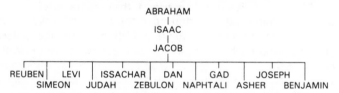

As with Abram, Jacob matured so much that God saw fit to change his name to one that had a deeper significance. The name 'Jacob' means 'following after', descriptive of his birth. It also means 'supplanter', descriptive of his cunning acquisition of the birthright. God's new name for him, 'Israel', means 'ruling with God', or 'prince with God', and this describ-ed his personal faithful life, besides being prophetic of God's purpose for him and his descendants. Modern Israelis say that it means 'fighting for God', and tend to forget the implications of 'ruling with God'.

The Hebrew Inheritance

Both Abram and Sarah were of the same family, descended from Eber (Genesis 11:16). Eber, in turn, was descended from Shem, son of Noah—hence the general appellation of Semites. Isaac was guided by God to marry into the same family group, as was Jacob in later years. While this was not close inbreeding, it was establishing a pattern of definite family characteristics, a gene pool that dominated future generations.

However, Jacob's twelve sons were by four wives, only two of whom were from the same family group. The background of the handmaids is not known. Thus a dilution of the family strain had begun. Of the wives of Jacob's sons, only two are known. Joseph's was a high ranking Egyptian woman, while Judah had a son by Tamar, who was presumably a local woman. It may be assumed that the other sons also married local women. Thus the initial Hebrew characteristics were diluted as the infant nation of Israel began to take shape. To what extent there may have been further inter-marriage with strangers in Egypt is not recorded.

The point to notice is that for three generations there were a series of divinely controlled marriage relationships that established the characteristics of the race that developed from them. The extensive inter-marriage that came later did not efface the dominant genes that gave the race its 'Jewishness'. This genetic inheritance has been identified by medical science and used to establish the claims of individuals to be of Jewish stock:

> "It is reassuring to know that modern science gives evidence of the integrity of the Jewish race down so many centuries. We need not be disconcerted, however, to learn that not all who call themselves Jews are 'of Abraham': that, too, we could have predicted from Scripture. In the end, however, though the Jews are 'beloved for the fathers' sakes', God looks not on outward appearance, nor on genetic characteristics—nor circumcision, nor Israeli citizenship—but on the heart. 'The LORD knoweth them that are his'" (*The Christadelphian*, 1985, p. 348).

Birth of a Nation

The proud sons of Jacob who freely roamed the hills of Canaan with their flocks were doubtless irked at having to make the journey to Egypt to beg for food. They were certainly humiliated by the 'Egyptian' official who fulfilled their needs. After finally migrating to Egypt under Joseph's protection, and in the divine purpose, they lost the freedom of the hills, but prospered at first in Goshen. Years passed, and with a change in the Egyptian hierarchy, they were out of favour, and in real trouble. Their great numbers were now regarded as a menace

26

by the Egyptians, who had only recently thrown off the Hyksos interlopers. Lest the Hebrews should seek to take over control, the wily Egyptians subjected them to slavery and the first recorded attempt at genocide.

Rameses II in his War Chariot, 1285 B.C. An inscription of his boasts that— "Israel is annihilated, Israel will have no posterity"

This turn in the lives of the people of Israel left them but little time to reflect on their ancestry or their inheritance. They became a dispirited people. Yet there were some who had retained a knowledge of the God of Abraham and of the promises to their fathers. The identity of Israel as a people had been blurred, but not lost. This is evident from the meeting of Moses and Aaron with the elders of Israel (Exodus 4:29-31). As Levites, the two brothers had the respect of the elders.

Eventually the plagues upon Egypt made an effective division between Israel and their taskmasters. The rabble of slaves became united in a remarkable consensus of opinion, such as the nation has not had since that day. This was tested and proved by the events of the Passover, when Israel was finally severed from Egypt by God in a terrible and dramatic way. The Exodus ('coming out') followed, in which the birth of the nation took place. Israel was born of water, and of the spirit. They were baptized in the Red Sea and in the divine cloud that hid them from their foes. It was a miraculous birth, with the power of God very evident to all who had the perception and the faith to see it. There have been many mass migrations of a people elsewhere, but never one like this one, accompanied by such signs and wonders.

Many thousands, perhaps millions, of Egyptians and their livestock perished as the destroying angel smote that nation (Exodus 12:29). Pharaoh himself and his host were drowned in the Red Sea (Psalm 136:15). It is well named the Sea of Destruction by the Arabs to this day, for it not only destroyed the Egyptian forces, but it also destroyed the bondage in which the people of Israel had been enthralled. The nation was reborn to begin a new phase in God's purpose for the descendants of faithful Abraham.

The Red Sea

Wherever the Red Sea is mentioned in the Bible it is a translation of the Hebrew *Yam Suph*. While *yam* means 'sea', *suph* does not mean 'red'. The Hebrew for red is *adam*. So why has *suph* been translated 'red'? Several English versions now render it 'Reed Sea'. Is this really what was intended? Reeds do not grow in salt water, there are no reeds in the Red Sea, nor in the salt lakes from which it has receded.

But *suph* is the word used for the 'flags' or 'reeds' in which the baby Moses was hidden on the banks of the fresh-water Nile. (*Suph* also has this meaning in Isaiah 19:6.) In these contexts the Hebrew word appears to have been derived from the Egyptian word for 'papyrus' — *twf* (pronounced 'thoof'). This is the reason why some translators conclude that *Yam Suph* must mean 'Reed Sea'.

But, as in other languages, a word may have more than one meaning. There is also a word in Hebrew derived from the Aramaic *sup*, with the meaning of 'end' or 'finality'. Thus *Yam Suph* could mean the 'sea of the end', or 'the sea of finality'. Significantly, this is very similar to the Arabic name 'Sea of Destruction'. In complete contrast the ancient Egyptian's name for it was 'the pale green sea.'

Erythra Thalassa

Maybe the clue as to how the Red Sea got its strange name could be found in the Septuagint translation of the Holy Scriptures into Greek, where *Yam Suph* is rendered *Erythra Thalassa*. This does literally mean 'Red Sea'. From this it was rendered into Latin as *Mare Rubrum*, and so into English as 'Red Sea'. But why did the translators into Greek render it as *Erythra Thalassa*?

There seems to be a reasonable explanation connected with the much sought after valuable purple-red dye that was obtained from certain marine snails in a few coastal locations. This trade was mainly in the hands of Phoenicians, but the Greeks also had one or two coastal locations where these murex snails were found, and they discovered that there was a good supply on the coast of India. Hence Greek traders daringly crossed the vast Indian Ocean (as we call it) for supplies of this red dye. The Greek for 'red' is *erythra*, hence the Indian Ocean came to be known as the 'Red Sea' or *Erythra Thalassa*. Not only the ocean, but its arms, the Persian Gulf and the Red Sea, carried the same name for the Greeks. For example, Josephus states (*Antiquities* 1.1.3) that the rivers Tigris and Euphrates flow into the *Erythra Thalassa*, meaning the Persian Gulf, a branch of the Indian Ocean.

However, the name gained a secondary meaning, because of the extreme dangers which the great endless ocean presented to sailors of those days. It became known as the ocean without end, or the ocean which was the end of the sailors who ventured across it, in other words 'Sea of Destruction'.

A Trial of Faith

For the people of Israel these events were a trial of faith. Especially was this true of Moses who led them. His preparation for this gigantic task had been ordained by God, and had taken eighty long years; first as an adopted prince of Egypt for forty years, trained in all the arts of leadership by the world's top nation; then another forty years as a shepherd in the wilderness, learning the skills of living in an inhospitable land, and of caring for a flock. What an extraordinary contrast! The man who emerged from this schooling was the man whom God had specially prepared to lead Israel out of bondage and then to teach them what it meant to be a holy nation. Moses needed to be a man of skill, a man of great faith and of unusual humility.

As for the people, while their response to the emergency of the Passover and the Exodus was a faith born of desperation, their human weaknesses soon came to the fore amid the difficulties of the wilderness of Sinai. Their faith in Moses as the divinely chosen leader wavered with the occasion; their faith in

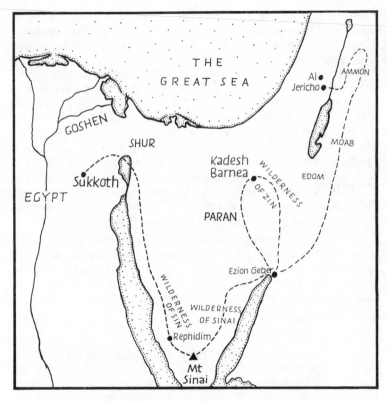

*The Exodus from Egypt through the Wilderness
to the Borders of the Land*

God was very weak, or indeed completely lacking at times, in spite of the evidence of His presence in the cloud by day and the pillar of fire by night. Israel, called to be a holy people, did not allow the divine influence and protection to transform them into a devoted nation. While individual characters responded, the nation did not. They soon forgot the misery of their slavery, and even longed to return. Miracle after miracle failed to convince them that God was with them in a very practical way. Water for their thirst, grazing for their flocks, manna for their nourishment, clothes that did not wear out, shoes that lasted a lifetime and many other benefits, were all taken for granted without thankfulness. How easy it was to do this! How typically human they were! Are we so much better?

At Sinai

Israel emerged from Egypt freed from the slavery to their taskmasters, but not free from slavery to their natural lusts and passions. They had a vague awareness that they were a people with a heritage. They were bound by close family relationships, unlike the Egyptians. But although a group of families, they were not quite a nation yet. The God of Abraham, who had brought them out of Egypt by a wondrous series of miracles, was not yet a truly living God to the people. At Sinai, this was to be remedied. Their flight from the reach of Egypt was halted at Sinai deliberately, while the God of Israel spoke to the people through the mediation of Moses. The Almighty revealed Himself as one who is "merciful and gracious, longsuffering, and abounding in steadfast love and faithfulness, keeping steadfast love for thousands, forgiving iniquity and transgression and sin." This was so unlike the characters of the pagan gods of Egypt, as interpreted by their priests, from whom there was no mercy and no forgiveness. Yet, the God of Israel "will by no means clear the guilty" (Exodus 34:6,7). As the Apostle Paul was to comment centuries later: "Behold therefore the goodness and severity of God: on them which fell, severity; but toward thee, goodness, if thou continue in his goodness" (Romans 11:22).

To Moses on Mount Sinai, God unfolded a code of laws for His people. These gave them guidance, which, if followed, would ensure their happiness and well-being. These instructions are usually described as 'the Law of Moses'. It was God's law given to the people through Moses. It is usual for Jews to refer to this as *Torah*, a term which is also used to describe the five books of Moses. Centuries later the Psalmist could say: "The law of the LORD is perfect, converting the soul" (Psalm 19:7). It is easy to appreciate the value of such a divinely devised law, but not as easy to keep it!

The Law of God

While the natural man is irked by restrictions of any kind, and law is generally seen as restriction, yet the purpose of God's law (and some human laws) was for the well-being of His people.

31

Only one who knows the human mind, as the Creator knows it, could legislate for true happiness.

BIBLE WEIGHTS AND MEASURES

Weights	*Metric*
Gerah	just over 0.5 grams
Shekel (20 gerahs)	just over 11.5 grams
Mina (50 shekels)	just over 571 grams
Talent (60 minas)	just over 34 kg

Liquid Capacity	*Metric*
Hin	about 3.8 litres
Bath (6 hins)	about 23 litres
Cor (10 baths)	about 230 litres

Dry Capacity	*Metric*
Omer	about 2.25 litres
Ephah (10 omers)	about 23 litres
Homer or Cor (10 ephahs)	about 230 litres

Lengths	*Metric*
Handbreadth	about 7.5 cm
Span	about 22.25 cm
Cubit	about 44.25 cm

The Ten Commandments, if kept conscientiously by all mankind, would ensure a world of peace, plenty, purity and prosperity. While given specifically to Israel by Moses from God, the principles of the commandments can be applied with benefit by all men everywhere. Jesus Christ endorsed them and confirmed that God spoke through Moses (Mark 12:29), and that Moses spoke to Israel and wrote down the law for future generations (John 5:46). Indeed, Jesus' respect for God's law was such that he did not transgress it in any way at all, thus demonstrating that although it was not easy to keep, and no man ever had, yet he kept it in spite of innumerable temptations.

Besides the basic laws for human conduct and worship, the law through Moses contained extensive instructions for the precise manner of Israel's worship, with an emphasis on the need for divine forgiveness upon confession of one's error. As it was pointed out centuries later by the Apostle Paul: "If it had not been for the law, I should not have known sin" (Romans 7:7). "It is written, 'Cursed be every one who does not abide by all things written in the book of the law, and do them.' Now it is evident that no man is justified before God by the law; for 'He who through faith is righteous shall live.' But the law does not rest on faith, for 'He who does them shall live by them'" (Galatians 3:10-12).

Thus the fact that no Jew was able to keep the law in every respect should have made the people more fully aware of God's mercy in having made provision for forgiveness, something that is unique among world religions. But their response seems to have been minimal. Instead, a system was developed whereby selected features of the law were ostentatiously kept, while other aspects were neglected. A philosophy of self-righteousness developed out of this system, which in later years was roundly condemned by Jesus. The beautiful law, which none could keep, should have brought every Jew to his knees in humility seeking for God's mercy: "God, be merciful to me a sinner" (Luke 18:13).

Skill in the Wilderness

Yet there were men and women who worked hard to follow the divine instructions that came through Moses. They willingly wove tents; they gladly gave their ornaments of gold and silver; they used their skills to construct the Tabernacle, the Ark of the Covenant, the hangings, the embroidery, the golden vessels and even the carts on which the heavy items were to be transported. These skills must have been used under very difficult wilderness conditions.

Bezalel was divinely chosen and endowed to lead the construction of these articles, and to instruct others. Is it possible that he, and perhaps some of his fellow workers, had been craftsmen in Egypt? Maybe not all the slaves were making bricks. Possibly some may have been craftsmen making furniture, or even chariots. That Egypt had highly skilled wood-workers using tools similar to those commonly in use today is very clear from some of the wall paintings that have been discovered in ancient tombs. The items of furniture found in

33

some of these tombs were beautifully made and are an eloquent testimony to the skills of the time.

The wood used for furniture found in these tombs was similar to that which Bezalel was instructed to use for the Tabernacle. It was Acacia wood, which still grows in Sinai. The Hebrew name for it is 'shittah' (plural 'shittim'). This wood is extremely durable, immune to insect infestation, but quite difficult to prepare. Three varieties of Acacia still grow in Sinai. There may have been other varieties in those days. The felling of the trees, their transport to the camp of Israel, the sawing and shaping to the specifications that God gave to Moses must have occupied many men for many days. But the fact that the woodwork, the weaving, the tapestry, the metal work and the preparation of oil and incense were all completed, suggests that there were men and women who were obedient and faithful at that time.

Kadesh Barnea

The forty years in the wilderness were not all spent in moving around from one camp to another. Most of the time the people were encamped around the great plateau known as Kadesh Barnea, also called Mishpat ('Fountain of Judgment'). This area is some 40 miles south-west of Beersheba. It can be visited today on an Israeli military road. There are a number of springs in the area, which is also crossed by several wadis.

Here there was, and still is, a supply of brackish water, similar to the 'bitter' water that Israel complained of at Marah. The source of this water in Sinai has been investigated by geologists who describe it as 'fossil' water, which exists in colossal quantities soaked in the porous rock. It is neither rain water nor sea water. It has been suggested that it may have been laid down at the time of the Flood! Its brackish taste is due to the absorbed minerals including Epsom salts.

From here the spies set out, probably as a rather pompous delegation to view the land. They returned with ample evidence of its fruitfulness, but full of fear of its inhabitants.

The End of the Road

The last part of the journey, to the east of the Dead Sea, was a very difficult route. The opposition of the inhabitants of that countryside was only part of the problem. The terrain was rough, with steep ravines to cross. One wonders how the ox carts bearing the Tabernacle were manipulated.

By this time, forty years after leaving Egypt, very few who had escaped from slavery still survived. It was now a young nation led by a very old man. Moses was allowed to view the Promised Land from the heights of Mount Nebo, then he died aged 120 years. His very able assistant, Joshua, took the lead. Trans-jordan having already been conquered, the nation crossed the Jordan river by another miracle. It would appear that a minor earthquake blocked the river at a place called Adam ('red earth') at precisely the time for the people to cross. The miracle was in the timing of the earthquake by the Almighty. Similar blockages of the flow of the river have occurred in recent times, but these were not miracles.

A Successor to Moses

Joshua was a man of tremendous faith and energy. With God's help he led the nation to victory over the many little city-states. It is noticeable that he avoided the cities of the Philistines. The lists of the nations that God wished to be eliminated do not include this people. In Joshua 10 there is a detailed record of the lightning campaign in southern Canaan, the area that was to become Judah's portion. Why were the cities of the Philistines left alone? Surely possession of their coastline would have been desirable? May it be that Joshua was mindful of the relationship and the covenant between Abraham and Abimelech "not to deal falsely with my offspring or with my posterity" (Genesis 21:23). This covenant of peace had been renewed by Isaac (Genesis 26:28). In view of the antagonism that developed centuries later, one wonders whether Abraham and Isaac really did the right thing to make an alliance with a godless people, even though it seemed a sensible thing to do at the time.

It seems probable that these cities of Canaan had already been weakened by Egyptian military incursions during the reign of Thuthmose III whose troops bore an emblem of a hornet (Joshua 24:12). The faith that led Joshua to a victorious occupation of the land was no longer evident when he had passed from the scene. The nation alternated between a state of chaos and short-lived success.

ISRAEL

The Division
of the Land
by Joshua
to the Twelve
Tribes of Israel

Judges and Kings

When a strong man (or woman) arose to lead them they won victories, but then lapsed into a lawless state. The people seemed to forget that God was still their king, even when they were being led by such a faithful man as Samuel. So God gave them a giant of a man to be their king, named Saul. His kingship was to teach the people a lesson of the folly of trusting in a faulty human king (1 Samuel 8:11-18). It also filled the years before a king of the appointed line of Judah could be installed. Judah's bastard son, Pharez and his descendants in the royal line could not take office until the tenth generation (Deuteronomy 23:2). David was of the first generation who could take office as king. The little genealogy at the end of the book of Ruth illustrates this point. Of all the sons of Jesse, David was "a man after God's own heart", in spite of his occasional lapses (1 Samuel 13:14).

The Golden Years

The example of godliness set by David, the faith that he exuded, the courage that he displayed, the leadership that he undertook, the appreciation of God's love and care that he showed, and the fact that God saw fit to use him as a vehicle for prophecy, all combine to make David a model and an example for all time. The fact that he also had failings enabled him to show to others that God is able and willing to grant forgiveness to the repentant sinner.

While David's mind was fully conscious of the great and precious promises that God had made to the fathers of the nation, his mind was not anchored in the past. As a prophet he foresaw God's ultimate purpose with His people, and with all the nations. Under divine guidance he wrote amazingly detailed

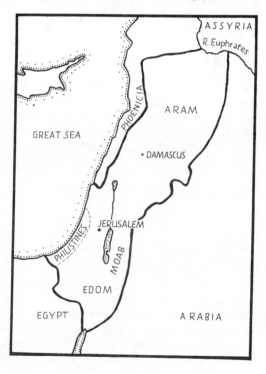

Israel at its Fullest Extent under Solomon — "From the River to the Border of Egypt"

37

prophecies of the rôle of his illustrious descendant who was to be born 1,000 years later. That David should call this descendant "my Lord" was surely proof of David's humility in spite of his position of high honour as king of God's chosen people, reigning over the Kingdom of the Lord (1 Samuel 12:12; 1 Chronicles 28:5).

The reigns of David and his son Solomon were the high peak in the history of Israel. David prepared for, and Solomon built, the very beautifully proportioned Temple that stood on the highest part of mount Moriah, above the little walled city of Jerusalem. Its simple design was a contrast with the extravaganzas that were erected to the heathen idols of other nations. It was unique.

But Solomon had not the humility of his father. He had been born 'with a golden spoon in his mouth'. While he started very well, he was a cunning politician and a very shrewd business man, with a tremendous sense of self-confidence. By making many marriages of convenience with princesses of neighbouring kings, he gained control of the whole of the area that had been promised to Abraham, from the river of Egypt to the great river Euphrates. But his ambitious schemes led him to be oppressive of the people, and the introduction of idols to please his foreign wives angered the God of Israel over whose kingdom he had been placed on trust. On his death there was rebellion and the kingdom was split.

Divine Correction

The southern kingdom of Judah, based around Jerusalem, retained the kings of the royal house of David. The northern ten tribe kingdom of Israel (sometimes called Ephraim) suffered a series of kings of fortune, who, in their anxiety to prevent their people from defecting to Judah, led them astray by introducing false forms of worship.

Thus Israel quickly became an idolatrous nation. Abraham who was styled "the father of the faithful" had a nation of "children in whom is no faith". Since "without faith it is impossible to please God" the faithless nation was removed from their land, but not before they had been warned and pleaded with for many years by God's faithful prophets.

RISE AND FALL OF THE KINGDOM

Enemies	BC	Kings	Prophets	Kings	BC	Enemies

THE UNITED KINGDOM

Enemies	BC	Kings	Prophets
Philistines	1050	Saul	Samuel
	1011	David	Nathan
	971	Solomon	Gad
			Ahijah

THE DIVIDED KINGDOM

Enemies	BC	JUDAH	Prophets	ISRAEL	BC	Enemies
Shishak	931	Rehoboam		Jeroboam I	931	
	913	Abijam		Nadab	910	
	910	Asa		Baasha	909	
Zerah				Elah,Zimri	886	
				Tibni,Omri	885	
	870	Jehoshaphat	Elijah	Ahab	874	Benhadad
			Micaiah			
			Elisha	Ahaziah	853	Shalman-
				Joram	853	eser III
	848	Jehoram				
	841	Ahaziah		Jehu	841	Hazael
	841	Athaliah				
	835	Joash				
Hazael			Joel	Jehoahaz	814	Benhadad II
	796	Amaziah		Jehoash	798	
	767	Uzziah	Jonah	Jeroboam II	782	
			Hosea			
			Amos	Shallum	753	
Rezin				Menahem	753	Tiglath
				Zechariah	752	Pileser III
	740	Jotham		Pekahiah	740	
	732	Ahaz	Micah	Pekah	732	Shalman-
			Isaiah	Hoshea		eser V
					722	Sargon II
Sennacherib	716	Hezekiah				
Tirhakah						
Esarhaddon	687	Manasseh				
Ashur-banipal	642	Amon	Nahum			
	640	Josiah	Zephaniah			
Necho			Jeremiah		612	Nineveh fell
	609	Jehoahaz	Huldah			
Nebuchad-nezzar	609	Jehoiakim	Daniel			
	597	Jehoiachin	Habakkuk			
	587	Zedekiah	Obadiah			
	586		Ezekiel			
Babylon fell	539					

ISRAEL

The northern kingdom of Israel was thus the first to receive the divine rebuke. The cruel armies of Assyria were the instruments that God used. They had no pity on their captives and made sure that their captives would have no opportunity to return home. Yet, in spite of the terrible lesson that Israel was taught, Judah failed to get the message. The prophet Isaiah repeatedly warned them of the consequences:

"God said, 'Here am I, here am I', to a nation that did not call on my name. I spread out my hands all the day to a rebellious people, who walk in a way that is not good, following their own devices; a people who provoke me to my face continually."

(Isaiah 65:1-3)

The Holy Land and the Holy City were being defiled by an unholy people, and they too were removed from their inheritance.

*Ptolemy of Egypt
(305-283 B.C.)*

Judah went into captivity 150 years after Israel. The Babylonians had superseded the Assyrians as the dominant power. Four times they raided Judah and took captives, but to no effect, and on their last raid destroyed Jerusalem and the beautiful Temple. However, Judah's captivity was comparatively short. When, as had been foretold by God's prophets, Babylon was overcome by the Medes and Persians, a change took place in the fortunes of the captives from Judah (Ezra 1:1-4). Thousands were allowed to make *aliyah* to Jerusalem with instructions and the wherewithal to rebuild the city and the Temple. The

Antiochus Epiphanes of Greek Syria (175-163 B.C.) who desecrated the Temple and whose defeat is celebrated at the Feast of Dedication each Kislev 25 for eight days

40

little state of Judea then became a buffer state between the great powers to its north and south. At first it was Persia versus Egypt and then Greek-Syria versus Greek Egypt. Eventually the Jews managed to establish, for a short time, an independent Hasmonean state under the leadership of the family of the Maccabees, only to fall eventually to the expanding Roman Empire.

	MAIN EVENTS BETWEEN OLD AND NEW TESTAMENT RECORDS
B.C. 445	Rebuilding of walls of Jerusalem completed
B.C. 334	Army of Alexander the Great took Jerusalem
B.C. 320	Ptolemy Soter (of Egypt) conquered Judea
B.C. 250	Completion of Septuagint translation of Hebrew Scriptures
B.C. 198	Antiochus Epiphanes (of Syria) captured Judea
B.C. 168	Revolt of Jews against desecration of Temple by Antiochus
B.C. 165	Establishment of semi-independent Judea under Maccabees and re-dedication of the Temple
B.C. 143	Independent Judea under Jewish Hasmonean dynasty
B.C. 130	Jerusalem besieged by Antiochus Sidetes, but not taken
B.C. 96	Jewish civil war raged around Jerusalem
B.C. 67	John Hyrcanus regained control for the Jews
B.C. 63	Roman army under Pompey captured Jerusalem
B.C. 40	Jerusalem plundered by invading Parthian army
B.C. 37	Herod the Great appointed king of Judea by Rome
B.C. 37-31	Cleopatra, Queen of Egypt, tried to annexe Judea
B.C. 19	Herod began reconstruction of the Jerusalem Temple
B.C. 4	Herod the Great died; replaced by Archelaus, Herod's son
B.C. 4	Jesus born in Bethlehem, presented at Jerusalem Temple

The Nation's Last Days

It was while occupied by Roman troops, under a king appointed by Rome, that Jesus (Yeshua) of Nazareth was born in Bethlehem. They were times of great frustration and stress for the people. The Jews were a fiercely independent people, resentful of their pagan oppressors. King Herod, who was half Jew, half Edomite, tried to appease the nation by an extensive building programme. This included the plan to enlarge and beautify the Second Temple and extend the Temple Mount so that it would accommodate the great multitudes of pilgrims who came for the appointed feasts.

Some of the Jewish authorities found it prudent to cooperate with the Romans. But there were others who maintained a guerrilla war with the foreigners which necessitated the presence of increasing numbers of the hated Roman troops. Thus resentment was building up. The nation was longing for a liberator to arise and lead them to independence.

When the common people thought that Jesus might lead them against their oppressors, they besought him with the cry of "Hosanna" ('Pray save us') thinking that he would respond and become their national saviour. His name Yeshua ('Yah saves') may have contributed to this impression. When it was realised that this was not his mission, many of them in disappointment were ready to join in the demand for his death. He was regarded as another false messiah, as indeed he is to this day by most Jews.

But, a few weeks later, the people of Jerusalem had an opportunity to change their minds concerning Jesus, and in the following years many did so. The little community of believers in 'The Way' that Jesus had opened for personal salvation developed in Jerusalem and quickly spread far and wide in the Roman Empire before the Jews in Judea were liquidated and Jerusalem was smashed in A.D. 70.

The End of an Era

The factual history of the people of Israel ends there in the Bible record. But Israel's history in the centuries to come was written beforehand in the divine prophecies which revealed that a devastating dispersion would take place before there could be a glorious future for the nation. In summary, their 2,000 years of existence to this time had seen them twice evicted from their homeland, twice they lost their independence, twice the Temple was destroyed by pagan invaders. They had entered the Promised Land en masse as a nation under God's guidance, they had forfeited their inheritance because they had repeatedly broken their part of the covenant, they were exiled from their land in bits and pieces to be scattered among one hundred nations world-wide, some as slaves, mostly as refugees seeking asylum.

By all normal standards these calamities would have been the end of the identity of Israel as a nation. But they were not to be the end for very good reasons. The nations that dispossessed them, enslaved them, despoiled them, slew them and persecuted them all disappeared. They are all past history. But Israel is still identifiable, having persisted in spite of their scattering to all parts of the earth. They were and still are the people of God's covenant with Abraham, which has not been abrogated, nor has it been forgotten, but is awaiting fulfilment in all its details by the specific descendant ('seed') of Abraham who was promised so long ago. The covenant can be fulfilled by no other than the Son of Abraham whom God provided in due course by another miraculous birth: Jesus the Messiah.

JERUSALEM—'THE EYE OF THE STORM'
HIGHLIGHTS OF ITS 4,000 YEARS OF HISTORY
The dates B.C. are approximate only

B.C.

1800	Reference in Egyptian Execration Texts to 'Rushlumin'
1800	Salem visited by Abram when Melchizedek was its king (Genesis 14:18)
1350	The city mentioned in the Tel Amarna tablets as 'Urusalim'
1240	Jerusalem attacked by the tribe of Judah (Judges 1:8)
1000	Jebus captured by David's forces led by Joab (2 Samuel 5:6)
954	The Temple built by Solomon, completed and dedicated (1 Kings 8)

43

ISRAEL

925	Jerusalem plundered by Shishak's Egyptian army (1 Kings 14:25)
845	Jerusalem plundered by Philistines and Arabs (2 Chronicles 21:16)
790	Jerusalem plundered by Joash of Israel (2 Chronicles 25:23)
730	Jerusalem successfully defended by Ahaz (2 Chronicles 28:21)
701	Hezekiah defended the city with divine aid (2 Chronicles 32:21)
686	Assyrians attacked city taking Manasseh captive (2 Chronicles 33:11)
608	Pharaoh Necho took tribute from Jehoiakim (2 Chronicles 36:3)
606	Babylonians took spoil in Jehoiakim's 11th year (2 Chronicles 36:7)
597	Babylonians took spoil in Jehoiachin's 1st year (2 Chronicles 36:10)
586	Babylonians destroyed both city and Temple (2 Chronicles 36:19)
536	Cyrus decreed rebuilding of city and Temple (Ezra 1:2)
535	Rebuilding of Temple begun, but abandoned (Ezra 4:4)
518	Rebuilding work resumed (Ezra 6:14)
514	Rebuilding of Temple completed (Ezra 6:15)
445	Rebuilding of Jerusalem's city walls completed (Nehemiah 6:1)
334	Army of Alexander the Great took the city
320	Jerusalem conquered by Ptolemy Soter of Egypt
198	Jerusalem taken by Antiochus the Great of Syria
168	Jerusalem freed by the Jews under Judas Maccabeus
168	Temple desecrated by Antiochus Epiphanes of Syria
165	Jerusalem re-conquered by the Jews under Judas Maccabeus
165	Temple re-dedicated as remembered at Ḥanukkah, Festival of Lights
130	City besieged by Antiochus Sidetes of Syria, but not taken
96	Jewish civil war raged around the city
67	Hyrcanus took control for the Jews

63	Roman army under Pompey captured Jerusalem
40	Jerusalem plundered by invading Parthian army
37	Herod the Great made king of Jerusalem and Judea by the Romans
19	Herod began reconstruction of the Jerusalem Temple
4	Archelaus (Herod the Ethnarch) ruled after his father
4	Jesus (born in Bethlehem) presented at the Temple

The dates A.D. may be taken as reasonably accurate

A.D. (or C.E.—common era)

30	Jesus of Nazareth died at Jerusalem
66	Jewish revolt: Romans looted city, but were repulsed
70	Roman army under Titus destroyed city and Temple
132	Bar Kochba led Jewish rebellion against Romans
135	Jerusalem devastated and 'ploughed as a field' by Hadrian
135	Hadrian's edict that no Jew should live in Jerusalem
135	City rebuilt by Romans as Aelia Capitolina with pagan temples
261	Invasion by Kingdom of Palmyra
335	Roman emperor Constantine allowed 'Christian' shrines built
335	Constantine forbade Jewish pilgrimage to Jerusalem
363	Emperor Julian attempted to rebuild Temple, prevented by earthquake
529	Jerusalem attacked by the Samaritans
614	Persian army under Chosroes II captured city
629	Byzantine army under Heraclius recaptured city
637	Moslem army led by Omar captured Jerusalem
691	Moslem Dome of the Rock completed by Abd el-Malik
996	The Fatimids of Egypt invaded and took city
1012	Egyptians ordered all houses of prayer to be burned down
1016	Dome of the Rock destroyed by earthquake
1071	Seljuk Turks conquered city
1098	Mamelukes, led by Afdal, took city for Egypt
1099	First Crusade, Jews massacred, Kingdom of Jerusalem established
1187	Crusaders driven out by Saladin at head of Moslem army

ISRAEL

1202	Fourth Crusade established Latin Kingdom of Jerusalem
1217	Fifth Crusade recaptured the city
1244	Tartar army took city from Crusaders
1249	Syrian forces took city from Tartars
1250	Jerusalem captured by a Mongol army
1260	The city again came under control of the Mamelukes
1517	Ottoman Turks took over control of the city
1536	Jerusalem's walls rebuilt in present form by Suleiman
1665	Sabbatai Zevi proclaimed himself Messiah at Jerusalem
1689	The city deserted due to famine
1799	City prepared for attack by Napoleon, prevented by Britain
1824	Revolt against Turks by inhabitants of Jerusalem
1827	First visit by Sir Moses Montefiore from England
1832	Jerusalem occupied by Egypt, supported by France
1835	Sultan of Turkey formally revoked Hadrian's edict of A.D. 135
1839	First British Vice-consulate established in Jerusalem
1840	Egyptian occupation ceased
1848	First Post Office opened in Jerusalem by Austrians
1863	First newspapers published in the city
1877	First Municipal Council appointed in Jerusalem
1892	Jaffa-Jerusalem Railway opened by a French Company
1914	'The Language War'—Babel or Hebrew
1917	Jerusalem taken from Turks by General Allenby's British troops
1921	Arab riots in Jerusalem and elsewhere
1923	Jerusalem and Palestine came under League of Nations British Mandate
1929	Riots in Jerusalem
1936	Riots of Jews versus the Mandatory Power of Britain
1948	Jerusalem a divided city in War of Independence
1967	Six-Day War: Old city cleared of Jordanian presence

2

THE JEWISH RELIGION

THE Jewish religion is the oldest of the world religions that acknowledge the One Most High Creator God. Jewish society is organised on the civil and ecclesiastical beliefs and practices provided in the laws and ritual given to Moses at Sinai and in the wilderness. The concept of Israel as ''the chosen people'' is based on their descent from Abraham, Isaac and Jacob, to whom God gave great and precious promises, and on the intervention of God in their distress in slavery in Egypt, and on the giving of divine laws for their guidance through Moses.

Torah ('the teaching') in the first place refers to all the laws given through Moses, but may also refer to all of Moses' writings, the Pentateuch. The term has been used of all the Hebrew Holy Scriptures, although these are more correctly termed the *Tanakh*. The term refers more to the content of the books than to the books themselves, and may be stretched sometimes to include the oral law, the rabbinical extensions of the law that are alleged to date from the time of the divine revelation to Moses.

בְּרֵאשִׁית בָּרָא אֱלֹהִים אֵת הַשָּׁמַיִם וְאֵת הָאָרֶץ: וְהָאָרֶץ
הָיְתָה תֹהוּ וָבֹהוּ וְחֹשֶׁךְ עַל־פְּנֵי תְהוֹם וְרוּחַ אֱלֹהִים
מְרַחֶפֶת עַל־פְּנֵי הַמָּיִם: וַיֹּאמֶר אֱלֹהִים יְהִי אוֹר וַיְהִי־
אוֹר: וַיַּרְא אֱלֹהִים אֶת־הָאוֹר כִּי־טוֹב וַיַּבְדֵּל אֱלֹהִים בֵּין
הָאוֹר וּבֵין הַחֹשֶׁךְ: וַיִּקְרָא אֱלֹהִים ׀ לָאוֹר יוֹם וְלַחֹשֶׁךְ
קָרָא לָיְלָה וַיְהִי־עֶרֶב וַיְהִי־בֹקֶר יוֹם אֶחָד: פ

Genesis 1:1-5 in the Hebrew Bible

THE SHEMA
THE JEWISH CONFESSION OF FAITH
"Hear, O Israel, the LORD our God is one Lord"

The basic tenets of the Jewish religion may be summarised as follows:

1. The Shema. That God is One, is Creator, is Spirit, is Eternal and that He alone is worthy to be worshipped.
2. The Torah. That God communicates with man and seeks to guide him through His laws and through His prophets.
3. That God is concerned about man and seeks a response in love, rewards good and punishes evil.
4. That Israel are God's chosen race through whom He seeks to send a blessing on all nations, through the Messiah.
5. That death is real, and that there will be a resurrection for those who have kept the law of God.

JEWISH RELIGIOUS LITERATURE

The Siddur: The Jewish Holy Scriptures (The Tanach), in particular the Torah (The Books of Moses) and the Psalms, form the basic Jewish religious literature. To the practising Jew, the next most used work is the Jewish Prayer Book (The Siddur). The prayers reflect many of the primary Jewish tenets such as the concept of the One God, Israel the Chosen People, the divine source of the Torah, God's goodness and the Hope of the Messiah. The prayers consist more of praises than petitions and more thanksgiving than asking.

The Talmud: Next to the Torah, the written law, as given to Moses by God, is the Talmud comprising Jewish teaching, tradition and Biblical interpretation sometimes spoken of as the Oral Law. For centuries this has been handed down by word of mouth from teacher to pupil and from father to son—hence the *Oral* Law—but it was finally written down as the Talmud ('instruction'). It was probably this mass of oral law that was mentioned disapprovingly by Jesus as the 'traditions of men' (Mark 7:3-13). The Talmud consists of two parts, the Mishnah and Gemara.

The Mishnah: After the Roman desolation of Jerusalem and scattering of the people, the Jews who were left gave themselves to a deeper study of the Jewish law and way of life. Much of this was written down, and about A.D. 200 a leading rabbi—Judah the Prince—made a collection of these writings, carefully edited them and compiled the Mishnah ('repetition'). This is an orderly arrangement under six categories of laws: (1) Agricultural; (2) The Sabbath and Festivals; (3) Marriage and Divorce; (4) Civil Law; (5) Temple Ritual; (6) Personal Purity.

Preparation of unblemished, almost transparent parchment (from sheep or goat skin) for use in Torah scrolls and similar 'holy' uses

The Gemara: After the Mishnah was completed, it was supplemented by scholarly discussions on all manner of subjects that were debated in the rabbinical schools. To complicate matters, there are two forms of the Talmud. One was the unfinished work of the academies in Palestine, the other the authoritative work of Babylonian Jewish scholars during the third to the fifth centuries A.D. known as the Amoraim ('speakers'). The latter Talmud is the one in use today.

The Midrash: The Midrash ('inquiry') is a large commentary on the Holy Scriptures, compiled over a period of many centuries up to the 11th century A.D. The Haggadah is the aspect of Midrash which illustrates its ethical teaching with parables and folklore, while the Halachah consists of detailed legal discussions and pronouncements on this work. The Midrash may have been more influential on Jewish thought than any of the above mentioned works.

Rashi: Rashi is an acronym for Rabbi Solomon ben Isaac, a famous French Jew of the 11th century whose commentary on the Talmud, referred to as *'Tosafot'* ('additions'), makes plain sailing of difficult passages, and is still quoted extensively.

Mishneh Torah: Perhaps the greatest Jewish sage of the Middle Ages was the Spanish born physician Moses Maimonides (known as the Rambam) who wrote the Mishneh Torah, a compilation and exposition of Jewish law in fourteen volumes. However, he sought to reconcile Judaism with Greek thought, as also did the Jewish philosophers Saadiah, and Solomon ben Gabirol. On the other hand Yehuda Halevi attempted to free Jewish thought from Greek philosophy.

The Shulchan Arukh: Rabbi Joseph Karo (of Spain) wrote a masterly compilation of the whole of Jewish law and thereby established a standard for Jewish religious behaviour for all Jews. It means 'the table prepared'. To this day it remains the authoritative guide for orthodox Jews the world over.

The Targums: The Targums ('interpretations') are a series of translations and paraphrases of the Hebrew Holy Scriptures into Aramaic, a language used by the Jews of the captivity and after, and used by Jesus in speaking to the common people. Also known as Syro-Chaldaic.

RELIGION IN DAILY LIFE

JEWISH life from the cradle to the grave is closely based on the religious beliefs as taught in the Torah. The life-style, the liturgy, the calendar, the festivals, the ceremonies and the diet all have to conform.

The child of a Jewess, whoever the father, is by tradition to be regarded as a Jew by birth. A male child is normally circumcised at eight days to relate him to the covenant that God made with Abraham. A boy is regarded as becoming responsible to

Bar Mitzvah of Ethiopian Boy at the Western Wall

keep the law at age 13, when his coming of age is celebrated at a ceremony known as his Bar Mitzvah ('Son of the commandment'). A similar ceremony for a girl at age 12 years and one day has recently been introduced—her Bat Mitzvah ('Daughter of the commandment').

Children are taught in the law to care for their parents in old age. After death, burial must take place within 24 hours in consecrated ground. Following a death seven days of deep mourning are observed by the family. Cremation is not normally practised.

A major part of the religious observances is the keeping of the appointed feasts and holy days of the Hebrew calendar. The regular Sabbath observance and the careful watching for the New Moon are regular reminders of the divine creation of life, the heavens and the earth. The three major divinely appointed feasts, Passover, Shavuot and Sukkot were each a memorial of a very significant national event, in which God's concern for Israel was evident.

To these feasts have been added two man-made events, Hanukkah and Purim, memorials of turning points in the nation's history. One day each year of fasting was divinely appointed, the Day of Atonement, or more correctly Yom Kippurim ('Day of coverings') when a consciousness of sin was aroused, and its forgiveness sought. Tradition has added other fast days in memory of disasters, the Fast of Ab, the Fast of Gedaliah, and others.

The Temple and the Synagogue

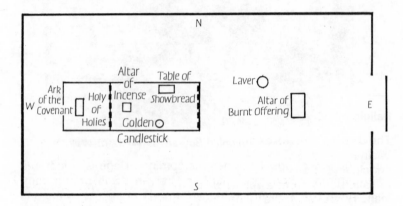

Plan of the Tabernacle

The centre of Jewish religious life was at first the Tabernacle, then the Temple at Jerusalem. When the nation went into exile to Assyria and Babylonia, at first assemblies were held in houses, then in buildings that were the forerunners of the synagogue. All Jewish religious services are required by rabbinical law to have a quorum of not less than ten responsible males, known as a *minyan*. The meeting places where enough Jews lived in the cities of their dispersion became the traditional place for worship, teaching and cultural life. The word synagogue is Greek for 'bringing together'.

After the final dispersion of A.D. 70, and the destruction of the Temple for the second time, the synagogue became ever more important in Jewish life. The office of priest (*cohen*) ceased with the fall of the Temple and the leadership and tuition of the religious Jew became the responsibility of the rabbi (master) who was well versed in the Torah.

THE SEVEN TEMPLES OF THE LORD

1. The Tabernacle in the Wilderness (Exodus 40:18)
2. The Temple of Solomon (1 Kings 6:1-7)
3. The Temple rebuilt by Ezra (Ezra 4:1)
4. The Temple rebuilt by Herod (Luke 1:9)
5. The Temple of Ezekiel's Prophecy (Ezekiel 43:10)
6. "For we are the temple of the living God" (1 Corinthians 3:16)
7. "For its temple is the Lord God the Almighty and the Lamb" (Revelation 21:22)

Religion in Business

The Jewish law is very clear in its insistence on honesty in all business transactions. A just weight and a just measure is a principle that applies in many ways. Jewish law forbids a Jew to take usury from a fellow Jew, that is, taking interest on a loan. However, there is no law to hinder the taking of usury from a Gentile. The mediaeval Christian church took the same line and forbade Christians to take usury of a Christian. Partly for this reason the Jews of the diaspora became usurers to fill the gap in the economy, and took usury readily from their Gentile neighbours. The invasion of Britain in 1066 by William of Normandy was financed in this way by Jewish usurers, and a Jewish presence in Britain probably dates from this time. Many other royal ventures were financed in 'Christian' Europe in a similar way. The Jewish reputation as a usurer* was popularised by Shakespeare's character of Shylock. In more recent times the business of usury has become known as banking, and Jews have taken a major part in this profession.

---

*Thus in the *Shorter Oxford English Dictionary*, 1933 edition: "Jew . . . Applied to a grasping or extortionate usurer . . ." In Roget's *Thesaurus*, 1936 edition, under the entry "Lending", there is the following group of associated words: "lender, pawnbroker, moneylender, usurer, Jew, Shylock; under "Parsimony", the following: "miser, niggard, skinflint . . . harpy, extortioner, Jew". Modern dictionaries tend to be somewhat less offensive.

Unorthodox Jewry

That all Jews were not orthodox, or even religious at all, becomes evident from the record of the Holy Scriptures at a very early date. From the incident of the golden calf onwards, there were many who disdained God's way. After the division of the united kingdom, the inhabitants of the northern kingdom of Israel were deliberately encouraged to desert their former faith and place of worship for a form of idolatry.

With the return of the exiles from Babylonia, and the attempt to restore Jerusalem as the centre of Jewish religion, it took Ezra to introduce a new way of keeping the old law. Indeed, Ezra is known as 'the father of Judaism', and it was he who purged the people, and urged them to reform their ways, and 'get back to the Torah'. During the difficult days that followed when the Jewish hold on the land was tenuous, and any thought of idolatry had been knocked out of the Jewish mind, a sect arose which developed into the Pharisees. To them a strict observance of the Torah was everything. They furthered the introduction of the synagogue, seeing it as a means of reducing the influence of the priests. By the First Century A.D. there were hundreds of synagogues in the city of Jerusalem. The Pharisees' grip on the minds of the people was almost complete. Yet there were unorthodox Jews such as the Sadducees, the Essenes and others, who resented the power of the Pharisees.

To increase their power over the people the Pharisees extended the law, made traditions and additions which became "burdens grievous to be borne" (Luke 11:46). With the destruction of Jerusalem, the power of the Pharisees was inherited by the rabbis, and Judaism became the religion of the Jews. This still had its foothold on the Torah, but was developed in such a way that man's interpretation became more important than God's Word. It is doubtful whether Ezra would have approved of the way in which the reform movement that he started finally developed.

Proselytes

The Jewish people as a nation have not set themselves out to convert Gentiles to their ways. Nevertheless there have been examples in history of Gentiles being attracted to the Jewish

6. Grandfather and Children at the Western Wall:
''Grandchildren are the crown of the aged'' (Proverbs 13:6)

7. Sukkot—Feast of Tabernacles: "You shall take the fruit of goodly trees (an 'etrog', citrus fruit), branches of palm trees . . leafy trees (myrtle), and willows . . and rejoice before the Lord" (Leviticus 23:40)

8. Young and Old—A Yemenite Jew and Children: "And the streets of the city shall be full of boys and girls playing" (Zechariah 8:5)

9. An Italian Jewess reading a Bilingual Prayer Book:
''In the morning my prayer comes before thee'' (Psalm 88:13)

faith, and accepted into the nation. Early examples are Caleb, Rahab and Ruth. Such people exhibited an Abrahamic faith in God's promises to the nation. The mixed marriages that Ezra had to condemn were certainly not the result of making proselytes or converts to the Jewish faith.

Yet there must have been a time when a Jewish missionary effort was made, for it was condemned by Jesus in very strong terms: "Woe to you, scribes and Pharisees, hypocrites! For you traverse sea and land to make a single proselyte, and when he becomes a proselyte, you make him twice as much a child of Gehenna as yourselves" (Matthew 23:15).

With the advent of the Roman Empire, and the wide dispersion of Jews within its boundaries, there was something about the Jewish faith that gained favourable attention from their Gentile neighbours. There developed a large number of people who were sympathetic to the Jewish way of life. Perhaps it compared favourably with the violent pagan way of life. Perhaps Jewish stedfastness to their peculiar standards drew favourable attention. However, there were, during the last two centuries B.C. and the first two centuries A.D., a large number of pagans who sympathised with Jewish views, some of whom were known as 'God-fearers' and who took instruction in the Jewish faith at the synagogues.

Archaeological evidence of these God-fearers and their practical support for Jewish activities has come to light at Aphrodisias in Asia Minor. A large marble slab lists 54 names of *kai hosoi theosebeis* ('and those who are God-fearers') who had been contributors to the erection of a building which was probably to be used as a Jewish 'soup kitchen' for the relief of needy citizens. The same description has been found on another inscription at Miletus. Maybe some of these 'God-fearers' eventually became proselytes, but there is a mass of literary reference to them suggesting that they were 'halfway' Jews, who had a knowledge of the Jewish Scriptures, which they heard read in the synagogue, believed in the One God of Israel and may have kept certain other features of the Jewish way of life. As Paul's missionary journeys testify, they were being prepared to receive the Gospel message that so many of the Jews refused to accept.

THE HEBREW HOLY SCRIPTURES

THE Hebrew Holy Scriptures, or Bible, or Tanakh, as used by Jews, has all the books of the 'Old Testament', but many of them are in a different order. The traditional three sections of the Hebrew scrolls are: (1) The Torah; (2) The Nevi'im, and (3) The Kethuvim. The word Tanakh is an acronym of these three words.

1. The Torah ('teachings') comprises the five books of Moses, also known in Greek as the Pentateuch.
2. The Nevi'im ('prophets') includes Joshua, Judges, Samuel, Kings, Isaiah, Jeremiah, Ezekiel and the twelve minor prophets (but not Daniel).
3. The Kethuvim ('writings') include all the remaining books concluding with Chronicles.

The Roman Apocryphal books are not included in the Hebrew Tanakh.

Scripture Readings

Although the Jews have been called 'the people of the book', in that God's Word was written, guarded and preserved by the people of Israel, the reading and study of it has been left to a minority. The Jews are not Bible readers any more than nominal Christians are Bible readers. During the centuries of their dispersion, only the few who could read Hebrew were able to read the Holy Scriptures. Even for religious Jews, the reading of a portion of the Torah, followed by a few verses of the Nevi'im, at the synagogue services was probably the only exposure to the Word of God that they would receive. Additional readings on feast days included the smaller books of Ruth, Esther, Lamentations, Song of Songs and Ecclesiastes. Thus, large parts of the Scriptures were never read in public. Even the sacred words that were read would not be intelligible unless the hearer had a knowledge of Hebrew. The Jews of the dispersion were therefore in the hands of the rabbis for their understanding of the law and the prophets.

Translations

Translations of a part, or maybe the whole of the Scriptures were made at an early date. The first were probably into

Aramaic, the spoken tongue of the common people after the exile. There are several known as the Targum, but as they are really transliterations, they are not very helpful in establishing the Hebrew text. In the third century B.C. when many Jews were living in Greek-speaking lands, the Septuagint version of the Holy Scriptures in the Greek language was made. This was reputedly produced by 72 Jewish elders at Alexandria, Egypt, for the library of Ptolemy. Many copies were soon in circulation in the Greek-speaking world.

Even though the Jewish synagogue services retained the Hebrew version, the rabbis insisting that Hebrew was the only holy language, and that to translate into another tongue would debase the Holy Scriptures, the Septuagint version was widely known and used by the First Century A.D. There is evidence that some of the Apostle Paul's quotations were taken from the Septuagint version, as would be appropriate seeing that he wrote in the Greek language to Greek-speaking believers.

Among Jews of the dispersion, until recent times, Hebrew has remained the language of Holy Scripture. During the last century a Yiddish translation was made for European Jews. Yiddish is an expressive language comprising a mix of Jewish, German and Slav words, widely used in eastern Europe at one time, and still used in some Jewish communities to a limited extent. Versions in German (for the Ashkenazim) and in Ladino (for the Sephardim) were also produced.

English Versions

Then, in the mid 19th century, as a result of mass migration from eastern Europe into English speaking countries, and the adoption of the English language by many of the refugees, the need arose for a translation into English by Jews for Jews. In England Dr. A. Benisch produced a version, followed by another by Dr. M. Friedlander. But neither of these had a wide circulation. Then an American Jew, Isaac Leeser, produced a version which was accepted by all the synagogues in America and many elsewhere. But it was soon realised by Jewish scholars that this work could be improved upon. After twenty years of work by a group of rabbis and doctors of the law, the Jewish Publication Society of Philadelphia issued the result of their labours in 1917: *The Holy Scriptures according to the*

Masoretic Text. This version is very similar to the King James Version, using similar language but without some of the archaisms. These translators acknowledged that they were grateful for access to the English versions of Wycliffe, Tyndale, Coverdale and others, and were obviously influenced by them.

The division into chapters and verses follows that of the King James Version with minor exceptions. The use of the letter 'J' is retained, even though there is no such letter in Hebrew. The English spelling of Hebrew names is retained, but, as might be expected, the name 'Jehovah' is not used. A footnote to Exodus 6:3 reads: "The ineffable name; read Adonai, which means 'The Lord'." The words LORD and GOD in capital letters, as in the King James Version, are used where the Tetragrammaton (YHWH) occurs in the Hebrew.

In Britain, the Chief Rabbi, Dr. J. H. Hertz, produced a version which is virtually the Jewish Publication Society translation with his own extensive and very interesting commentaries added. The Soncino Press also issued a sumptuous edition with extensive commentaries based on the traditional expositions of the rabbis of old time. Some of the comments are valuable helps to an understanding of passages that involve Jewish customs and modes of thought, while others tend to be fanciful and highly speculative.

New English Versions

In New York, a modern version has appeared known as the *City Bible*, while in Jerusalem another modern version has appeared known as the *New Israel Version*, confusingly shortened to N.I.V. Recent quotations in the *Jerusalem Post* column headed 'Tora Today' have been from the last named version. These give the impression of being rather liberal.

The Jewish Publication Society of Philadelphia has produced what is described as the most important translation of the Scriptures by Jews for Jews since the Septuagint (2,250 years ago). This version disclaims any influence from Christian translations. It was completed in 1985 and is beautifully printed and presented as *Tanakh—A New Translation according to the Traditional Hebrew Text*. It claims to be a triumph of Biblical scholarship and accuracy. The use of well chosen contemporary language makes for clarity, ease of reading and comprehension. There is no commentary but brief notes indicate where the original Hebrew is uncertain, and where there are variant readings. It must be said, however, that there does appear to be evidence of bias by the translators in a few passages that are seen by Christians to be specific prophecies of the Messiah.

The Christian New Testament

For centuries the New Testament has been shunned by most Jews as being spurious and contrary to their interests. It was, and still is regarded as the book of their persecutors. They tend to associate Christians with the Crusades, the Inquisition, the Holocaust and all the repression that they have suffered during the long centuries of their dispersion.

However, there has been evidence of a change in recent years. Some Jews have read the New Testament with interest, even if very critically. Classes are held in Jerusalem to point out the alleged errors and discrepancies in the Gospels and Epistles with a view to enabling Jews to refute Christian missionaries.

In spite of this understandable prejudice, several eminent Jews have expressed their opinion that the character of Jesus is a credit to his Jewishness. They realise that for a Jew to have the worldwide influence that has been exercised by Jesus, is something to be proud of. Some Jews even accept that Jesus was a great prophet, misunderstood at the time. Even so, it is still maintained that he was a false Messiah, and that the resurrection could not have taken place, but was a trick arranged by the disciples.

A very small minority have recognised that Jesus of Nazareth was indeed the promised Messiah, and look for his return.

A KINGDOM OF PRIESTS

THE first mention of a priest in the Bible is of Melchi-zedek, the priest of the Most High God at Salem, to whom Abram paid tithes (Genesis 14:18). That is not to be taken as meaning that there were no priests before this time. The word 'priest' is derived from a word meaning 'elder'. The Hebrew word is *kohen* (also *cohen*), signifying one in authority.

The office of priest was to represent his family to God, and God to His family, as both intercessor and mediator. For this reason the priest offered sacrifices to God as an acknowledgement that erring humans are worthy to die the death of the animal sacrificed. The sacrifice provided a covering for sin (Genesis 3:21), even as Adam and Eve were taught when they had sinned.

It seems likely, therefore, that Melchi-zedek was the elder of his family of Semites, and was perhaps even Shem himself, who was contemporary with Abram (Genesis 11:11). He was certainly Abram's superior, his mentor and intercessor. Abram, Isaac and Jacob all offered sacrifices as elders of their families. Of Jacob's family it would appear that he had intended that Joseph, the eldest son of his first love, Rachel, should be priest to his family—if the exotic garment that he made for him was indeed a priestly robe. But Joseph's rôle as intercessor for his family came about in a way that Jacob could not have foreseen. Joseph in power in Egypt was literally God's mediator to provide for the family, and to plead on their behalf.

Moses and Aaron

In Egypt, years later, the brothers Moses and Aaron, of the tribe of Levi, seem to have been looked up to by the other men of Israel. It was Moses of the tribe of Levi who led the people out of their bondage; it was Moses of the tribe of Levi who received instructions for the nation from God, and represented the nation to God as he pleaded for them. Aaron was the appointed spokesman and so it was not surprising that Aaron and his sons were appointed priests of the Most High God (Exodus 28:1).

The next evidence of the Levites coming into prominence was when Moses called on them to support him at the time of the golden calf incident (Exodus 32:26). From this time on, the Levites were given special duties. Aaron's family, in spite of

Aaron's rôle in this sad affair, were to be the priests of the nation, and the Levites were to construct the Tabernacle (a portable Temple), guard it, minister for it, and transport it.

Postage Stamps illustrating the Ark and the Altar

The Levites

Levi means 'joined'. Although the name was bestowed on the child by his mother in the hope that she, Leah, would be joined to her husband by producing a third son, yet the name was most appropriate for the rôle of the tribe in Israel's national worship. The Levites were the tribe who were selected to join Israel to their God. In the course of time this family failed to fulfil this function, even though some of its members were faithful from time to time. Like priest, like people, was a principle that shows how great an influence the priesthood had in the attitude of the nation to divine matters.

When the people of Israel reached the Promised Land, the Levites were not given a portion, but were scattered throughout the nation. Although they were to attend to the service of God in the place which the LORD would choose, this was not a continuous attendance, but was by rota. Thus most of the year the Levites were living in and among the cities of the people. No doubt this was intended as an infusion of a good influence on the nation. The Levites were to be the instructors of the children and the people in the divine laws and requirements, in the hope that Israel would be a holy nation, devoted to living in the way that God had ordained for their blessing and happiness.

TRADITIONAL JEWISH SYMBOLS

ARON HAKODESH: The Ark or box in which scrolls of Torah are kept in a Synagogue.

BATIM HOUSES: The little leather boxes containing miniature scrolls for Phylacteries (or *Tephillin*).

DREIDEL: A small spinning top inscribed with an anagram for Hanukkah.

GREGGERS: Rattles used at Purim when name of Haman is mentioned.

MENORAH: The seven-branched lampstand as used in the Temple, now the emblem of Israel, and small editions used in homes.

MEZUZAH: Small container containing Scroll, placed on doorposts (Deuteronomy 6:9).

NER TAMID: The everlasting light kept burning in the synagogue in front of the Ark, symbol of the light of the Torah.

OMER: The yield of a sheaf of barley at the Feast of First-fruits.

SKULLCAP: Worn by orthodox Jewish males, traditionally to differentiate them from the shaven crowns of priests.

STAR OF DAVID: Six pointed star, traditional flag of Israel, not used until middle ages.

TALLIT: Prayer shawl having four corners with *Tzitzit* (tassels).

TEPHILLIN: Phylacteries, little leather boxes (*Batim*) in which are miniature scrolls of part of Torah. Worn on the head and arm during morning services (Deuteronomy 6:8).

TZITZIT: Tassels or fringes on the four corners of a *Tallit*, originally having a blue cord entwined (Numbers 15:38).

YAD: 'Hand', the pointer used by reader of Scroll of the Law.

National Influence

In fact God's purpose for His people went further than this. He revealed to Moses:

"You have seen what I did to the Egyptians, and how I bore you on eagles' wings and brought you to myself. Now therefore, if you will obey my voice and keep my covenant, you shall be my own possession among all peoples; for all the earth is mine, and you shall be to me a kingdom of priests and a holy nation" (Exodus 19:4-6).

Just as the Levites were to be a good influence among Israel, so the nation of Israel were to be a good influence among the nations of the world, a kingdom of priests for all people. Ideally, they were to be an example to other nations, so that the heathen around them would see the blessings that came upon a godly nation (Deuteronomy 4:6-8). This way the nations could be taught that 'ruling with God' was the way to human happiness, peace and prosperity. In this way they could fulfil an incipient realisation of being a blessing to all nations.

But this did not come to pass. Psalm 106 recounts the disastrous waywardness of the chosen people:

"They despised the pleasant land, having no faith in his promise. They murmured in their tents, and did not obey the voice of the LORD" (Psalm 106:24-25).

The failure of Israel as a nation to 'rule with God' either in their personal life or in their national life finally ended in their expulsion from the Promised Land. They failed to keep their part of the covenant with God, and lost their land inheritance.

A New Nation

God's covenant and purpose remained steadfast, even if it had been thwarted by the negative response of the chosen people. So few members of the nation responded in faith, that the prospect of conveying a blessing to all nations was out of the question. In His patience and foreknowledge God had provided for this eventuality, and intervened by sending His only begotten Son, Jesus of Nazareth, born to Mary. He was of the royal line of Judah, and legal heir to the throne of Israel (Luke 1:32).

Although his enemies thought they had ended his brief career by cruel crucifixion at the hands of the Romans, this was by no

means the end of God's purpose for His sinless Son. Because he was without personal sin, death could not hold him, and he was raised to life and immortality to await the fulfilment of his divine mission. The resurrected Jesus was the first of a new creation, the last Adam, born out of death by the power of faith. By his sacrifice he had opened up a new and living way to God, whereby men and women of faith could receive remission of sin and enter the family of faithful Abraham by adoption. Both Jews and Gentiles could embrace the Abrahamic faith by (1) faithfully believing God's Word; (2) repenting of past sins; (3) seeking forgiveness; (4) baptism as a symbol of burial with Christ and rebirth to a new life, and (5) living faithfully thereafter.

Thus a new nation of priests had been created to supplement and complete the work that Israel had failed to do. This was not based on physical descent, but on an attitude of mind. Just as there had been some of natural Israel who had a willing heart (Exodus 35:5), and had a heart filled with wisdom (Exodus 35:35), and who served the LORD with a perfect heart (1 Chronicles 28:9), and like the Psalmist had "a broken and contrite heart" (Psalm 51:17), so there were Gentiles who embraced the Hope of Israel who sought adoption into the family of those who seek to 'rule with God' in their lives, and who look for the fulfilment of the promises to Abraham in the land and in the blessing to all nations.

The New Priesthood

Just as Jesus was not of the sons of Aaron, nor of the tribe of Levi, yet filled the office of a mediator between God and man, and an intercessor for man with God, so a new generation of priests came into being. This is likened to the order of priesthood of Melchi-zedek, whose office preceded that of the Levites by many centuries. He had combined kingship with priesthood. Jesus of the royal line of Judah has a similar rôle (Hebrews 7:17), as clearly foretold by his royal ancestor David (Psalm 110:4).

"Therefore, holy brethren, who share in a heavenly call, consider Jesus, the apostle and high priest of our confession" (Hebrews 3:1).

He is the high priest of the new order of priesthood:

"Since then we have a great high priest who has passed through the heavens, Jesus, the Son of God, let us hold fast our confession" (Hebrews 4:14).

The Apostle Peter extends this conception of a new priesthood to those who have put their faith in Abraham's Messiah, "to be a holy priesthood, to offer spiritual sacrifices acceptable to God through Jesus Christ" (1 Peter 2:5). "Our confession" is the confession of our faith in the promises of God, beginning with those to Abraham and concluding with the outworking of those same promises through Abraham's Messiah, Jesus Christ. The Apostle John, to whom Jesus revealed the future, extends the identity of all who make this confession as "a kingdom, priests to his God and Father" (Revelation 1:6). This same idea is extended in the beautiful song of the redeemed:

"Worthy art thou to take the scroll and to open its seals, for thou wast slain and by thy blood didst ransom men for God from every tribe and tongue and people and nation, and hast made them a kingdom and priests to our God, and they shall reign on earth" (Revelation 5:9,10).

This is confirmed in the vision of John as he was shown the condition of the redeemed in the millennial kingdom:

"Over such the second death has no power, but they shall be priests of God and of Christ, and they shall reign with him a thousand years" (Revelation 20:6).

Thus the new priesthood will ultimately fill the office that the Levitical priesthood failed to fill. The office of priest is to represent God to man, by teaching man what he needs to know in order to become God-like, and representing man to God as his intercessor. While this is the rôle of Jesus in heaven today, there is a place for men and women of faith to share in the worldwide office of teachers, advisers and leaders in the divine way now, that they may be qualified to share in Messiah's benign government when he is established as king-priest in fulfilment of the covenant to Abraham.

ISRAEL

The popular conception of the office of a priest may be based on the current use of the word to describe clerics of the churches of Christendom. On the other hand, it might be coloured by the pictures of the priests of pagan lands and their horrific customs. From the divine point of view the office of a priest was perfectly illustrated by the behaviour of Jesus of Nazareth as he visited the towns and villages of Judea and Galilee.

First and foremost he was a teacher. Wherever he went he taught, often by means of vivid parables, sometimes by issuing challenges, and always by his exemplary way of life. Always he magnified God's Word, always he honoured his Heavenly Father. Thus he presented to his followers a perfect example of a God-like man. Surely this is the pattern for the office of a priest, to be followed by those faithful ones who aspire to be among the number who are to be made "a kingdom, priests to our God".

THE JEWISH CALENDAR

THE Jewish calendar as used today was devised by the famous scholar and rabbi Hillel II in A.D. 360.

The Year

Jewish years are counted from the assumed date of creation. However, this way of reckoning only came into use during the 10th and 11th centuries A.D. Compared with the chronology of Ussher, as used in some Bibles, the Jews would appear to have lost about 240 years. For example A.D. 1988 corresponds with the Jewish years 5748/5749.

The Bible counts years from the Exodus, or from the years of reigning kings. When the Temple was destroyed, a new chronology was started. In the modern State of Israel, suggestions have been made for a new chronology to be started from 1917, when the land was freed from the Turks, or alternatively from 1948, when the State of Israel was established.

It is usual for Jewish publications printed in English to use the dates that are commonly in use, but to refer to them as B.C.E. (before Christian era), or C.E. (common era).

The Months

The names of the months on the Jewish calendar are a reminder that for over 1,000 years there was a virile Jewish community living in Babylonia. The months bear the names that the Babylonians used. Most of the original Hebrew names have been lost except the four months named in the Bible (Abib, Ziv, Ethanim, Bul)—see chart.

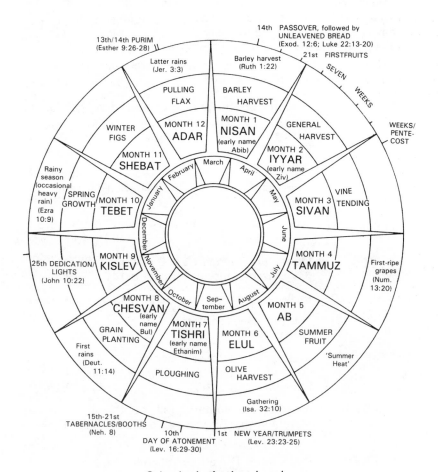

Calendar in Ancient Israel

67

Jewish months all begin with the new moon, and may be 29 or 30 days in length. Twelve lunar months total 354 days. To adjust this to the solar year of 365 days, an extra month is added at approximately three year intervals. The extra month is known as Ve-Adar, or Adar II, and is inserted to follow the month of Adar on each leap year. Thus the Jewish calendar varies from the Gregorian calendar in common use, but is so adjusted that it corresponds with it every 19 years. (By contrast, the Moslem calendar is based on the lunar year of 354 days and is not adjusted for solar time. Thus a Moslem date for a holy day moves all around the seasons in the course of time.)

The names of the months are all derived from the names used during the Babylonian captivity:

NISAN   (March-April) Beginning of sacred year (Exodus 12:2); commemorates Israel's birth as a nation. Biblical name Abib 'sprouting' (Nehemiah 2:1; Esther 3:7). *(30 days)*

'IYYAR   (April-May) means 'brightness', the freshness of spring and sunshine after rain. Biblical name Ziv (1 Kings 6:1). *(29 days)*

SIVAN   (May-June) means 'bramble month' (Esther 8:9). *(30 days)*

TAMMUZ   (June-July) named from Syrian idol, whose fast day was this month (Ezekiel 8:14). *(29 days)*

'AV or 'AB   (July-August) 'verdure' (Ezra 7:9). *(30 days)*

ELUL   (August-September) 'gleaning' (Nehemiah 6:15). *(29 days)*

TISHRI   (September-October) 'beginning'. Commencement of agricultural and civil year. Biblical name Ethanim (Ezra 3:1-7). *(30 days)*

CHESVAN   (October-November) 'fall of the leaf' (also Marchesvan). Biblical name Bul (1 Kings 6:38). *(29 days)*

CHISLEU   (November-December) 'chilly' (also Kislev) (Nehemiah 1:1; Zechariah 7:1). *(30 days)*

TEBET	(December-January) 'shoots of trees' (Esther 2:16). *(29 days)*
SHEBAT	(January-February) (Zechariah 1:7). *(30 days)*
'ADAR	(February-March) 'magnificent' (from profusion of flowers) (Ezra 6:15; Esther 3:7; 8:12). *(29 days)*
VE-ADAR	Intercalary month inserted about every three years to justify lunar year with solar year. *(30 days)*

The Days

Each Jewish day begins at sunset and lasts until the following sunset. Hence "the evening and the morning were the first day" (Genesis 1:5). The days of the week do not have names, except the seventh day which is known as Shabbat meaning 'cessation', a constant reminder of the creation work.

Jewish		*Gentile*
Yom Rishon	(Day First)	Sunday
Yom Sheni	(Day Second)	Monday
Yom Shlishi	(Day Third)	Tuesday
Yom Revi'i	(Day Fourth)	Wednesday
Yom Hamishi	(Day Fifth)	Thursday
Yom Shishi	(Day Sixth)	Friday
Shabbat	(Cessation)	Saturday

The Holy Days

The God of Israel communicated with His people whom He had created from the very first day of life. He desired His people to be aware of Him, to honour Him, to appreciate His consideration for them and to reciprocate His love for them. The Seven Holy Days in the life of Israel were ordained to be appointments for the people to meet their God—the word translated 'feast' is *moed*, which means 'appointed' (the word for a gluttonous feast was quite different)—reminding them of what their Creator had done for them and was prepared to do for them in the future. They also served as a reminder that they also had obligations to the One who had given them life and the means to sustain life.

To the holy days appointed by the LORD, other days have been added to commemorate certain events, either by rejoicing, or by fasting and mourning. Two days for rejoicing have been added during this century. Passover (Pesach), Sukkot (Tabernacles) and Hanukkah (Feast of Dedication or Lights) are week-long events, others are one or two-day events. Details are shown on the Chart of Holy Days, with a comparison of the Jewish dates and Gregorian dates.

These Holy Days were not secular holidays, but were intended to promote a happy and lasting close relationship between God and man, in particular between God and the people of Israel.

The Purpose of the Seven Holy Days

1. Shabbat (The Sabbath): The seventh day of the week set apart as a day of rest in commemoration of the completion of the creative work of the Almighty (Leviticus 23:1-3). The prophet Isaiah describes the point of view of the LORD who ordained this Holy Day:

> *"If thou call the sabbath a delight, the holy of the LORD, honourable; and shalt honour him, not doing thine own ways, nor finding thine own pleasure, nor speaking thine own words: then shalt thou delight thyself in the LORD; and I will cause thee to ride upon the high places of the earth, and feed thee with the heritage of Jacob thy father . . ."*
> (Isaiah 58:13,14). .

How thankful we should be that this pattern of each week was set by our Creator at the beginning of life upon earth. The seventh day as a day of rest is typical of the final purpose of God with faithful men and women in that He has provided a "sabbath of rest" of a thousand years following the six thousand years of man's hard labour, when Israel's Messiah shall reign over all nations in a world at peace.

Our Lord Jesus fulfilled the sabbath in his own life in that he made *every* day of his life holy to the LORD. At his return he will fulfil it finally in his millennial reign as King of kings when "all men shall know the LORD".

2. Pesach Hag ha-Matzoth (Passover; Feast of Unleavened Bread—Greek, *Pascha*): divinely ordained as Israel prepared to leave Egyptian slavery (Exodus 12:6). The people were told to slay a lamb or a kid of the first year, one without blemish, on the 14th of the month Abib (later renamed Nisan).* The blood of the lamb was to be smeared on the lintel and sideposts of the door, using a bunch of hyssop. This was to indicate to the angel whom God would send to administer the final tenth plague on Egypt, the slaying of the firstborn of both man and beast, that the household were under God's protection, being people of faith. The angel of death would 'pass over' all such houses. This event was a miracle in that it proved that the divine instructions were effective for all who had faith in them, while the faithless and Godless people of Egypt suffered the loss of their firstborn.

The unleavened bread (*matza*) was a dry food suitable for their hasty departure, but also had a deep significance. The Feast of Unleavened Bread, called 'bread of affliction' lasted until the 21st of Abib. Bread was normally made by keeping a small amount of dough from one baking to the next, which became sour. This fermentation was added to the next batch and served to lighten it in the way that yeast is used today. Just as the leaven spread rapidly through the dough, so it is a type of the contagious nature of sin (1 Corinthians 5:8).

Although the keeping of Passover as an appointed assembly for the whole nation was to be annually (Deuteronomy 16:1), there is no evidence that it was kept until Israel entered the Promised Land. As the miraculous supply of manna, that fed them in the wilderness, ended, they kept this feast using the grain of the land (Joshua 5:10). The special mention of the Passover festivals held in the reigns of Hezekiah and Josiah, suggests that its observance had been slack in previous years (2 Chronicles 30:1; 2 Kings 23:22).

In the First Century A.D., Passover was the occasion of a massive pilgrimage of Jews from all over the world to Jerusalem.

---

*The Law of Moses made provision for a late Passover to be kept four weeks after the appointed time, on the 14th of Iyyar, if for some good reason the 14th Nisan could not be observed. This was permitted in Numbers 9:9-11 and an example of how it was used occurs in 2 Chronicles 30:2-5.

Passover Meal—A Yemenite Family celebrating the Passover seder

The historian Josephus estimated that 2½ million Jews were present at the Passover of A.D. 66. Since the destruction of the Temple in A.D. 70, Jews have not offered blood sacrifices. Passover has been made into a formal celebration that has lost much of its meaning. Yet it still includes significant rites that are kept without the participants realising the typical meaning to which the New Testament draws our attention. A Jewish booklet explains that: "Culture and people have changed since the day of the Red Sea. The teaching which it conveys has not changed—that freedom is the foundation of life, and justice the condition of freedom." It is a tragedy that freedom is seen as freedom to please self, and the real lesson of dependence, reliance and faith in the One God of Israel has been lost.

A Passover meal was eaten by Jesus of Nazareth and his disciples, who with a multitude of others had made the journey specifically to keep the feast. The Passover lamb was a prophetic symbol of the Lamb of God who was to be slain for the redemption of His people from sin (symbolised by Egyptian bondage). As the Passover lambs were being slain in Jerusalem on Nisan 14, Jesus was dying on the tree, his life blood shed for the remission of sins. Thus the faultless Son of God was providing slavation for God's adopted firstborn—all who are to become heirs of the Abrahamic promises by faith.

3. Firstfruits: There were presumably no grain harvests in the wilderness of Sinai, but provision was made in the Law for a memorial thanksgiving for the firstfruits of the barley harvest to be kept each year when Israel reached the Land. This was held on the third day after Passover, during the Feast of Unleavened Bread. Even if the barley was not quite ripe, a sheaf was to be cut and offered to the LORD as a thanksgiving (Leviticus 23:10-14). Thus the feast was to be a reminder early in the year that "the LORD will provide" (Deuteronomy 26:1-11).

The prophetic type of this ordinance pointed forward to the provision that the LORD would make of a firstfruits from the dead in the person of the resurrected Lord Jesus, who himself rose from the dead on the third day after Passover. As Paul points out, he was "the firstfruits of them that slept" (1 Corinthians 15:20). On the occasion of the offering of the sample sheaf of barley, the Law made no provision for the usual sin offering, but the sheaf was to be burnt before the LORD, a prefiguring of the completeness of the sacrifice of Jesus.

Present-day Celebration of the Festival of Firstfruits: 'Hag ha-Bikkurim'

73

4. Shavuot: (Feast of weeks; Pentecost—Greek, *Pente*, 'fifty'): Fifty days after the offering of the firstfruits of the barley another harvest festival was divinely ordained for the wheat harvest (Leviticus 23:15,16). The offering this time was to be in the form of two loaves made of finely sieved flour; this time it was to be leavened and made to a precise shape and weight. These were offered as a burnt offering together with seven lambs, one bullock and two rams. The typical significance of this feast is pointed out by Paul in 1 Corinthians 15:23: "Christ the firstfruits; afterward they that are Christ's at his coming". Shavuot therefore presents a type of the completed harvest of "them that are Christ's" at the Day of Resurrection. The loaves in the type are not without leaven because none is sinless, two loaves representing Jew and Gentile, yet offered as a burnt offering because devoted to the LORD's service.

Many Jews regard Shavuot as a celebration of the giving of the Law in Sinai (Exodus 19,20). However, the record states that Israel came to Sinai in the third month after leaving Egypt, and this surely indicates that the giving of the Law could not have been only 50 days after leaving.

5. Rosh Hashanah (Jewish New Year; Feast of Trumpets): Ethanim 1 was to be kept as a sabbath, with a ceremonial blowing of trumpets all day long. It has now become the Civil New Year, just six months after the Bible New Year on Nisan 1. The original trumpets were made of silver, but were later replaced with ram's horns known as the 'shofar'. Trumpet blowing may have more significance than might appear at first. The Psalmist said:

"Sing aloud unto God our strength: make a joyful noise unto the God of Jacob. Take a psalm, and bring hither the timbrel, the pleasant harp with the psaltery. Blow up the trumpet in the new moon, in the time appointed, on our solemn feast day" (Psalm 81:1-3).

"Blessed is the people that know the joyful sound (R.V. trumpet)*: they shall walk, O LORD, in the light of thy countenance"* (Psalm 89:15).

This is the sound that is awaited by the faithful of all generations:

"For the trumpet shall sound, and the dead shall be raised incorruptible, and we shall be changed" (1 Corinthians 15:52).

The secular Jew regards this day as 'the new year of nature'. A typical New Year greeting, either by word of mouth or by a greeting card is, 'May you be inscribed for good, and be well over the fast' (the last wish being a reference to Yom Kippur in ten days' time). The religious Jew sees it as a time to look forward to the consummation of the Hope of Israel, but clouded by the heart-searching that precedes the Day of Atonement. A custom that has arisen is for the penitent Jew to go to the seaside, or a river side, recite the Tashlikh, "Thou wilt cast all their sins into the depths of the sea" (Micah 7:19) and trust that his sins will be forgiven on the Day of Atonement.

'Tashlikh' ("Thou wilt cast . . .") Ceremony, enacted at 'Rosh Hashanah', or New Year festival

6. Yom Kippur (Day of Atonement; Tishri 10): A divinely appointed day, not for feasting, but for prayer, fasting and self-affliction. Its observance is announced in Leviticus 23:27 without any obvious historical reason for the choice of this day for this purpose. However, the Hebrew term is in the plural, *Yom Kippurim*, meaning 'Day of Coverings'. This could be a significant clue as to its origin.

It has been suggested with good reason that this day is intended as a memorial of the day when the first-ever sacrifice was made by the LORD God for the sinful and ashamed Adam and Eve. Thus they were provided with literal coverings for their nakedness (one for each) (Genesis 3:21). The plurality of the coverings is also a reminder that all Adam's descendants need coverings. (See *The Christadelphian*, September 1983, p. 332, for a exposition of this subject.) The 'Day of coverings' speaks not only of man's need for forgiveness, but of the amazing willingness of the Almighty to forgive sin by providing the coverings that man is unable to provide for himself.

This understanding of the 'Day of coverings' points forward to the day when the returned Jesus will provide permanent coverings for all his faithful people, when "this mortal shall put on immortality".

"He who conquers shall be clad thus in white garments, and I will not blot his name out of the book of life" (Revelation 3:5).

Jewish tradition confirms the association of this day with the day that Adam and Even had their nakedness covered. The religious Jew may even precede this day with a rigorous self-examination, and confession of sins for the previous week, but this was not ordained by God. The practice of the modern religious Jew of fasting from food and drink for 24 hours (from sunset to sunset) is not a requirement of the divine ordinance, but a product of rabbinical interpretation—"a burden grievous to be borne" of man's invention.

7. *Sukkot* (The Feast of Booths, or Tabernacles; Tishri 15-21): A divinely ordained major feast at the time of the year when all the harvests of grain and fruit had been gathered in (Leviticus 23:34-43). It was designed as a joyous occasion of thanksgiving to the LORD for all His bounty through the year. Of seven days' duration while the people lived in booths made of branches of trees, it was a reminder of the temporary nature of their housing in the wilderness journey.

It is doubtful whether this feast was kept before the Land was reached, and it does not appear to have been kept regularly after Joshua's time. In Nehemiah's time this festival was observed after a long time of neglect (Nehemiah 8:17). As the third harvest festival of the year it symbolised God's purpose finalised at the end of the millennial reign of our Lord. The dwelling in booths is a reminder that although God provides our daily food from the bounty of the earth, this life is not our final dwelling, but that like Abraham we should be looking for "a city that has foundations" (Hebrews 11:10).

Today, religious Jews tend to make little temporary 'summer houses' of plywood, or anything available. Sprigs of willow are nowadays flown from Israel for the occasion, each branch sealed in a plastic bag. In the first century, the feast had already been formalised and commercialised. Jesus visited Jerusalem for this feast as recorded in John 7, and his reference to "living waters" may have referred to a custom of drawing water from the Pool of Siloam to take up the hill to the Temple for various ceremonies.

Zechariah prophesies that this feast will be kept by all nations in the restored Kingdom of God (Zechariah 14:16). It will be as a sequel of the Messianic influence in that millennial age that God's great harvest of faithful men and women will be gathered in, when the final symbolism of this feast will be realised. It has been suggested that the various branches used in making the booths indicate the symbolism of the feast — palms for victory, olive branches for peace, pines for beauty, willow for security and myrtle for divine generosity.

This is the third of the major festivals appointed by God, and the seventh of the Holy Days — six feasts and one fast.

FEASTS AND FASTS OF ISRAEL AT A GLANCE

Nisan	14	Fast of the Firstborn (in memory of Egypt's firstborn)
	14	Feast of Passover (Pesach) (deliverance from Egypt)
	15-21	Feast of Unleavened Bread
	17	Feast of Firstfruits of Barley
	27	Fast of Yom ha-Sho'ah (in memory of the Holocaust)
Iyyar	5	Yom ha-Atzma'ut (Israel Independence Day, May 14)
	18	Lag be-Omer (The Counting of the Omer) (The Scholars' Feast)

Sivan	6	Shavuot (Feast of Weeks, or Pentecost)
Tammuz	17	Fast of Tammuz: in memory of (1) Romans breaching of Jerusalem walls; (2) Moses breaking the Tablets of the Law; (3) Cessation of daily sacrifices (Zechariah 8:19)
Ab	9	Fast of Ab: in memory of (1) Destruction of First Temple, 586 B.C. and of Second Temple, A.D. 70; (2) End of Bar Kochba's Revolt, A.D. 135; (3) Expulsion of Jews from Spain, A.D. 1492 (Zechariah 8:19)
Tishri	1-2	Feast of New Year, Rosh Hashanah, Feast of Trumpets
	3	Fast of Gedaliah (Jeremiah 41:1-3; Zechariah 8:19)
	10	Yom Kippur (Day of Coverings, or Atonement) (Leviticus 23:23)
	15-21	Feast of Booths (Sukkot)
	21	Hoshana Rabba
Kislev	25	Hanukkah (Feast of Dedication, or Festival of Lights)
Tebet	10	Fast of Tebet (Beginning of Nebuchadnezzar's Siege) (in memory of all unknown victims) (Zechariah 8:19)
Shebat	15	Tu bi-Shebat (Festival for New Year of the Trees)
Adar	13	Fast of Esther (Esther 4:16)
	14-15	Purim (Festival of Deliverance from Haman's Plot) (Esther 4:11-17)

Traditional Jewish Holy Days

To the divinely appointed feasts and fast, over the centuries the Jews have seen fit to add traditions that have survived the dispersion and are still on their calendar.

Rosh Chodesh: The Day of the New Moon, the first day of each month which begins with the appearance of the first faint sliver of the new moon. This is heralded by the sounding of the shofar. The Biblical New Year begins with Nisan 1, and all the annual Holy Days are calculated from this date (Exodus 12:2).

Fast of the Firstborn: A tradition that is held prior to the Passover in memory of the slaying of the firstborn of Egypt (Exodus 12:29). Not divinely ordained, but observed only by some firstborn Jews after reaching maturity. The father fasts for young children.

Yom ha-Atzma'ut: Israel Independence Day. Held on Iyyar 5 to commemorate the Declaration of Independence made on May 14, 1948 when Israel became an independent state. A time of national rejoicing, when the nation takes pride in its own strength.

Lag be-Omer: Held on Iyyar 18, 33 days after the second day of Passover. The tradition is that it celebrates a short-lived victory over the Roman forces under Hadrian by Bar Kochba in A.D. 132. Others have suggested that it celebrates the first day when manna fell in the wilderness. In spite of the uncertainty, it is celebrated with joy.

Fast of Tammuz: Held on Tammuz 17, this day commemorates the sad day when the walls of Jerusalem were breached by Nebuchadnezzar about six months after he had begun the siege. Special synagogue readings are taken from Exodus 32:11-14 and 34:1-10; Isaiah 55:6—56:8.

Tisha be-Ab: The Fast of Ab. Another traditional day in memory of the destruction of the Temple of Solomon by Nebuchadnezzar, and the Temple of Herod by the Romans, both events being at about the same time of the year. Held on Ab 9.

Fast of Gedaliah: Another fast day that dates back centuries to the assassination of Gedaliah by Ishmael as recorded in Jeremiah 41:2. By tradition this is dated on Tishri 3.

Simchat Torah: The Rejoicing of the Law. On the day following Sukkot, Tishri 22, the rota of Scripture readings in the synagogue is completed and is begun anew, an occasion for rejoicing.

Hanukkah or Channukah: The Festival of Dedication, or Festival of Lights. Held on Kislev 25, this tradition is in memory of the re-dedication of the Temple in 164 B.C. after it had been desecrated by the Greek-Syrian tyrant Antiochus Epiphanes.

The festival lasts eight days, and an eight branched lampstand is used (*menorah*). John 10:22 is a definite reference to this feast, and it may be that Jesus' description of himself as the light of the world (John 8:12) was also on the occasion of this feast.

Tebet 10: A fast day to commemorate the beginning of the siege of Jerusalem by Nebuchadnezzar.

Tu bi-Shebat: The New Year of Trees held on Shebat 15 is a recently devised celebration of the planting in Israel of many millions of trees. This has been a salient feature of the re-occupation of the Promised Land and a reversal of the spoiling of the Land over the centuries by its oppressors. The city of Jerusalem is now completely surrounded by forests.

Fast of Esther: This traditionally commemorates Esther's fast as recorded in Esther 4:16 and is held on Adar 13.

Purim: Festival of Hadassah. Two days of celebration, Adar 14 and 15, in memory of the deliverance of the Jews in Persia from the plot of Haman, by the bravery of Esther (Hadassah) (Esther 9:19).

NOTES

The Four Fasts of Tammuz, Ab, Gedaliah and Tebet 10 were already being kept by the Jews in captivity in the time of Zechariah (Zechariah 8:19). The commemoration of disasters in this way did not have the divine approval.

Wedding Fasts: It is traditional for Bride and Groom to fast on their wedding day—not very popular with modern Jews.

Sabbath: If a fast day falls on Sabbath, it is observed next day.

HOLY DAYS	1988	1989	1990	1991	1992	1993	1994	1995	1996
Pesach (Passover), Nisan 15	Apr. 2	Apr. 20	Apr. 10	Mar. 30	Apr. 18	Apr. 6	Mar. 27	Apr. 15	Apr. 4
Yom ha-Atzma'ut (Independence), Iyyar 5	Apr. 22	May 10	Apr. 20	Apr. 19	May 8	Apr. 26	Apr. 16	May 5	Apr. 24
Lag be-Omer, Iyyar 18	May 5	May 23	May 13	May 2	May 21	May 9	Apr. 29	May 18	May 7
Shavuot (Pentecost), Sivan 6	May 22	June 9	May 30	May 19	June 7	May 26	May 16	June 4	May 24
Tisha be-Ab, Ab 9	July 24	Aug. 10	July 31	July 21	Aug. 9	July 27	July 17	Aug. 6	July 25
Rosh Hashanah (New Year), Tishri 1	Sep. 12	Sep. 30	Sep. 20	Sep. 9	Sep. 28	Sep. 16	Sep. 6	Sep. 25	Sep. 14
Yom Kippur (Atonement), Tishri 10	Sep. 21	Oct. 9	Sep. 29	Sep. 18	Oct. 7	Sep. 25	Sep. 15	Oct. 4	Sep. 23
Sukkot (Tabernacles), Tishri 15-22	Sep. 26	Oct. 14	Oct. 4	Sep. 23	Oct. 12	Sep. 30	Sep. 20	Oct. 9	Sep. 28
Simchat Torah, Tishri 23	Oct. 4	Oct. 22	Oct. 12	Oct. 1	Oct. 20	Oct. 8	Sep. 28	Oct. 17	Oct. 6
Hanukkah (Dedication), Kislev 25 for 8 days	Dec. 4	Dec. 23	Dec. 12	Dec. 2	Dec. 20	Dec. 9	Nov. 28	Dec. 18	Dec. 6
New Year for Trees, Shebat 15	Feb. 3	Jan. 21	Feb. 10	Jan. 30	Jan. 20	Feb. 6	Jan. 27	Jan. 16	Feb. 5
Purim (Feast of Esther), Adar 14	Mar. 2		Mar. 10	Feb. 27		Mar. 7	Feb. 25		Mar. 5
Purim (on leap years), Ve-Adar 14		Mar. 21			Mar. 19			Mar. 16	

PRINCIPAL JEWISH HOLY DAYS ON GREGORIAN CALENDAR

Note: Above dates apply to Feast Days in the Diaspora, hence discrepancies with dates on page 78

3

THE JEWISH DISPERSIONS

"Who gave up Jacob to the spoiler, and Israel to the robbers? Was it not the LORD, against whom we have sinned, in whose ways they would not walk, and whose law they would not obey?" (Isaiah 42:24).

B Y any reckoning, 2,500 years of dispersion, persecution, misery and outrage is a long, long time. The wonder of it is that over all those centuries the identity of the people of Israel has not been lost. Many have tried hard to forget who they are and seek assimilation with the nations around, thinking that this would shake off their persecutors. Some nations have tried to assimilate the Jews, in which case they have maintained their separateness. Thus, in whatever part of the dispersion, they are still the Jews, the people of Israel, the people of God's displeasure *and* the people of God's promises.

The Lost Tribes
The stories about the 'lost ten tribes' are a fiction that has been used at various times to assert that (1) the Japanese, (2) the Maoris, (3) the Red Indians, or (4) the British constitute some of the tribes of Israel that cannot be accounted for. There is no basis for any of these fantasies. However, there does seem to be one small group that were lost by assimilation. At an early time, a few Jews went to China, perhaps in the silk trade, maintained their separateness for centuries but have now virtually vanished.

There is evidence that groups of traders were planted as colonies in Egypt, Ethiopia, Yemen and probably India as early as the time of the kings David and Solomon. Some of these became permanently separated from their nation, yet kept their identity and their faith based on the copy of the Law (Torah) which they had taken with them. Their dispersion was voluntary and was an indication of ancient Israel's far flung commerce.

The First Mass Dispersion

The first national mass dispersion was the result of divine anger with the rebellious and Godless northern ten tribes of Israel. Under Jeroboam and subsequent leaders they had been severed from the appointed centre for divine worship at Jerusalem for political reasons. This separation inevitably resulted in apostasy and eventually paganism. In spite of the warnings of God's prophets about the consequences of their infidelity, very few took heed. The kings and people were given about 200 years to change their ways, but to no effect.

The human instrument of divine wrath was the cruel army of the Assyrian Empire. One of their most arrogant and inhuman kings was described after his death in a satyrical poem by the prophet Isaiah as "the man that made the earth to tremble, that did shake kingdoms; that made the world as a wilderness, and destroyed the cities thereof; that opened not the house of his prisoners" (14:16,17). It is almost certain that this dread king can be identified as Tiglath-pileser of Assyria (verse 25), also named Pul of Babylon (verse 4) who died the same year that king Ahaz died (verse 28). This man was the only king of both Assyria and Babylon (1 Chronicles 5:26).

Jehu prostrated before Assyrian Monarch Shalmanezer III (Black Obelisk in British Museum): The only known portrait of a Jewish king

The Assyrian treatment of their captives was to take them away and dump them in a far-off land in order to break their spirit. Thus Israel of the ten tribes was deported to places from which they had

83

no way of returning to their homes. This took place during the 7th century B.C., and for the majority of their descendants there has not yet been any opportunity to return. It is noteworthy that a similar ruthless and heartless way of dealing with opponents has been used by the 'latter day Assyrians', who consign them to the frozen wastes of Siberia.

The Second Dispersion

For over a century after Israel's captivity, the southern kingdom of Judah remained independent. On one occasion the Assyrian menace was thwarted by the faith of good king Hezekiah. On his behalf, the all-powerful God of Israel intervened by sending His angel to decimate the Assyrian army, probably by plague. In course of time that threat was replaced by another, the Babylonian. Judah had not taken heed to the terrible lesson of Israel's infidelity. The obscene idols of the heathen were erected in Jerusalem. The faith shown by Hezekiah was forgotten. The kings were untrustworthy puppets of the Babylonians. As if to give time for a change of heart, the Babylonian threat was applied a little at a time. They took captives in a series of deportations before finally sacking Jerusalem.

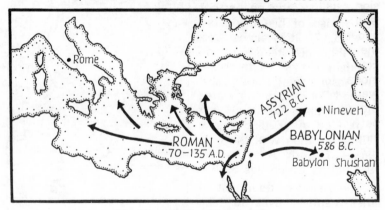

The Three Major Dispersions

The Babylonians were a powerful and relentless foe, but they were not as fiendishly cruel as their predecessors, the Assyrians. Their policy was to take only captives who could be used profitably. They even trained them for the service of their new masters. Thus it came about that Daniel and his fellow captives were cared for and given instruction with a view to them taking official duties. Daniel, although still a captive, was soon elevated to a position of great responsibility, as vizier of the province of Babylon (Daniel 2:48).

Partial Restoration

Judah's captivity in Babylon was relieved 70 years after the first group of exiles had been taken away. This was the result of the fall of the city of Babylon, which was taken in one night by the forces of the Medes and Persians. The attitude of the new Persian overlords to the captives was to make allies of them, to repatriate them and make them into 'buffer states' around the empire. Thus it came to pass that thousands of the people of Judah were sent back home by royal decree to rebuild Jerusalem and the Temple. The royal coffers even financed the project. This partial restoration under the leadership of Ezra was in fulfilment of the divine purpose that had been spoken by the prophet who had seen the dispersion (Jeremiah 25:11).

There were still many thousands in far-off lands. Their dispersion was to last for many long centuries. The Jews back in the land were not free men for long. The comparative freedom under the Persians gave way to a new and cruel dominance by the Greek successors of Alexander the Great. The Greek Empire was divided between rival generals who became the monarchs of each part. To the north of Israel, governing Syria, were the Seleucids — men with a cruel streak in their nature. To the south, governing Egypt, were the Ptolemies. Judea was between the two great powers who each vied for control of the land-bridge between them. At one time Ptolemy compelled 30,000 Jews to settle on his borders as a first line of defence. At other times the Seleucids sought to quell the Jews by desecrating the Temple.

Such treatment roused a brave family of Jews to resist this kind of oppression. Known as the Maccabees, or Hasmoneans, they did succeed in attaining a measure of autonomy for a century. Then the Romans came on the scene and found that they had taken on the control of an uncooperative people. To maintain control they had to keep Judea more heavily occupied with their legions than any other of their frontier provinces. Thus, at the beginning of the First Century A.D. Judea was governed by a half-Jew, Herod, appointed by Rome, was heavily patrolled by Roman troops, and was seething with discontent. It was during a time of great national unrest that a Jewish infant was born, who was to change the world.

Jews of the Roman Empire

The record in Acts 2:8-11 reveals that the Jews were widely dispersed in the Roman Empire by that time. They had come to Jerusalem to keep the appointed assembly from all points of the compass. They had adopted the language of the peoples among whom they lived. They had the means to make the tedious journey across land or sea to the centre of their hopes. In the early days of the Roman Empire, Jews were favoured because of their business acumen. Jewish communities in Roman cities were allowed to build synagogues and to talk about their faith. The Hebrew Holy Scriptures in both Hebrew and in Greek were widespread.

The Jews of the Roman Empire were mainly engaged in trade, for every Jewish boy had to learn a practical skill, even if he was intending to enter a profession, or become a rabbi — for example, Saul of Tarsus (the apostle Paul). Although he was a scholar and a Pharisee, he had learned the art of a tentmaker. The Jews within the Roman Empire maintained close ties with those living beyond its boundaries, especially those living in Babylonia, where great numbers still lived. The authority of the Palestinian Jewish sages was recognised by the exiles in Babylonia, even though a national frontier and many miles of desert divided them. Thus the Jews became a sort of state within the State, and could not be ignored by Rome. Indeed special legislation was passed in their favour.

The Third Dispersion

The Gospel record reveals that an uneasy relationship had developed between Rome and the Jews in Judea. By A.D. 66 Jewish opposition reached new heights and Rome was determined to put an end to the problem for all time. The Jews had not drifted into paganism this time, but were strongly influenced by Greek thought and philosophy. Judaism had

10. **The Wilderness of Zin:** "... a land whose stones are iron, and out of whose hills you can dig copper" (Deuteronomy 8:9)

11. South-eastern Corner of the Walls of Jerusalem—showing Stones of Herod's Time: "It has taken forty-six years to build this temple . . ." (John 2:20)

12. **Al Aksa Mosque, part of the desecration within the area of the Temple Mount:** "When ye therefore shall see the abomination of desolation . . . stand in the holy place . . ." (Matthew 24:15)

13. Market Scene in Jerusalem: "Let not the buyer rejoice, nor the seller mourn, for wrath is upon all" (Ezekiel 7:12)

become debased into a mere formality. Many of its prac-
titioners, such as the Pharisees, were happy to cooperate
with the Roman administration, since it was to their personal
advantage. The frustrations of the people were whipped up by
the Zealots who fondly imagined that they could throw off the
yoke of Rome.

By A.D. 66 the mood was at fever heat. Rome stepped in
with augmented forces. After numerous battles, eventually the
city of Jerusalem was surrounded. Factions among the Jews
within the city increased the misery. Those who escaped found
no mercy. Thousands were crucified outside the walls. Others
were split open in case they had swallowed their gold before
they escaped.

'Iudaea Capta' — Vespasian's Medal
celebrating the Destruction of Jerusalem

All the horrors told in such grim detail in Deuteronomy 28
came to pass. Why did this sorry state of things develop so
dramatically? For the reasons given in the same chapter, the
same reasons that brought about the former dispersions.
Although the people of Israel had a form of Godliness and made
a show of religion, they did not live as they professed. This time
it was not idols of wood or stone, but idolatry of pride and
selfishness. Once again they killed God's messengers who
called upon them to repent and change their way of living. Thus
came to pass the third dispersion by Rome. Jerusalem and its
Temple were destroyed again, thousands killed and the captives sold into slavery. This was 40 years after the death of
Jesus, just one generation later in A.D. 70.

Among the hills and caves some of the Jews had hidden, and
over the next sixty years a renewed resistance movement

Detail from the Arch of Titus in Rome, celebrating his Victory over the Jews in A.D. 70

developed. This underground movement even minted a coinage of its own. The Zealots were well trained and organised, but were not obvious as legions of soldiers would have been. Eventually the Romans decided that it was time to step in again and finally settle their Jewish problem. The forces of the Jewish leader, Bar Kochba, were finally defeated, their last stand being at Bethar. This last war against the Jews by the emperor Hadrian was rounded off by Hadrian's Edict, in which it was forbidden for any Jew to live in or around Jerusalem. This was in A.D. 135, just over a century after the death of Jesus.

The Emperor Hadrian, who finally broke the Jewish Resistance in A.D. 135. The man who sought to erase Jerusalem from the face of the earth is now portrayed in the Israel Museum in Jerusalem!

Aelia Capitolina

Not only were Jews forbidden to live in their Holy City, but the name of the new Roman city built on the same site was changed to Aelia Capitolina, and the province of Judea was re-named Palestina. This was in an attempt to blot out all memory of the Jewish occupation of the land. Yet a few still remained, mainly in the hills of Galilee. One remote village in those hills still claims to have been inhabited from that time to the present without a break, by a family of people all named Cohen.

These times and these events were carefully chronicled by that extraordinary man Flavius Josephus (his real name was Yosef ben Mattityahu ha-Cohen), who had been a Jewish leader fighting the Romans. When taken prisoner he was spared because of a bold prophecy that he made, which happened to come true. The Romans commissioned him to be their historian of Jewish affairs. His *Antiquities* and *The Jewish War* are very extensive records that throw light on the final dispersion of his nation in gruesome detail. It is possible that he may have indulged in a measure of exaggeration, but his main history is reliable. It is noteworthy that he makes a brief reference to the existence of Jesus Christ.

Commenting on the tragedy of this nation, the historian A. J. Toynbee wrote: "The concept of being God's chosen people resulted in a false self-confidence which led to their ruin." He called this the "idolization of an ephemeral self" (*A Study of History*, p. 310).

The Roman Diaspora

The Romans replaced the Jews of Judea with Syrians and Arabs. But the hill country of Galilee recovered from Hadrian's 'final solution' and very soon normal living and trading resumed. This area saw the Jewish way of life continue peaceably for the next two centuries. The tens of thousands of Jews dispersed far and wide in the Roman domains were mainly engaged in trade. They were officially recognised by the authorities as being a different people, and they were exempted from military service.

At the same time there was within the Empire a revaluation of spiritual and religious values by thoughtful people, who came to appreciate the Jewish worship of One God who heard prayer and offered a hope beyond death. The contrast with the Roman and Greek pantheon of crude gods who had all the human weaknesses and lusts was so great that many people became attached in a loose way to the Jews and are known to us as the 'God-fearers'. There is some evidence that they kept the Jewish sabbath and food laws. They were supporters of the Jews at the time when the first Christian missionary journeys were being undertaken, but appeared to be more receptive of the Gospel message than the Jews. Thus the dispersion of the Jews indirectly aided the spread of Christian teaching (see Acts 10:35; 13:16,26,43; *Encyclopaedia Judaica* (1971), Vol. 10, p. 55; Josephus, *The Jewish War*, 7.45, and *Antiquities*, 14.110).

In later years, when the Roman emperors sought to find a scapegoat for their own misfortunes, Jews, God-fearers and Christians were all bunched together for persecution. Christians were regarded as a sect of the Jews and were included in the anti-semitism that began to develop. Josephus wrote in his *Against Apion*, ''Some people have entrusted the supreme political power to monarchies, others to oligarchies, yet others to the masses. Our lawgiver, however, gave his constitution what may be called a 'theocracy', placing all sovereignty and authority in the hands of God'' (2.16).

The Wider Dispersion

There were many Jews beyond the borders of the Roman Empire. From Assyria they had moved north into the Caucasus and the steppes of Russia. For several centuries Judaism was the adopted faith of the Khazars, a nomad Tartar people who befriended Jews and adopted Jewish ways. Marco Polo, the Venetian explorer of the 14th century, commented on Jewish commercial activities in China. Others were in the oriental spice trade; long before Europeans ventured so far, Jewish traders were involved in the exchange of goods between east and west.

The dispersed people did not follow Abraham's nomadic way of life but, if possible, sought a settled city life. Yet, seldom could they settle for long; persecution forced them to move on. As God had foretold: ''There shall be no rest for the sole of your foot'' (Deuteronomy 28:65). This divine curse became depicted in the legend of 'The Wandering Jew'. The nations saw him as this mythical, tragic figure; one who trudged the byways of Europe without respite, chased from one place to the next. In 1916, *The Jewish World* related the case of a Russian Jew, Nathan Cohen, who migrated to Brazil. He was refused permission to land, and was then shunted back and forth between various American ports, none being willing to accept him. After wandering on the high seas for some 40,000 miles he was, at last, allowed to land at New York, where he died within hours.

Second Class Citizens

In countries where they were allowed to stay, almost without exception measures were taken against them. This might begin by denying the normal rights of citizenship, barring them from official positions, boycotting their shops, burning their books, closing schools to their children, looting their goods, enforcing the wearing of a distinctive mark on their clothing, or even burning their synagogues. Such harassment was worse in Christian countries than in Moslem lands. In Europe they were often forced to live in a *ghetto*, a specified area of the city. The first of these was in Venice—hence the Italian name for a Jewish enclave. This practice spread all over Europe. In some instances it became a prison; at the same time it could be a fortress. Thus their enemies ensured that they were a people that lived alone.

Life was not so restricted in Moslem lands: even though the Jews were regarded as despised 'cousins', they were not hated as were Christians. When the Moors overran Spain, the Jews in Spain had a golden age, wielded considerable political and financial power and produced a number of great scholars. During this period they developed a distinctive culture which spread among Jews in other Moslem Arab countries. They became known as Sephardim (the Jewish name for Spanish).

When eventually Christian armies drove out the Moors, the Jews were subjected to the Spanish Inquisition and either driven out, murdered or offered conversion. Some who were in high office chose conversion and became known as Marranos ('pigs'). For those who fled, Palestine and Turkey were the favoured destinations, where their skills were welcome.

Notable Exceptions

In spite of the disadvantages of being a Jew, there were some remarkable success stories from time to time. There were several notable physicians: perhaps the best known was Maimonides, who began life in Spain and eventually became court physician to Saladin in Cairo. It is claimed that the first man to step ashore in America was a Jew who accompanied Christopher Columbus. In almost every century some have managed to amass sufficient wealth, or to manage other people's wealth, so that they could become lenders of money. The invasion of Britain in 1066 by William of Normandy was financed by Jewish usurers. European monarchs seem to have been very dependent on Jews to organise their finances, mint their money, or make them loans.

During the last century great Jewish banking houses were established, the most notable being the House of Rothschild based on five cities in Europe. Also during the past century, Jews have risen to high rank in both European and American politics. With the increase in scientific knowledge, Jews have been foremost in almost every field of science. Albert Einstein comes to mind at once. Many names in the world of music are renowned—Mendelssohn, Strauss, Solomon, Irving Berlin and Eddie Cantor, to list but a few in varied spheres. Among outstanding political figures, Karl Marx, Trotsky and Benjamin Disraeli had tremendous influence over the lives of millions. The list of Jews of outstanding ability could fill pages.

In two countries it has not been a crime to be a Jew: in Holland and the United States of America. Here the natural abilities of the race have been permitted to develop and encouraged, with consequent benefit to these nations. Indeed, it is the success of the Jews in these lands that has caused them to hesitate to return to their homeland. The situation (as these words are being written) would seem to be that they have only returned to the land when forced to by circumstance. Millions in the diaspora, living in comfort, hesitate to share the hardships of beleaguered Israel, but are ready and willing to provide financial support for those who have made the move. Thus the commercial riches of the many are helping to provide for the penury of the few. This seems to be essential for the time being.

Effects of Dispersion

As a result of the three major dispersions—Assyrian, Babylonian and Roman—and the frequent movements resulting from persecution, the Jews have been scattered into all corners of the earth. There was no longer any unity of language, of customs, of attitudes or even of appearances. This diversity was evident before the third exile had begun. At that memorable Pentecost at Jerusalem recorded in Acts 2, the visiting Jews expressed their amazement at the gift of tongues given to the apostles: "How is it that we hear, each of us in his own native language?" (verse 8). This diversity has been even more evident among those who have returned during the past century. Even in the Promised Land, the language groups have tended to keep together; add to this the differences in colour and culture, and one has today a much greater problem in unifying the nation.

Unifying Influences

A reverence for the Torah, whether or not they professed religion, has been one major unifying influence. In every land of the dispersion, the scroll of the Torah has been revered, even if not obeyed. The Jews have always had a fiercely independent spirit, and a craving to be able to exercise it in the Land of their Fathers. At the back of their minds has been the Messianic hope, although many are not clear whether to believe in a personal Messiah, or a national one.

The great unifying influence of this century has been the restoration of the Hebrew language. From being a scarcely used 'tongue of the prophets', only for prayer and reading the Holy Scriptures, it has now become the daily language of several millions, having been adapted and enlarged to meet today's needs. Thus these unifying influences are still keeping the Jews separate, "not reckoned among the nations" (Numbers 23:9).

The Jews have always cherished the thought of being a chosen people and a people that dwells alone, yet have wanted to live in the style of other nations. This tendency first came to light in the days of Samuel, when they wanted a king to lead them into battle, having forgotten that whenever God had led them into battle they had won.

Ashkenazim and Sephardim

Not least of the problems of unification in recent times has been the two very different cultures in which the diaspora have lived

93

The Pale—Area of Russia to which Jews were supposed to be restricted

for centuries. Those living in the lands of Christendom, mainly in Germany, Poland and Russia, are known as the Ashkenazim (Hebrew meaning 'German'). Their outlook on life has been conditioned by the violent manner of their repression. They have tended to become subservient, law abiding and rather negative in outlook. The Zionist movement began in people of this background. They sincerely wished for their return to the land to be legal and peaceful. They were never aggressive, but were prepared to defend themselves and their property.

The Sephardim (Hebrew meaning 'Spanish') mainly came from Moslem countries, including Spain, which was ruled by the Moslem Moors for centuries. Their attitude to life has been influenced by the Arab attitude to them. They learned that they had to stick up for themselves, even to be aggressive at times. Their outlook was more positive. They saw Arab acquisitiveness as something to be resisted, and at times they would take the initiative to forestall aggression.

The first refugees to return to Palestine were all from the European background, the Ashkenazim. It was they who established the State of Israel. Zionism was initiated by them. But when the State was established and Arab fury knew no bounds, a torrent of the Sephardim flooded in, ejected from the surrounding Moslem lands. They soon became the majority in

Israel with a resultant change in the policy of the government. The humble spirit of the early settlers gave way to the more assertive spirit of the newcomers. As the Arab opposition grew, so did the determination of the Jews to resist aggression and defend their hard-won land.

Perhaps this description of the two cultural backgrounds is over-simplified, but the basic difference in outlook has to be taken into account when noting the changes in policy since statehood.

The Land that was Desolate

We have looked at the story of the people very briefly. The story of the land is also a sad one. Going back to Roman times, Judea was under the rule of Rome for 677 years, and was a neglected land after the dispersion. As Christendom spread, there was some interest in Jerusalem as a place of pilgrimage for both Jew and Christian. In the 4th Century, the Roman emperor Julian (the apostate), wanted to prove that the Bible was false and re-establish paganism. He ordered a temple to be built at Jerusalem, knowing that it was not the time that the Bible said one would be built. His men began to build but an earthquake destroyed their work and the plan was abandoned in A.D. 363. Julian died while making war with Persia.

For the next 447 years the Arabs had control of the land and city. Although the Koran says: "Make war upon those who have been given scripture . . . until they pay the tribute readily", nevertheless a few Jews did live there as a despised people. The situation was to change dramatically when the Crusaders from Europe drove out the Arab Moslems and set up the Kingdom of Jerusalem for 192 years. They were merciless to the Jews and slaughtered them, as they had done as they marched through Europe to liberate the Holy Places. Christian shrines and places of pilgrimage multiplied without much regard to the authenticity of the site.

Eventually the Mamelukes from Egypt ejected the Crusaders, and during the two centuries of their rule, it again became a place of refuge for Jews. In the meantime Jerusalem had been turned into a Moslem shrine, the Dome of the Rock had been built on the Temple Mount and Jewish access to the site of their Temple was restricted.

ISRAEL

The Turks

The Ottoman Turks were the next on the scene, ruling the Holy Land for four long centuries. Sometimes, at the whim of the Sultan, the Jews were ill-treated. At other times they welcomed Jewish refugees from other lands. The Holy Land was regarded as a useless part of the province of Syria. The few Jews living there were to be found in four 'holy' cities: Safed and Tiberias in the north, and Hebron and Jerusalem in the south. These were religious Jews who did not work for a living but devoted themselves to studying the Torah. They only survived by the generosity of their brethren in the diaspora who contributed to a fund for their support called the 'Haluka'.

As the Turkish Empire was declining, two rival European powers were fearful of Russia's designs on the Middle East. Both Britain and France were competing for control of the area. Napoleon took Egypt from Turkey and advanced into Palestine. Britain and Turkey made a strange alliance to oppose him and defeated the French forces at Akko (Acre) in 1799. Shortly afterwards Britain took Egypt, a significant move that eventually led to the British occupation of Palestine over a century later. Although the French had commercial interests in Palestine, the railway and chemical works, it was evidently not in God's purpose for them to remain.

No Longer Desolate

Towards the end of the 19th century, a few hard-working refugees settled in the land. In the diaspora Jews had not been farmers, but these pioneers got to work on the soil of their Promised Land. This caused some of the religious Jews to take up the challenge, and a small colony was formed on the Golan. This was one of the first to receive financial help from Christadelphian funds (see Chapter 11 for more on this theme).

Eventually it took World War I to prepare the land for the mass return of the people, by eliminating the Turkish presence. The giving of the Mandate to Britain opened up the land by giving it an administration which was at first favourable to the idea of a Jewish national home. A groundwork of law and order was firmly established, under which agriculture, industry and education rapidly developed. But the numbers of Jews permitted to return was strictly limited owing to Arab pressure and envy. It took World War II to prepare the people for the land by forcing thousands out of the countries of their dispersion. With eventual independence, the thousands became millions. And so it came to pass that, as Isaiah had prophesied 2,500 years before: "Your land shall no more be termed Desolate" (Isaiah 62:4).

The Diaspora Today

As this is being written, two-thirds of the known world population of Jews are not living in their land. Millions still live in Russia, and even more in the United States of America. There may also be many others whose roots are in Israel. An organisation known as Amishav is dedicated to bringing back the scattered remnants of the nation. They claim that there may be 21 million people in the world, who are not known as Jews, but whose roots are Jewish. There is uncertainty about the details of their genealogy, yet it is notable that many believe in the One God, keep laws similar to the Torah, and consider themselves to have descended from Abraham.

Among these, perhaps the most numerous are the Pathans of Pakistan and Afghanistan, the Shinlung of Burma and the Chiangmin of the Chinese-Tibetan border. There are unknown numbers of the Spanish Marranos in Central and Southern America. These were Jews who 'converted' under the pressures of the Spanish Inquisition, but still retained features of their Jewishness. The 30,000 Chuetas of Majorca may have had a similar origin. Thus the world total population of people of Jewish origin may be double the number of known Jews. They may be numbered among the friends of Israel, whether they return to the land or await the call of their Messiah. There could be some surprises when the facts come to light!

PERIODS OF MAJOR PERSECUTION
(Approximate dates)

Egyptian	1500−1470 B.C.	Crusades	1096−1271
Assyrian	850−722 B.C.	Spanish	1478−1820
Babylonian	586−536 B.C.	Poland	1648
Greek	223−165 B.C.	Russia	1871−1906
Roman	66 B.C.−A.D. 135	Germany	1936−1946

4

ZIONISM AND ALIYAH

FOR centuries Jewry had been scattered, battered, dispirited and dispersed across the continents. Now and again a few Jews had made their way to Palestine for various reasons. The Spanish Rabbi Moshe ben Nahman encouraged Jewish settlement in the land. Many years after his time, the Spanish Inquisition drove some to go to the land of their fathers. From time to time a number of self-proclaimed Messiahs arose and subsided. But one of these did raise hopes in the 17th century. A Jew of Smyrna, Sabbatai Zevi, made the claim so convincingly that many Jews followed him. His fame spread far and wide, even to Britain. In Pepys' diary for 1666 we read: "I am told for certain . . . of a Jew in town, that in the name of the rest do offer to give any man £10 to be paid £100 if a certain person now in Smyrna be within these two years crowned . . . as king of the world, and that this man is the true Messiah." However, to the chagrin of his followers, Zevi was converted to Islam and died ten years later.

The Messianic Hope

Many of these false Messiahs had plans to lead the scattered Jews back to Jerusalem. The ideal of the Promised Land for the Chosen People never really died. At some time it was encapsulated in a prayer which included the words: "I believe with faith whole and entire in the coming of the Messiah, and even though he may delay, I shall nevertheless await his coming every day." The Jews, although homeless, alone among the nations had an understanding of what it means to have a purpose in life. This was consciously based upon the covenant to Abraham, Isaac and Jacob, the fathers of the race. Considering that the Jews had not had a sovereign state since the time of the last king of Judah, Zedekiah (about 587 B.C.), this was quite extraordinary. For some of those in the diaspora, their

98

exile and homelessness had lasted for over 2,500 years, and for others nearly 2,000 years. Meanwhile their homeland had been devastated by a succession of hostile powers. The long story of the dispersion was told in Chapter 3.

Beginnings of Zionism

It was not until the beginning of the 19th century that hope began to be raised again. *The Jewish Chronicle* (London) of Nov. 9, 1849, commented: "The European Powers will not need to put themselves to the trouble of restoring the Jews individually or collectively. Let them but confer upon Palestine a constitution like that of the United States and the Jews will restore themselves. They would then go cheerfully and willingly, and would there piously bide their time for a heaven-inspired Messiah who is to restore Mosaism to its original splendour."

The first stirring was in Eastern Europe. In Russia a conference was held in 1860 to discuss Palestine as a possible home for Jews. The next year a Zion Society was formed. In Poland a 'Lovers of Zion' movement began. One or two adventurous Jews made the long journey to spy out the land, travelling even further than Abraham to reach their goal.

A century later, David ben Gurion wrote: "Zionism derives from two sources. One is deep, irrational, lasting, independent of time and place, and as old as the Jewish people . . . the Messianic hope. The second source was a source of renewal and action, the fruit of realistic political thought, born of the circumstances of time and place . . . The charter of liberation enunciating the Rights of Man and Nation which the French Revolution bequeathed on Europe, the national revival movements which developed among several European peoples . . . the new means of transport . . . the rise of the working class . . . the mass migration from Europe to overseas countries, all helped to bring about a new direction in Jewish thought . . . The Messianic hope, which for scores of generations had worn a religious garb and had appealed to a force above Nature, now changed its religious and passive form and became political and national" (*Israel Government Year Book*, 5714, page 5).

The Golden Door

Their dream of liberty was enshrined in a poem by Emma Lazarus, the Jewish poetess who felt for the millions who were suffering such persecution in the Old World. Her poem was engraved on the base of the Statue of Liberty in New York harbour:

"Give me your tired, your poor,
 Your huddled masses yearning to breathe free,
 The wretched refuse of your teeming shore,
Send these, the homeless, tempest-tost to me.
 I lift my lamp beside the golden door."

Literally millions of Europe's persecuted Jews made the voyage past that statue and found a pleasant land, but not the Promised Land. Yet the fruits of their labours were to play a very significant part in aiding others who eventually reached the land of Palestine.

Sir Moses Montefiore

Two highly esteemed British Jews came on the scene during the 19th century. Both were to give financial backing for a start to be made with organised settlement in the land. Baron Lionel Rothschild, a British banker, who came to be known as 'the Great Benefactor', and Sir Moses Montefiore, who was a financial adviser to Queen Victoria. The pioneer work of these gentlemen has been largely overshadowed by later developments. However, they laid the difficult foundations on which others built.

*Sir Moses Montefiore
on his 100th Birthday*

100

When Sir Moses was over 90 years of age, in a conversation with a relative of his, he recalled how his interest in the land had started. Just married, he and his wife were reading about Elijah the prophet. They both agreed that it would be interesting to visit Carmel and the scene of the Tishbite's exploit. "I promised that if ever we should have leisure, I would take Lady Montefiore to the East. That night I dreamed that I saw in front of me a venerable man, whom I knew to be Elijah the prophet. He pointed to Jerusalem, which I recognised in the distance, and said only these words — 'Possessor of all things'. I awoke, and then dreamed this a second time, and then again a third time. The dream made so strong an impression on me that I resolved the first thing I would do, when I had time, would be to go to the Holy Land and see if there really was work to be done there for me, aye, and for you too."

Practical Beginnings

In 1827, Sir Moses made his first visit to Jerusalem. His experiences of that year coloured the whole of his life thereafter. He and his wife were warned by the British Consul at Alexandria that if they entered Palestine, he might prepare for death and she for the worst fate that could befall a woman. But their desire to visit the land was invincible. The plague was raging in Jerusalem. They stayed only a fortnight, but what they saw of the condition of the unhappy Jews, oppressed, plundered, starving, and diseased, but rich in an imperishable hope and consoled by glorious memories from history, was enough to inspire the visitors with the devotion of a lifetime. Again and again they returned. Seven visits were made from 1827 to 1874. Every time they brought new blessings to the unfortunate people who lived in tombs and caves around the ruins of the Temple. Britain opened a consulate in Jerusalem in 1839, and British influence gradually ameliorated the political condition of the Jews. The charity of the West, largely organised and directed by Sir Moses, provided a better water supply, schools, gardens and houses for those inhabitants whom he had found on the first visit to be living like conies in the rocks.

British Approval

In Britain, attitudes to Jews had improved. They were admitted to Parliament, and some held high office, even Prime Minister.

ISRAEL

There was an awakening interest in Palestine, ever since Napoleon had been defeated in his attempt to occupy it. *The Birmingham Post*, Oct. 24, 1884, featured an article about Sir Moses: "Montefiore has done his utmost to encourage agriculture in Palestine, and although his efforts have been slow in producing successful practical results, they bid fair to bear fruit at last. At 100 years of age, he is found capable of signing many letters a day, all of which he reads with the most scrupulous attention. He is still very enthusiastic in his great dream of re-establishing the Jewish Empire and restoring Jerusalem in all its gorgeous magnificence as its capital." Besides this energetic gentleman's visits to the land, he went to Morocco, to Constantinople, to Moscow in pursuance of his life's ambition to promote the cause of his less fortunate fellow Jews. He was the first to put his money where he heart was, the first actually to found a colony. In 1852, he built the almshouses in the Bethlehem Road, Jerusalem, which still bear his honoured name. In Britain he pressed for full civil rights for all Jews, and himself became Sheriff of the City of London.

Early Colonies

In 1848, before there was any colonization of the land, John Thomas, on the basis of his understanding of the Scriptures, wrote: "I believe there will be a pre-adventual limited coloniza-

Baron Edmond de Rothschild—known to Palestine Jews as 'The Unknown Benefactor'

tion of the country by the Jews . . . and that the prosperity of this colony . . . will be the cause of the country's invasion by the Russian 'clay', styled Gog by Ezekiel."

The next meaningful event was in 1856, when the Sultan of Turkey formally rescinded the Edict of Hadrian (A.D. 135) which had forbidden Jews to live around Jerusalem on pain of death. The same year, Sir Moses organised the first planting of a citrus grove. Now that the way was clear for the legal establishment of more colonies, Baron Edmond de Rothschild founded Mea Shearim ('The hundred gates')

102

and Nahalath Shebah ('The sevenfold heritage'). These and many other early colonies were around the Jerusalem area.

In the 1880s Christadelphians had begun collecting funds to help the colonies of refugees in Palestine. 150 acres of land in Upper Galilee was purchased at Yanna; cash was provided for the purchase of tools for other colonies, and large quantities of clothing were despatched. Mr. Laurence Oliphant acted as agent for these activities, for until 1887 no Christadelphian had visited the land (see Chapter 11).

The Zionist surge was yet to come. Indeed the term 'Zionism' was not coined until 1890 by Nathan Birnbaum. A useful preliminary to the developments that were about to take place was the mapping of the land by the Palestine Exploration Fund, begun in 1865 but not completed until 1878 by Lieutenant Kitchener (later Lord Kitchener).

Rise of Anti-Semitism

It is necessary, first of all, to look at the effect of the Franco-Prussian war of 1870-1. The beginnings of a renewed anti-semitism began in both countries about this time. In Russia, pogroms had been a regular feature for some time and in 1881 reached a peak, being deliberately organised by the Czar's government. These vicious attacks on Jews spread to Poland. Tens of thousands were murdered, tens of thousands fled, mostly to America, but some to Palestine. Golda Meir, in her fascinating auto-biography *My Life*, vividly described a pogrom in her village, when defenceless people and children were brutally attacked for no reason other than that they were Jews. She narrowly escaped with her life. At this time, a Jewish doctor, Leon Pinsker, wrote *Auto-emancipation*, which sought to stir Jews to help themselves and try to regain their self-respect. A number of spontaneous movements erupted. In Russia, probably the earliest of these was Dabiu, an abbreviation of the Hebrew for "Tell the children of Israel and let them go forward" (Exodus 14:15). Other early movements were Bilu, "Sons of Jacob, let us arise and go" and Hibbat Zion, 'Love of Zion', with the slogan 'To Palestine'. The wave of emigration which these stimulated is generally spoken of as The First Aliyah (1882-1904).

ISRAEL

These early arrivals in the land did not find "the land of milk and honey" of their dreams. These 'Halutzim' (pioneers), at great cost in life and labour, did slowly make the deserted land to bloom again. Eventually orange groves, vineyards, farms and forests sprang up where wilderness and swamps had been before. But the Zionist surge was still to come.

The French Catalyst

Moses Hess, in 1862, had written *Rome and Jerusalem*, a manifesto of Jewish nationhood. He favoured France as the champion of a Jewish renaissance, probably because of the world-wide effects of the French Revolution on public opinion. France was to be involved, but not for a few more years. Jews in France had full civil rights, yet still faced public anti-semitism. In 1894, a Jewish officer in the French army, Captain Alfred Dreyfus, was charged with espionage. Both public and official opinion was prejudiced against him. Although the real traitor, Major Esterhazy, confessed, the bias was so strong that at a second trial the Jew was again condemned. However,

Postage Stamp: Theodor Herzl

he was eventually set free. An Austrian Jewish newspaper reporter in Paris was so disturbed by this evidence of hatred for the Jews that he became obsessed with the idea that the Jewish problem must be solved by the Jews themselves. This reporter was Theodor Herzl. He wrote and published his ideas in *Der Judenstaat*, in which he outlined plans for a Jewish political state. "The idea which I have developed in this pamphlet is a very old one, the restoration of the Jewish State. The earth resounds with the outcries against the Jews, and their outcries have awakened the slumbering idea." Herzl pleaded with the Sultan of Turkey, with the Pope, with kings, presidents and politicians. His vision called for "a legally secure homeland in Palestine".

The French Rothschilds

The French branch of the Rothschild family quietly and effectively played a very large part in the early development of Jewish settlement in the land. Baron Edmond was only known to his many beneficiaries as the 'Unknown Benefactor', while his son James Rothschild was known by the initials of the organisation that he financed—PICA (Palestine Jewish Colonization Association). For 75 years these two men dipped very deep into their pockets, to the extent of many millions of francs, to buy land for settlement and to sustain uneconomic farming and industrial projects that kept the refugees at work.

Early Settlers in the Fields of Gedara, 1884

In 1907, they settled the debts of three of the pioneer settlements in Galilee, amounting to nearly three million francs. The fact is that most of the Jews were unaccustomed to agricultural work and preferred to supervise Arab labour rather than work themselves. They were described as 'sowers of pretension and reapers of credit'. Nevertheless the Rothschild millions supported the work from 1882 until 1957. This support was a vital element in the preliminary settlement of the land in preparation for the eventual establishment of the State of Israel. Activities that are now prosperous began as loss-making enterprises that had been propped up by the Rothschilds during their infancy. Thus, the Almighty has used the resources of Jews in the diaspora to facilitate the fulfilment of His promise to gather His people back to the land.

ISRAEL

Zionism

The next year, 1897, saw the first Zionist conference at Basle. Here the Zionist Movement was founded. Herzl called it 'The Jewish nation on the march'. But the nation did not march. Just a few Jews trickled. It was not until Russian pogroms were renewed in 1905 that a great tide of refugees, possibly 40,000, had the urge to escape to Palestine. Thus, Zionism was at first a movement of Eastern European Jews seeking a homeland.

As will become evident later, Zionism was to change direction as circumstances changed. From the very first, the movement was essentially one that put faith in the Jews' ability to solve the Jewish problem. It was totally lacking in confidence in God, or in His promises. While the Messianic hope hovered in the background, the motivation was material and political. Nevertheless, the movement was blessed, because it was fulfilling God's purpose for His land and for His people. Thus far, it was mainly Russian, Polish and Roumanian Jews who had returned. Their language was not Hebrew, but Yiddish. This was a strange dialect combining German, Hebrew and Slav words written in Hebrew characters. A few of these words have now come into general usage.

The Tongue of the Prophets

For centuries the Hebrew language had remained dormant, used only for the Holy Scriptures and for prayer. Jews normally used the language of the country in which they lived, for everyday use. Thus the average Jew had little or no knowledge of the Holy Scriptures. When it was read in the synagogue services it was in the tongue of the prophets, a language that was strange and only used by scholars. In 1888, a young Jew from Lithuania, Eliezer Perlman, was given the opportunity to learn Hebrew. In time he became totally engrossed in the determination to make it the tongue of his people for their everyday use. His ambition was that Jews, from whatever part of the world they came, should have a language in common. He saw this project as essential if ever the Land of their Fathers was to become a national home.

Changing his name to Eliezer ben Yehuda, he went to Jerusalem to begin his campaign for the Hebrew language. He edited a newspaper in Hebrew and began to introduce new words that he had adapted from original Hebrew root words. With a vigorous educational campaign, in spite of fierce opposition from religious Jews, he eventually made Hebrew into a language that could be used in the everyday life of a modern nation. By taking the basic three letter words of classical Hebrew and adding to them in the traditional way, he produced new words that were relatively easy to understand and to learn. Eliezer ben Yehuda was the father of modern Hebrew, which is now, a century later, the everyday language of several million people. Instead of being restricted to liturgical and religious purposes only, it is now the language of literature, of commerce and of everyday life in Israel.

There is no doubt that a common language for the Jewish people has been a powerful factor in the eventual establishment of the State of Israel. The updating of the language is now the duty of the Academy of the Hebrew Language.

Zionism and Rome

In 1904, Theodor Herzl had an audience with Pope Pius X. The relationship was a delicate one and was not helped by the Pope's words: ''We cannot prevent Jews from going to Jerusalem, but we could never sanction it . . . the Jews have not recognised our Lord; we cannot recognise the Jews.'' The attitude of Rome to the Jewish problem has altered little since that interview. Rome has not officially recognised the existence of the State of Israel, and has no diplomatic relations with it. The only suspicion of a change came in 1985 when the Vatican inspired a move to ask the Jews to forgive Christians for the wrongs that they had done them over the centuries.

The Second Aliyah

In 1905, there was a revolution in Russia. While it was quickly crushed by the Czar's forces, it sparked off another round of pogroms. This in turn gave impetus to the Second Aliyah (1905-14). During this period, tens of thousands of Russian Jews fled to the Land. Among them was a youth named David ben Gurion, who many years later was to found the State of Israel, just 50 years after Herzl envisaged it. Two other Jewish youths later told how they had walked all the way from Russia across Turkey and Syria, travelling mostly by night. Such was the urge for freedom that motivated those early pioneers.

In 1906, Britain proposed to make Uganda (a protectorate) available for Jewish refugees. When discussing this offer Chaim Weizmann is said to have asked Lord Balfour, ''Suppose I were to offer you Paris instead of London; would you accept?'' ''But Mr. Weizmann, we *have* London.'' ''That is true'', replied Weizmann, ''but we Jews had Jerusalem when London was only a marsh.''

In 1908, the Jewish National Fund began planting trees in Palestine in a big way, and the next year the foundations of the first new Jewish city were laid. It began as a suburb of Jaffa, but was planned for greatness and in time Jaffa became a suburb of Tel Aviv. At the same time Britain was becoming more involved in the Middle East. Napoleon's plans to dominate the area had been thwarted by Britain who now held Egypt as a British Protectorate. The Suez Canal was part of the lifeline of the British Empire to her dominions in India and the east, but Sinai and Palestine were still part of the shrinking Turkish Empire. The Turks had gained possession of the Holy Land from the Crusaders in 1187, and were to retain it until 1917. However, Turkey was not an ally of Britain, and in the event of war, was seen as a threat to the Suez Canal.

World War I

When World War I broke out, Turkey opposed the Western Allies. British troops advanced into Palestine from Egypt and eventually took Jerusalem on December 9, 1917, led by General Allenby. Significantly this was the 24th day of the 9th month (Kislev) (see Hosea 2:18). The capitulation of the city followed the dropping of leaflets by Bomber Squadron No. 14, and no shots were fired (see Isaiah 31:5). Later, a Christadelphian wrote to the General asking him if he knew that his action was a fulfilment of Bible prophecy. He replied to the effect that he knew he was doing the right thing, but he did not know about Bible prophecy.

That Britain would eventually rule Palestine seemed to have been assumed by most of the population. The departure of the dead hand of the Turks operated like the removal of a great weight from a compressed spring. The reaction was almost instantaneous. During the war the editor of *The Christadelphian* magazine had commented: "This colonization (of Palestine) now threatened with destruction would be very greatly extended under a British protectorate, and we look for such a protectorate as the outcome of the present war." At the conclusion of the war, the historian H. G. Wells wrote to a prominent Zionist, Mr. Israel Zangwill: "And now, what is to prevent the Jews having Palestine and restoring a real Judea?"

"To the English Command,

Since two days shells have fallen on some of the places in Jerusalem which is a holy sanctuary to all. The Ottoman Government, to safeguard the religious place from destruction, have withdrawn the soldiers from the city. Functionaries have been appointed to guard the church of the Holy Sepulchre and the Mosque Al Aksa and other religious places. It is hoped a similar treatment will be accorded them by you. I am sending this paper by Hussein Ben Husseinni, acting president of the Municipality.

(Signed) 'Izzat

Governor of Jerusalem"

Translation of letter sent to General Allenby commanding the British forces by the Turkish Civil Governor of Jerusalem

---

The Balfour Declaration

During the war, Britain had run into difficulties in the making of high explosives. Dr. Chaim Weizmann, a Russian Jew living in England, was a brilliant chemist. He discovered a better way of making acetone, vital to the production of explosives. For this practical contribution to the war effort, he was asked by Lord Balfour what he would appreciate as a reward. In reply he explained the concept of Zionism and asked for Palestine for his people. On November 2, 1917, before Britain had been given the Palestine Mandate,

Chaim Weizmann

Lord Balfour wrote the now famous Balfour Declaration in the form of a letter to Lord Rothschild, a foremost Zionist leader:

"His Majesty's government view with favour the establishment in Palestine of a National Home for the Jewish people, and will use their best endeavours to facilitate the achievement of this object, it being clearly understood that nothing shall be done which may prejudice the civil and religious rights of existing non-Jewish communities in Palestine, or the rights and political status enjoyed by Jews in any country."

Chaim Weizmann called it 'The Magna Carta of Jewish liberties'. But its ambiguous wording was to be the source of endless trouble. Zionists, of course, saw it as laying the foundation stone of a re-established Jewish Commonwealth. It gave them hope such as they had never had before.

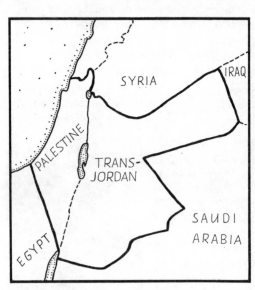

Area of Middle East mandated to Britain in 1920 and promised to the Jews. Subsequently Trans-jordan was given to Sheikh Abdullah in 1922

In the post-war allocation of spheres of influence over the conquered territories of the deflated Turkish Empire, the League of Nations proceeded to appoint Britain as the Mandatory Power for Palestine, in 1920—this in spite of French aspirations to the area. At the San Remo conference, 52 nations endorsed Britain's appointment to the vital territory, which included the whole of the land now occupied by Israel and the Kingdom of Jordan (see map).

MAIN COUNTRIES FROM WHICH JEWS RETURNED TO THE LAND		
Ashkenazim	Russia (until 1917) Poland Rumania	over
Sephardim	Iraq Egypt Morocco	50,000
Ashkenazim	Hungary Bulgaria	
Sephardim	Turkey Syria Iran Yemen Libya Tunisia	over 10,000

Great Men

Dr. Weizmann wrote a most interesting autobiography entitled *Trial and Error*, in which he told of the heights and depths of the Zionist Movement. It would seem that he knew that he was a man of destiny who would become the right man at the right time in the right place. Whether he could see the hand of God at work seems to be doubtful. The example of Theodor Herzl loomed large in his thoughts. When David ben Gurion came to look back on these times he wrote: ''Two great men rose in the cause of Zionism—Herzl and Weizmann. It is difficult to find in the history of any one nation, two men who had so powerful an influence over the lives of their fellows, yet who were so very different, not only in their capabilities, but in the relationship they bore to their people.''

Weizmann was working in Manchester when the leadership of the Zionist Organisation fell vacant. Berlin was the head-quarters of the Movement. He is reported to have said: ''The road to Palestine does not go through Berlin.'' As events turned out, it was his work in Britain that was to lead to British

111

cooperation and some real progress. At a Jewish conference in London, a speaker was reported to have said: "The Jewish revival was the most stupendous factor in Jewish life today, and the community that refused to take part in it signed its own death warrant." These remarks can only mean that there were many Jewish people who were not interested in the Zionist Movement, and did not want to be disturbed from their very comfortable Gentile homes. As it was to turn out later, there had to be two kinds of Zionists, those who wanted to return to the Land and those who remained in the diaspora and gave financial help from a Gentile base.

Controlled Immigration

On hearing of the plans under the British Mandate to open the land to a limited Jewish immigration, the Bishop of London said: "There could be no greater obstacle to Christianity than to have Palestine full of unconverted Jews." The Pope was also reported to be apprehensive. What would they do to the 'holy places'? Could he have been reading Ezekiel 11:17 and 18?

But although the door had been opened, all was not well within the Zionist Movement. In 1916, *The Jewish Chronicle* (London) published a very satirical definition of Zionism as a plan "to get a land that everyone wants for a people that does not desire it". At an American Zionist convention in 1916, an accusation of Godlessness was made against the Movement: "The keynote of Zionist meetings should be God. It would have been well if each session had been opened with prayer, for Zionism is hypocrisy unless God is in its thought, first, last and all the time." The fact was that Zionism was a materialistic and political movement that was being used by God to achieve a limited purpose. A history of Zionism was written by M. Sokolow, in which he made a complaint that the Biblical Israel that was to receive the blessings was too often spiritualised, while the Israel to receive the curses was always natural Israel. This inconsistency is written large in many Christian Bible commentaries, and in the teachings of the British-Israel people.

Rival Arab Claims

An Arab leader, the Emir Feisal, attempted to forestall the giving of the Palestine Mandate to Britain. He fancied himself as the head of a new Arab Empire. He claimed Mesopotamia, Syria, Lebanon and Palestine, with Damascus as his capital. The French, who had been given the League of Nations Mandate over Syria and Lebanon, made some quick moves and settled Feisal's pretensions. Clearly it was not in God's purpose for Palestine to be ruled by Arabs at this vital time. During the war, the Turks had been suspicious of Jewish loyalty and deported 11,000 to Egypt, including David ben Gurion. The war over, these now returned under British protection. The few Jews who had remained in the land had suffered terrible privations and many had died. The Jewish community in Palestine was reduced during the war from 85,000 to 56,000.

Sir Herbert Samuel

In 1920, Britain appointed a Jew, Sir Herbert Samuel, as the High Commissioner. The Jews of Jerusalem acclaimed him as if he were Messiah, saying that their redemption had come. However, Sir Herbert made a grievous mistake in choosing as official leader of the Arab community in Palestine, Haj Mohammed Amin El Husseini. This man was known as the Mufti. He proved to be a mischief maker. He caused endless trouble, eventually having to be expelled from the country, yet still able to rouse Arab opposition from a distance.

In 1921, Winston Churchill was British Colonial Secretary and in control of Palestine affairs. He was prepared to recognise the claims of another Arab leader, the Emir Abdullah, who had invaded, and wanted, all that part of the mandated territory east of Jordan. Churchill gave way to him and in so doing gave away four-fifths of the territory promised to the Jews. Yet later on, Churchill was foremost in espousing the cause for Jewish settlement in Palestine. He warned that if Britain continued to appease Arab demands, it "will cast our country, and all that it stands for, one more step downwards in its fortunes". How true that was to become!

When the League of Nations confirmed the establishment of Abdullah in Trans-jordan, Woodrow Wilson, president of the U.S.A., protested that nobody had a right to alter boundaries of the land that had been given to the Jews; but his protest was ignored. Even though the major part of the total area had thus been given to the Arabs, they were not satisfied, opposed all

Jewish settlement, excluded them entirely from the Trans-jordan, and threatened to push them into the sea. The Emir became king, and the Hashemite Kingdom of Jordan was form-ed. The Arab claim to Palestine was based on the McMahon letters to Sherif Hussein of Mecca which promised Arab control of vast areas that had been under the Turks. But as McMahon pointed out in a letter to *The Times* (July 23, 1937), Palestine was never in the territory promised to the Arabs.

British Partiality

Even with British troops in the land, the Jews often had to work under the protection of their own guards. It was like the time of Nehemiah when ''each with one hand laboured on the work and with the other held his weapon''. Many workers died in a vicious tit-for-tat war. Yet Jews were still buying land, mainly in the Sharon plain, Esdraelon and up-per Jordan valley. This land had often been badly neglec-ted, yet high prices were asked. The land soon respond-ed to the efforts of the newcomers, even though agri-culture was a novel experience for them. Palestine did not

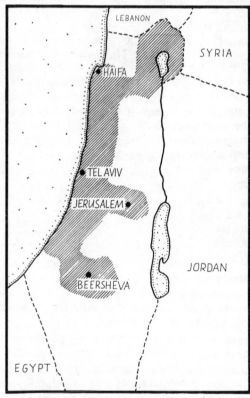

Agriculturally Fertile Areas of Palestine settled by Jews

have a ready made economy, and at first there was difficulty in finding employment for the many refugees. Some did not stay, as they did not wish to take menial tasks. Any such vacancies were soon filled by Arabs at low wages, and Arabs from nearby lands began to filter in. While the numbers of Jewish refugees permitted to enter was severely curtailed and controlled, there was no such restriction on the immigration of Arabs. In fact there was a partiality shown by the British all the time they had the Mandate. The facts and figures that prove this have now been published in a book by Joan Peters entitled *From Time Immemorial*. This book refutes the myth that the Arabs have an 'inalienable right to Palestine' as so often claimed. Whenever Arab protests about Jewish progress were made to the British authorities, further restrictions were imposed on Jewish immigration, but never on Arab infiltration.

The Fifth Aliyah

By the 1930s, millions of European Jews were trying to escape from Russia and Germany. Limited numbers were allowed to enter the land legally, but America was the only place open to the vast majority. In May 1939, the British Government stated that it was not their policy that Palestine should become a Jewish state. Immigration was actually curtailed at the very time when the Jewish mass flight from Nazi Europe was at its height. This sparked off increased opposition to the mandatory authority in the Land. In spite of British vigilance, a total of 142 ships succeeded in beating the blockade. Other immigrants were smuggled in by air and overland, making a total of at least 122,000 who reached their goal before the outbreak of World War II.

World War II

As war loomed, the Arabs were persuaded that the best way to obtain their demands would be to take sides with Germany. The British sought to counter this by issuing a White Paper that gave in to many of the Arab demands. But this did not quell Arab violence; the British forces in the land were unable to maintain peace. It was at this time that a British Officer, Charles Orde Wingate, showed himself to be a Zionist sympathiser. He actively organised and improvised the Jewish defences and taught the settlers the arts of self-defence. The

League of Nations devised plans to partition the land with a small Jewish state and an Arab one alongside. But neither would agree. Meanwhile other nations were closing their doors to immigration and pressure mounted even higher for access to Palestine. By 1941, the pressure was so great that a secret Jewish organisation, the Palmach, was formed to smuggle refugees into Palestine and safety.

'Aliyah Bet' (Illegal Immigrant) Ships defied British Blockades both before and after World War II. Refugees landed on the beaches and merged with welcoming crowds to avoid deportation

Millions of Jews were trapped in Europe like animals in a cage. Thousands tried to escape and crowded into unseaworthy ships, hoping to reach the Promised Land. Some ships sank on the way; others were turned away when they reached the coast of Palestine. On July 17, 1939, it was reported: "2,550 refugees are adrift in four ships; refused permission to land at any port, they have been cruising for four weeks and food is running short. On another vessel, plague broke out among the packed passengers and the vessel was quarantined. After fumigation it was sent out to sea again." Nobody wanted to know about the plight of millions of people. Some of the sad story is told in the book *Exodus*, which makes grim reading.

Palestine the Strategic Base

Britain's real interest in Palestine all along had been its value as a strategic military base. "In the Near East there is not so much a line of defence as a group of defended localities . . . Palestine is the main strategical base, retention of which is of supreme importance. It is the main pillar supporting the central arch of Imperial Defence." *The Palestine Journal* in 1940 said: "The Jews are the only people in the Middle East with the mechanical ability on which a serious munitions industry could be founded." Within ten years there was indeed a serious munitions industry in the land, formed out of Jewish necessity.

With the outbreak of war, 136,000 Palestine Jews offered their services to Britain, in spite of the cruel restrictions that had been imposed. As the war raged, Palestine remained a bastion of Britain's defences.

Hitler's Fury

In Europe, even while the war was in progress, Hitler's hatred of the Jews was intensified and concentration camps were built, not only for German Jews, but for those of the lands that the German army overran. The concentration camps were turned into extermination camps. A realisation of what was really going on did not come to the world's notice until the war was ended. Then it became known that over 6 million had died from starvation, torture, by murder and in the gas

Badge identifying a Jew ('Jude') under Nazi Oppression

chambers. Hitler's plan was to remove all Jews from the face of the earth. He succeeded in eliminating about one-third of the total world population of the race. This is known to history as the Holocaust.

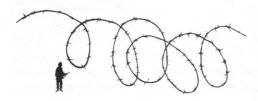

When this war was finally over, the pressure from refugees was maintained. The British still resisted appeals to allow more

117

*Arrest
of Jews
in the
Warsaw
Ghetto,
1943*

than the quota to land. An enquiry was instituted that was hoped would "make possible the abandonment of that administrative separation between Palestine and Trans-jordan". But before the enquiry could be held, the British Foreign Secretary, Ernest Bevin, "decided to avoid any risks and took the bold step of announcing the forthcoming granting of independence to Trans-jordan"—this in spite of the fact that it had been designated to the Jews by the Balfour Declaration.

Exodus

A state of confrontation developed between the British occupying forces and the Jewish refugee organisations, which had become well trained smugglers of refugees. The crisis came with the turning away of the ship 'Exodus' with 4,500 people on board. This was so insensitive in the eyes of the world that the name of Britain began to stink. This event appears to have been the catalyst that caused Britain to decide to relinquish the Mandate. Palestine was no longer seen by the British Labour government as a vital defence post. The insoluble nature of the Jewish problem outweighed all other considerations. Why should not the Jews solve their own problem—if the Arabs did not solve it for them? In any case, Arab supplies of oil were more important than refugees of a despised race.

Before the British occupation forces abandoned the territory the Jews found themselves fighting both British and Arabs.

14. Lone Tree in the Desert:
''Like a root out of dry ground'' (Isaiah 53:2)

15. Engedi—The David Spring: "The burning sand shall become a pool, and the thirsty ground springs of water" (Isaiah 35:7)

16. Safed in Galilee:
"A city set on a hill cannot be hid" (Matthew 5:14)

17. Jerusalem from the South: ''The Lord will inherit Judah as his portion in the holy land, and again choose Jerusalem'' (Zechariah 2:12)

18. Awassi Sheep at Sunrise: ''I will be the shepherd of my sheep, and I will make them lie down, says the Lord God'' (Ezekiel 34:15)

*Immigrants
arriving at
Haifa Port*

Some of the Jewish defence forces, the Irgun and Haganah
went on the offensive to hasten the British departure. The
United Nations drew up more partition plans, promptly rejected
by both parties. Meanwhile, about 84,000 refugees arrived by
secret routes, but seven refugee ships sank with unknown loss
of life. In May 1948, the crisis reached white heat.

A Jewish State

The terrible events of the war, the horrors of the Holocaust, the
tragedy of drowning refugees who had been refused a
landing, all combined to force a reluctant world to grant, at last,
a Jewish State. Indeed, the 'dry bones' of Israel had been
coming together and now flesh was about to cover them. But
the State of Israel was not to be established by the United
Nations Organisation, although it gave assent to its formation,
even Russia agreeing. Israel's representative at the U.N. was
recommended to delay the formation of the State. He replied:
"We are aware of the dangers, but the danger of not taking
action outweighs the risks we are taking." When the new state
was attacked by all the surrounding Arab nations, the U.N. did
nothing to defend it. It was established in spite of U.N.
diffidence, and because of Jewish desperation, determination
and undoubted divine aid. However, the evidence of the divine
aid, which could be seen by students of Bible prophecy, was
neither seen nor appreciated by the Jews involved. They proud-
ly claimed that it was their own strong arm that had won them
the victory, when at last it came.

THE INCOMING WAVES		
		Total Population
FIRST ALIYAH		
from Russia and Roumania	1882-1904	
SECOND ALIYAH		
from Eastern Europe	1904-1914	85,000
THIRD ALIYAH		
from Eastern Europe	1919-1923	84,000
FOURTH ALIYAH		
from Poland	1924-1928	150,000
FIFTH ALIYAH		
from Germany	1929-1939	500,000
MASS MOVEMENT		
from Arab lands	1948-1950	1,203,000
These figures include the	1960	1,911,300
natural increase of the	1970	2,582,000
local population	1980	3,200,000

Note: From 1914 to 1919 population decreased—11,000 being deported and unknown numbers killed by the Turkish authorities in World War I.

Israel Proclaimed

With the declaration of the infant State of Israel by David ben Gurion on May 14, 1948, the most important event in Israel's long sad history since the final dispersion of A.D. 70 now took place. At last there was a homeland under their own control, although it was born of fire and blood. The official record of this great event reads thus:

"The 25 year old British Mandate ended midnight May 14/15, 1948, when British High Commissioner General Sir Alan Cunningham left, and all civil administration ended. The State of Israel had been proclaimed a few hours earlier at Tel Aviv. The armies of Egypt, Jordan, Syria, Lebanon and Iraq invaded Israel on three fronts. Prior to May 14 there had been fighting in three main areas—(1) Jaffa, surrendered to the Jews; (2) Safed in Galilee, surrendered by the Arab Liberation

120

Army; (3) the Tel Aviv-Jerusalem road, which had been blocked by Arabs at several strategic points, and the city of Jerusalem itself. David ben Gurion announced the name of the new state to be 'Israel', and was appointed Prime Minister and Minister of Defence at age 62. Israel's first act was to revoke the British order of 1939 that limited immigration. The British blockade of immigrant ships ceased'' (*Keesing's Archives*).

David ben Gurion

In his memoirs David ben Gurion recalled those days:

''On the day when the independence of Israel was proclaimed, no more than 6% of the Jews of the world lived there . . . The place of the land of Israel in the faith of Jewry and its national consciousness, and the singularly independent structure of the Yishuv here, its roots in the soil, the victory of Jewish labour . . . the Hebrew culture and language, the Yishuv's reliance on its own strength, and its awareness of its national mission, all of these made it competent to be transformed into the State of Israel, the joy, pride and ultimate hope of the Jewish people.''

One cannot help but notice the complete lack of recognition of the God of Israel in all this. ''Reliance on its own strength'' has been Israel's recipe for disaster time after time as the Hebrew Holy Scriptures so ably record. Yet still the lesson has not been learned!

The Dream Realised

Thus the Zionist dream of just 50 years earlier now became the reality of a political state of Israel. The question in everybody's mind was, ''Can it survive?'' The Arab confederacy was determined to sweep Israel into the sea. An Arab postage stamp of the time showed a map of Israel with a dagger piercing it, and blood flowing. However, in spite of Israel's self-confident Godlessness, such an early demise was not in God's purpose for His people. The several Arab leaders were all jealous of one another and actually hindered one another in their anxiety to be in the forefront of the expected Arab victory. But the Arab victory did not come.

To the student of Bible prophecy, watching from a distance, the hand of God was clearly evident in that the very few defeated the many; David defeated Goliath again. When it was over, it was sad to find that the victors denied that the hand of God was in the matter at all. All the credit was claimed for themselves.

SELF-DEFENCE FORCES

SHOMERIM — 'Watchmen', late 19th century, local defence groups of settlers.

HASHOMER — 'Watchmen', 1909-1914, defence organisations against Arab attacks.

HAGANAH — 'Defence', 1920-1948, comprehensive underground force which later became Israel's army.

IRGUN (Irgun Tzeva'i Le'ummi) — National Military Organisation, 1931-1948. Split from Haganah to go on offensive against enemy.

STERN GROUP — 1940-1942, split from Irgun to oppose British Mandate Administration.

PALMACH — 'Striking force', organised for War of Independence, 1941-1948, and to aid illegal immigration of refugees.

I.D.F. — Israel Defence Forces of Army, Navy and Airforce, formed 1948. A small regular force with many reserves.

Arab Opposition

There followed a flood of refugees from Arab lands. Within two years Israel's population doubled. Countries such as Morocco and Iraq, where Jews had lived for 2,000 years and more, were almost emptied. This influx from Arab lands changed the nation from having a majority of European (Ashkenazim) Jews, to having a majority of Sephardim (Jews from Arab and eastern lands). The policy of the State altered accordingly. From being the movement of a people with a Zionist vision, it became the movement of a people with practical down-to-earth plans to counter the Arab opposition. The Sephardim had centuries of hard experience in dealing with the Arab problem. The people with a vision were now mainly to be found abroad in the diaspora, where Zionism became more of a financing system to support those who had established the State.

Although there are said to be around 16 million Jews in the world, the majority being in America, yet Israel is now the most Jewish land on earth, with more Jews than non-Jews. It is becoming the custom for Jews, wherever they live, to identify with Israel to such an extent that when they speak of 'our government', they mean the government of Israel, even though they have no intention of living there.

Is Zionism Racism?

At first the U.N. sought to keep the peace between Jew and Arab. However, in 1975 the Organisation passed a resolution that equated Zionism with 'racism'. How strange that anti-semitism has not been so labelled! The old prejudices that have pursued the Jews into every land are still simmering. Aware of how easy it is to awake anti-semitism, the people of Israel, perhaps more than those of the diaspora, are trying very hard not to give offence. It is an almost impossible task, seeing that Soviet and Arab information services are constantly giving out warped news items that invariably show Jews, Zionism and Israel in a bad light.

Strange as it may seem at first glance, there are Jews in Israel who are themselves anti-Zionist. They see Zionism as a Godless political movement and will have nothing to do with it. Even stranger, the political system has given them a voice in the Knesset which they are not slow to use, and their views are spreading. Thus there seem to be signs that a religious revival may be on the way in Israel.

CHANGES IN JEWISH POPULATIONS ILLUSTRATING THE MASS MOVEMENTS OF JEWS DURING THE CENTURY 1880-1980		
	1880	*1980*
Europe	5,500,000	3,000,000
America	300,000	6,000,000
Israel	24,000	3,500,000
Rest of World	5,000,000	2,500,000

5

THE STRUGGLE TO EXIST: 1948-1988

ALTHOUGH the word 'Zionism' had been coined a few years before, the First Zionist Congress in 1897 at Basle was seen as a 'Jewish State on the way'. Theodor Herzl, who called this first conference together, wrote in his diary: "In Basle we established a Jewish State. If I were to say that aloud today, universal laughter would be the response. Maybe in five, certainly in fifty years, everybody will recognise it." The State was founded just fifty-one years later. Within fifty years the United Nations had approved the idea of a Jewish political state. This was at a time when the British Mandatory Administration in Palestine was in a dilemma. It was torn between its promise to provide a national home for the Jews, enshrined in the Balfour Declaration, and political commitments to the Arabs made in the McMahon letters.

When the British finally decided to pull out and leave the Jews to their fate, there were Jewish men and women of vision who were prepared and ready to take over control.

Overwhelming Odds

To the world, the Jewish immigrants had no hope of resisting the overwhelming superiority of the Arab forces arrayed against them. For years Britain had restricted Jewish immigration, while allowing unrestricted Arab infiltration, so that the country had an Arab 'fifth column' within its borders. However, the Jews were not unprepared. They had made plans to meet the contingency as best they could. They had been fighting Arab terrorists and the British occupying forces for some time, and so were not totally without skill or arms. The day of the British withdrawal was known beforehand and preparations were made accordingly.

Golda Meir was a 'mother' figure to the infant state, who was to become Prime Minister in later years. She recalled the events of the inauguration ceremony at which independence was proclaimed on May 14, 1948. In her autobiography, *My Life* (pages 184-5), she wrote: "I was so lost in my thoughts about the children (wireless operators in the desert) that I can remember being momentarily surprised

Golda Meir, 1898-1978

when the phone rang in my room, and I was told that a car was waiting to take me to the Museum. It had been decided to hold the ceremony at the Tel Aviv Museum on Rothschild Boulevard, not because it was such an imposing building (which it wasn't) but because it was small enough to be guarded easily . . . the floors had been scrubbed, the nude paintings on the walls modestly draped, the windows blacked out in case of an air raid, and a large picture of Theodor Herzl hung behind the table at which the thirteen members of the provisional government were to sit . . . ''

Independence

"A few minutes later, at exactly 4 p.m., the ceremony began. Ben Gurion, wearing a dark suit and tie, stood up and rapped a gavel. According to the plan, this was to be the signal for the orchestra . . . to play 'Ha-Tikvah'. But something went wrong and there was no music. Spontaneously we rose to our feet and sang our national anthem."

The refrain of Hatikvah has the lines:

"Yet is our hope not lost,
   The ancient hope
To dwell in the land of our fathers;
   In the city where David encamped."

The words of 'Ha-Tikvah' were written a century earlier by the secretary of Mr. Laurence Oliphant.

"Then Ben Gurion cleared his throat and said quietly, 'I shall now read the Scroll of Independence'. It took him only a quarter

*Opening verse
of the Israeli
National
Anthem—
'Ha-Tikvah'*

of an hour to read the whole proclamation. He read it slowly
and very clearly, and I remember his voice changing and rising a
little as he came to the eleventh paragraph: 'Accordingly we,
the members of the National Council, representing the Jewish
people in the Land of Israel and the Zionist Movement, have
assembled on the day of the termination of the British Mandate
for Palestine, and, by virtue of our natural and historic right and
of the resolution of the General Assembly of the United Nations,
do hereby proclaim the establishment of a Jewish State in the
Land of Israel—The State of Israel'.''

*David ben Gurion reading the Proclamation of Independence
of the State of Israel: May 14, 1948*

126

The State of Israel

"The State of Israel! My eyes filled with tears and my hands shook. We had done it. We had brought the Jewish State into existence—and I, Golda Meyerson, had lived to see the day." The Declaration of Independence went on to say that the purpose of the State was "for the full social and political equality of its citizens, without distinction of religion, race or sex, and the guaranteeing of freedom of religion, conscience, education and culture" and to "safeguard the Holy Places of all religions".

Golda Meir's recollections continue: "The long exile was over. From this day on, we would no longer live on sufferance in the land of our forefathers. Now we were a nation like other nations, masters—for the first time in twenty centuries—of our own destiny. The dream had come true—too late to save those who had perished in the Holocaust, but not too late for the generations to come . . . It seemed to me that no Jew on earth had ever been more privileged than I was that Friday afternoon. Then, as though a signal had been given, we rose to our feet, crying and clapping, while Ben Gurion, his voice breaking for the only time, read: 'The State of Israel will be open to Jewish immigration and the ingathering of exiles.' This was the very heart of the proclamation, the reason for the state and the point of it all. I remember sobbing aloud when I heard those words spoken in that hot packed little hall."

Appeal to the Arabs

"But Ben Gurion just rapped his gavel again for order and went on reading: 'Even against the violent attacks launched against us for months past, we call upon the sons of the Arab people dwelling in Israel to keep the peace and to play their part in building the state on the basis of full and equal citizenship and due representation in all its institutions, provisional and permanent.' And: 'We extend the hand of peace and good neighbourliness to all the states around us and to their peoples, and we call upon them to cooperate in mutual helpfulness with the independent Jewish nation in its land. The State of Israel is prepared to make its contribution in a concerted effort for the advancement of the entire Middle East.' Then something quite unscheduled and very moving happened. All of a sudden Rabbi

Fishman-Maimon stood up and, in a trembling voice, pronounced the traditional Hebrew prayer of thanksgiving. 'Blessed be Thou, O Lord our God, King of the Universe, who hast kept us alive and made us endure and brought us to this day. Amen.' It was a prayer that I had heard often, but it never held such meaning for me as it did that day.''

Rebirth of a Nation

It was indeed a day to be remembered. For so long it had been a hazy dream. Now it had come to pass. The world had not known by what name the new State was to be called. Ben Gurion had now made it known—''The State of Israel''. Not Canaan, not Palestine, for these had been the names of heathen people, but Israel, the name that God had given to Jacob so long ago; a name that has a divinely significant meaning, 'ruling with God'.

Here was a paradox. In the proclamation of the new state with this meaningful name, there had been no mention of God. It was a secular state. ''*We* had brought the Jewish State into existence''; ''Masters of *our own* destiny.'' The first time that God was mentioned was in that unscheduled prayer by the Rabbi. Thus was founded, in the midst of war, a Jewish secular state that bore the name that had been divinely bestowed upon the God-fearing father of the race, Jacob, re-named Israel.

The mood of the new nation was expressed very clearly by Ben Gurion in these words: ''Always we shall demand of the world what is justly ours. But morning and evening, day in and day out, we must remind ourselves that our existence, our freedom and our future, are in our own hands. Our own exertions, our own capacity, our own will, they are the key.'' What a contrast is this view of the situation with the assurance that ''He who scattered Israel will gather him'' (Jeremiah 31:10) and ''I will take you from the nations . . . and bring you into your own land'' (Ezekiel 36:24). From the time when the people of Israel demanded to be like the nations and have a king, to the present secular State of Israel, the Jews have not accepted the divine call to be the people of God, a nation based upon a faith like that of Abraham, who trusted God's Word, believed His promises and looked for a better country that God would provide.

The Politics of Israel

Early twentieth century Jewish politicians foresaw the Zionist state for which they worked as a bi-national democratic republic, with Jews and Arabs sharing power. Later, as the realities of the situation began to dawn, it was realised that such an ideal arrangement would be impossible, because of the growing hostility of so many of the Arabs. The voting system introduced when the state came into existence in 1948 was one of proportional representation. The temporary National Assembly that had formed the state was soon replaced by elected members of the Knesset ('the Assembly'), but at no time did the elections produce a majority party.

Thus, in order for a government to function, uneasy coalitions had to be made. The many minor parties, some having only one representative, each had to be courted. In consequence, they tended to offer cooperation on their own terms, and thus gain a disproportionate voice in matters of policy. For this reason, major parties have been unable to carry out the programme for which they were elected. The disadvantages of the proportional representation system have been shown in other ways. Every party, however small, is represented, but the voters do not have personal representation for their region, nor do they know what their favoured party will actually do, if it gains power. In practice, therefore, there is much dissatisfaction with the system, especially among supporters of the major parties, Labour and Likud (Conservative).

Jewish Opposition

There is a minority of ultra-orthodox Jews in the land who refuse to acknowledge the secular State of Israel. They refuse to pay taxes, vote for the Knesset, serve in the army, or acknowledge the state in any way. The view they take appears to be that it is the honour accorded to Messiah to re-establish the Kingdom of Israel as a theocratic state at his coming. They say that the forming of the republic was premature, atheistic, and quite deplorable.

Otherwise the Jews in Israel are solidly behind their government, while being highly critical of it. The Arab population is divided. Those who have worked with and for the Jews for many years, mainly 'Christians', have cooperated; but those who are newcomers, mainly Moslems, are antagonistic. In 1948, when the Arab armies were attacking the infant state, Arab residents in Israel were advised to get out of the way until the Jews had all been swept into the sea. They were promised that if they did this they would be able to go back and take over the former Jewish property when Israel had been destroyed. Even though the Arabs were repulsed, Israel accepted about 50,000 of the displaced Arab residents back. The Arab refugee problem of so-called Palestinians was created by the policy of the Arabs themselves for political purposes.

Arab Opposition

The Jewish people in Palestine under the British Mandate had been fighting for their lives against both Arabs and British for several years before they were able to take over the administration in this dramatic way. Even as Ben Gurion was reading the Proclamation of the State of Israel at Tel Aviv, the new nation was at war. Five Arab nations had conspired to try to eliminate the infant at birth. The United Nations Organisation had sanctioned the forming of the new state, but did not lift a finger to help it in its birth pangs. All it did was to make plans for further division of the land called Partition Plans. None of these was accep-

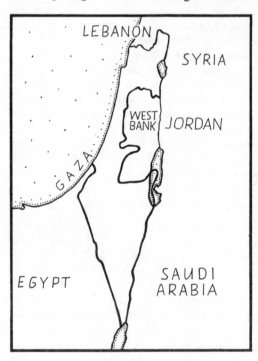

Israel's Borders after the 1949 Armistice — a very vulnerable fledgling State

table to either Jews or Arabs. Eventually, when the Arabs found that they could not overcome the spirited resistance of the Jews, an armistice was arranged. This ended the initial battle, but did not end the state of war, which has continued for 40 years. An uneasy period of limited hostility followed, punctuated by acts of violence by Arab terrorists from time to time. Egyptian Fedayeen ('self-sacrificers') infiltrated Israel from the Gaza Strip and from Sinai, killing and burning at will and then disappearing over the border. To try to settle this problem, Israel planned 'Operation Horeb', which in a few weeks at the end of 1948, drove Egypt out of a large part of Sinai. But Israel did not want the territory and returned it to Egypt after having quietened the menace for the time being.

Soviet Involvement

In the East-West 'Cold War' of the 1950s, the Soviet Union and the United States of America contended for the favours of the Arab nations who controlled much of the world's oil resources. Soviet 'generosity' supplied vast quantities of munitions to Egypt. This was manifestly the Russian way of trying to eliminate Israel by using a third party. In reply, Israel sought arms supplies, but Britain and the United States both refused to oblige. However, France came to the aid of the people under threat and supplied some valuable equipment. In July 1956 President Nasser of Egypt began his challenge by nationalising the Suez Canal and prohibiting the passage of traffic to and from Israel. Previously the Canal had been under the control of a French company and could be used by all nations. Nasser's action angered Britain and France, and a secret plan was made for a joint action by Israel, Britain and France to free the canal. The secret was so well kept that the Egyptian Intelligence Service was quite unaware of what was coming.

The Suez Crisis

Golda Meir later wrote her recollections: ''The Sinai Campaign began as scheduled, after sunset on October 29, and ended as scheduled on November 5. It took the Israel Defence Forces, made up of reservists travelling in a crazy assortment of military and civilian vehicles, less than one hundred hours to cross and capture from the Egyptians, the whole of the Gaza Strip and the Sinai Peninsula — an area two and a half times larger than Israel itself. We had counted on surprise, speed and utterly confusing the Egyptian army, but it was only when I myself flew to visit Sharm el-Sheikh at the southernmost tip of Sinai and toured the Gaza Strip by car afterwards that I really understood the extent of our victory—the sheer size and desolation of the territory through which those tanks, half-tracks, ice cream trucks, private cars and taxis had raced in under seven days. The Egyptian defeat was absolute. The nests of the Fedayeen were again cleared out. The elaborate Egyptian system to defend Sinai—the fortresses and the battalions concealed in the desert—was put totally out of commission. The hundreds of thousands of weapons and millions upon millions of rounds of ammunition—mostly Russian —stockpiled for use against us, were worthless now. A third of the Egyptian army was broken. Of the 30,000 Egyptian soldiers whom we found pathetically wandering in the sand, 5,000 were taken as prisoners to save them from dying of thirst (and eventually exchanged for the one Israeli the Egyptians had managed to capture). Although we had won our war against Egypt, the French and the British had lost theirs—due to some extent to their ineptness, but mostly to the overwhelmingly negative public reation in France and Great Britain to what was viewed as an imperialist assault on an innocent third party.''

Golda Meir's Plea

In spite of Israel's victory and conquest of Sinai, pressure from the United Nations compelled Israel to withdraw again from Sinai and the Gaza Strip without Egypt having been brought to the negotiating table. Russia made use of 'Israel's unrestrained aggression' to hide her own invasion of Hungary, and was clearly very upset that so much of the military material given to Egypt had fallen into Israel's hands.

At the end of 1956, Golda Meir was able to speak at the United Nations General Assembly, where she said: ''Israel's people went into the desert or struck roots in stony hillsides to establish new villages, to build roads, houses, schools and hospitals; while Arab terrorists, entering from Egypt and Jordan, were sent in to kill and destroy. Israel dug wells, brought water in pipes from great distances; Egypt sent in Fedayeen to blow up the wells and the pipes. Jews from Yemen brought in weak,

Immigrants tilling the stony hillsides of their new Homeland

undernourished children believing that two out of every five would die; we cut that number down to one out of twenty-five. While we fed those babies and cured their diseases, the Fedayeen went in to throw bombs at children in synagogues and grenades into baby homes.''

Arab Covetousness

The Arab enmity was not a natural phenomenon. It was deliberately stirred up and nurtured. Israel was seen as an out-post of Western 'imperialism' or 'colonialism', intruding into a vital area that could control the crossroads of the earth. The Arab nations each side of the coveted land were armed to the teeth by a major power that wanted them to do its evil work for it. The Palestinian refugees were deliberately kept apart from their brother Arabs in neighbouring lands for political reasons. They could easily have been re-settled in several of the Arab countries. But they were intended to be evidence of how badly Arabs were treated by Israel. The United Nations Organisation was called in to feed them. They were not allowed to integrate. They were victims of Arab strategy. They were deliberately incited against Israel. Most of them had infiltrated into Palestine while Britain was in charge. They had no 'inalienable right' to the land, as was claimed. In the refugee camps they were political pawns.

King Hussein of Jordan said in 1960: ''Since 1948, Arab leaders have approached the Palestine problem in a very irres-ponsible manner . . . they have used the Palestinian people for selfish political purposes." However, Hussein himself was under pressure from more powerful Arab leaders and was not in a position to try to sort matters out amicably.

Israel's Other Problems

Besides the constant threat to its borders, and the Palestinian problem, Israel had many other problems. At the formation of the State, a great flood of refugee Jews surged in. Many of these were from Arab lands, whence they had fled penniless. They had to be housed, fed, found jobs and assimilated into Israel's economy and culture. None was turned away, all found a welcome. These were mainly Sephardim, with a very different cultural background to the Ashkenazim who had founded the state. This fact in itself constituted another problem.

An army of reservists had to be kept trained and supplied, always at the ready. Saboteurs had to be spotted and their bombs defused, if possible. The diplomatic corps representing Israel to the nations, had to try to win and keep friends, promote exports and seek funds. The World Zionist Organisation, which had been formed to encourage Jews to make aliyah now had to raise funds to help finance the new state.

Relations with some of the 'third world' countries were cultivated, and Israel began to export Jewish skill and know-how, mainly in agricultural techniques. Israel had to develop an arms industry of its own, as other nations were reluctant to supply their requirements, and in time became an exporter of arms to other nations. Because other countries were reluctant to ship Israel's exports, Israel had to become a mercantile power with its own shipping lines that cover the world's oceans, and an airline that flies to major airports. For a country that covers little more than a large English county, Israel has made a significant impact on world affairs in a very short time.

Israel's commercial successes and military strength have given the people a measure of self-confidence and self-satisfaction that could be misleading. The aid that has been given to several small countries has even been claimed as a fulfilment of the promise that Abraham's seed should be a blessing to all nations!

Nasser's Opposition

During the 1960s, Syria, Egypt and Jordan were stockpiling Soviet-made weapons. Terrorists continued to plant bombs and kill civilians. Guns on the Syrian Golan Heights overlooking Galilee bombarded the settlements in the valley below from time to time. Snipers crept in to harass farmers and fishermen. In 1966, the Soviets accused Israel of preparing for war against Syria. This was the reverse of the facts. Nasser announced brazenly that "Egypt with all its resources . . . is ready to plunge into a total war that will be the end of Israel." He ordered the United Nations peace-keeping forces out of Sinai and massed his troops on the frontier. Syria and Jordan were alerted to make a simultaneous strike. The United Nations did nothing to avert the threatened war. Britain and the United States were sympathetic and worried about the threat to Israel, but did nothing. France, however, was not only sympathetic but offered to give help if war began, but cautioned Israel not to start it.

Again, Israel was alone, with well-equipped Arab armies all around. Nasser kept everyone in suspense. This gave Israel time to dig trenches, fill sandbags and organise its reservist army. The nation was united as seldom before. Political and social discontent vanished. Not one Israeli fled the country, but hundreds returned from abroad. Thousands of American Jews clamoured for permits to go and help. During this crisis the Ministry of Defence was given to Moshe Dayan, the man who had lost an eye in skirmishes with the British many years before. He proved to be a dynamic and dramatic leader, and quite fearless.

The Six-Day War

In June 1967, when the war finally broke out, the Arabs occupied all of Sinai, the Gaza Strip, the West Bank, the Golan Heights and the Old City of Jerusalem (within the walls). When the Six-Day War ended all these areas were in the possession of Israel. It could be asked: "If these areas were so precious to the Arabs, why did they start the war that lost them?" Israel's response to the initial attack was prompt. Within six hours of the first Arab attack, the Israeli air force had destroyed over 400 Arab planes, mostly on the ground. The same day, Israeli

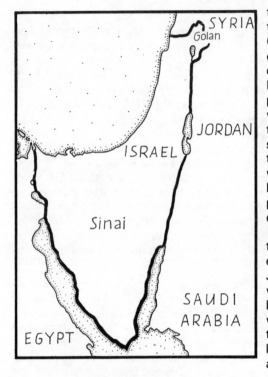

Israel after the 1967 Armistice — with more land than was wanted

tanks were well on the way to the Suez Canal, and were on its banks in four days. Most of Egypt's Soviet supplied equipment was taken, many thousands of their soldiers were captured and the whole of the Sinai Peninsula was occupied, including the oil fields. Egypt lost 10,000 soldiers in the desert. On the eastern front, the Jordanians shelled western Jerusalem, but within two days were beaten back to the River Jordan, losing the old city and the whole of Judea and Samaria (known as the West Bank to Jordanians). Then attention was turned to Syria. A very difficult two days sufficed and Syria begged the United Nations to arrange a truce.

It had been a lightning war, but a cruel one. Both sides suffered heavy losses. The question now was: Will the Arabs sit down at a peace conference to resolve the problems of the area?

No Peace

The Arab response was to reverse the facts and portray Israel as the aggressor. Their next step was to upstage a diplomatic war. It was not until 1968 that a strongly defined Palestinian identity was to emerge, twenty years after the Palestine Arabs had fled on instructions from the invading Arab armies. For the first time the claim was made for their 'inalienable right' to the land. On the other hand the Arabs of Israel's newly acquired territories could now explore western Jerusalem, visit Tel Aviv and the seaside without hindrance. Jews could now visit the Old City of Jerusalem, which they found to their sorrow had been utterly desecrated. Other places that could now be visited included Bethlehem, Hebron and Jericho. Excursions could safely go to the snows of Mount Hermon in the north, or the barren wilderness of Sinai in the south. The tension of the war was replaced by the euphoria of peace at last. But peace was not to last.

Moshe Dayan wrote: "Beneath me as I flew was a land without division between Arab and Jew, a land strewn with villages and cities, fields and gardens, a land bounded on the east by the River Jordan and on the west by the Great Sea, crowned in the north by the snowy peak of Mount Hermon, sealed in the south by the parched wilderness. Our land. The Land of Israel" (*Living with the Bible*, page 227).

An Arab summit conference issued its findings:

1. No peace with Israel;
2. No recognition of the State of Israel;
3. No negotiations with Israel.

But that was not all. It was demanded that Israel must give up all the area it had conquered, and be destroyed. "But if the Arabs had learned nothing, Israel had learned something." Israel was disappointed that their victory had not won them peace. The Arabs were disappointed at the disaster that had overtaken them, and were more bitter than before. Israel was ready for talks, but her neighbours would not talk. Israel could well have said: 'This is the new line of demarcation: sign here.' Instead she said, 'Let us negotiate'. A book was published by a satirical writer, Ephraim Kishon, illustrated by the cartoonist Dosh, with the title *Sorry We Won*. It seemed that whether Israel won or lost, they were the losers.

Rise of the Palestine Liberation Organisation

The so-called West Bank (i.e. of the Kingdom of Jordan) is the area correctly named Judea and Samaria. At first this was inhabited by Arabs. Israel permitted them to move freely across the Jordan and for Jordanian businesses to operate there. This freedom tended to encourage terrorists to enter the area and infiltrate into Israel. It was placed under military control, to the resentment of the inhabitants. The mountainous northern border with Lebanon also became a danger as terrorists crept across it, and rockets were fired at Jewish villages in Galilee from north of the border. The government of Lebanon was weak and unable to control much of the country, which was divided between several rival militias.

On the border with Israel, Arabs under the name of the Palestine Liberation Organisation (P.L.O.) had virtual control, terrorising the local people and threatening Israel. In the south, Egypt kept up a barrage of shells across the Suez Canal at the Israeli outposts on the east bank. The Six-Day War was over, but there was still a state of war all around the nation's borders. The army consisted of reservists who had civilian jobs, who wanted to get back home. This War of Attrition was maintained by Egypt during 1968-70. It was supported by thousands of Russian instructors and masses of Russian equipment.

But Israel could not afford to give in. Goaded into retaliatory action, Israel bombed Egypt extensively, bringing the reality of war to the civilian population. Israel's offers to negotiate were still scorned. A Jordanian newspaper said of Mrs. Golda Meir, Israel's Prime Minister: ''She believes that one fine day a world without guns will emerge in the Middle East. Golda Meir is behaving like a grandmother telling bedtime stories to her grandchildren.''

The situation was summed up by Moshe Dayan in this expression of self-confidence: ''We must face up to and not be deterred by the hatred of hundreds of thousands of Arabs around us who seek our destruction, and we must resolve never to divert our eyes lest our hands become weak. That is the decree of our generation, to be armed and ever ready, strong and firm. If the sword should slip from our grasp, then would our lives be cut off altogether.'' It was most noticeable that neither the Prime Minister nor her Defence Minister sought the protection of the God of Israel, nor even acknowledged Him.

Internal Problems

In August 1970, Nasser died, and Egypt agreed to a cease-fire. Russia continued to build up stocks of arms in Syria and Iraq. Israel had developed her own facilities for building tanks and warplanes. Her only outside supplier was now the United States, but even so, she had to beg for whatever she needed. Besides the enervating War of Attrition, there were many internal problems. Golda Meir had to tell the nation: "The government cannot do everything all at once. It cannot wave a magic wand and meet everyone's demands simultaneously, eradicate poverty without imposing taxes, win wars, go on absorbing immigration, develop the economy and still give everyone their due."

There was a relaxation of tension when Sadat replaced Nasser in Egypt, and when King Hussein turned the P.L.O. out of Jordan. But acts of terrorism grew more horrific, including the murder of Israelis abroad and the shooting of visitors to Israel. No Jew, at home or abroad, felt really safe. But, unlike some other countries, Israel never gave in to the demands of the terrorists. Austria, which had been the only official exit route for Russian Jews, became a victim of the terrorists who demanded that this escape route be closed.

The 'Yom Kippur' War

In 1973, the nightmare war broke out. From May onwards, reports had come in that Syria and Egypt were massing troops on their frontiers. Israeli reservists were called up. Nothing happened and tension was relaxed. By October there was evidence of more troop movements, but Israel's leaders did not suspect that war was imminent. On October 5 it was reported that the families of the Russian advisers in Syria were packing up to go home. The Israeli army and air force were put on high alert. The Arab press was again accusing Israel of massing troops against Syria.

The Israeli cabinet was divided as to whether a real emergency was developing. At 4 a.m. on the Day of Atonement (Yom Kippur), the Prime Minister was alerted that Egypt and Syria would strike that day. That day was to Jews the most solemn holy day of the year, and many would be fasting and at prayer in their synagogues. While Israel did have the capacity

Bombed Convoy of Syrian Armoured Cars abandoned in the Yom Kippur War

and the ability to make a pre-emptive strike, this would be seen by the world as aggression, and would be sure to alienate world opinion. The Yom Kippur War burst on the nation just after mid-day on both fronts at the same time. At first, things went badly for Israel. The enemy advanced. It looked like being a long war, and Israel needed supplies urgently. President Nixon of the United States personally urged the sending of ammunition, tanks, clothing, rockets and medical supplies. These were sent by a shuttle service of planes that sometimes arrived every fifteen minutes. When the war seemed almost lost, the tide turned. The Syrians were pushed back almost to Damascus, the Egyptians were chased over the Suez Canal almost to Cairo.

When a Christadelphian said to a Jewess, in commenting on the way that Israel had beaten back her enemies, "Hasn't God been good to you?", she replied angrily: "It's nothing to do with God, it's our strong arm that did it." Although a miracle had happened again, it was not seen in that light by most of the people of Israel.

Russian Supplies

The involvement of the Soviets in sending gigantic supplies of armaments to Egypt, Syria and Iraq was carefully monitored by Israel, whose secret service was second to none. In one day, in that crisis, 125 Russian planes landed in Syria, 58 in Egypt and 17 in Iraq. But when the Russians found that their clients had lost the war and were in a worse state than when it began, they initiated a campaign to sue for a ceasefire. The forces of Israel were in a position to press on. Damascus and Cairo could have been besieged, but Egypt staged a cunning diplomatic move by offering to lift the embargo on Middle East oil being sent to the United States in exchange for a quick ceasefire. The U.N. Security Council obliged, for this plan suited Russia also. While this did not entirely end the war, eventually Egypt agreed to negotiate. Syria kept up sporadic shooting and would not negotiate.

The Galilee Border
Activity now moved to the border with Lebanon. The situation in that beautiful country was very muddled. The country was divided between a number of rival factions which each had a private army. The P.L.O. had taken advantage of this situation to infiltrate southern Lebanon and terrorise the local people and fire rockets into Galilee. Israel had tried to control the situation by subsidising the South Lebanon Army, a nominally Christian militia who were sympathetic to Israel. Russia was supplying the P.L.O. with great quantities of munitions that were being hidden away in secret caches in Lebanon. Israel was aware of this build-up and decided to strike first.

To complicate matters, Syrian troops had already occupied part of Lebanon, saying that they intended to suppress the P.L.O. So Israel struck at suspected P.L.O. bases and then withdrew. Then the P.L.O. hijacked a bus in Israel and killed Israeli citizens. A tit-for-tat war developed which in 1982 became a full scale invasion of South Lebanon in an endeavour to oust the terrorists, who had virtually formed a state within the state, and were deeply resented by the local Lebanese. This operation was termed 'Operation Peace for Galilee', whose mountainous border with Lebanon was difficult to control effectively.

The Lebanon Quagmire
Lebanon was easy to enter, but proved difficult to leave. At first, many of the locals were sympathetic to the invaders, for they, too, were tired of the P.L.O. Initially, the Amal militia (Shi'ite Moslems) cooperated with Israel in disarming the P.L.O.

Then as the main body of the foe retired towards Beirut, Israeli troops followed, drawn into the quagmire. Beirut was half 'Christian' and half Moslem. But the operation of trying to separate the P.L.O. from the Lebanese was difficult. Inevitably many civilians lost their lives and much property was destroyed. This led to resentment, and was followed by a change of mind by the Shi'ites who became antagonistic, once the P.L.O. was dispersed. Many mistakes were made because of the difficulty of distinguishing friend from foe.

The P.L.O. was allowed to evacuate from Beirut, and a U.N. peace-keeping force was sent in. There was confusion as Israel began to withdraw. Lebanese groups fought one another. Suicide bombers destroyed both the Israeli and the U.S. headquarters in Beirut, killing hundreds. The Syrians became more firmly established but kept out of the fighting. In 1983 Israel and Lebanon signed an agreement, but this was abrogated the next year under Syrian pressure.

The outcome for Israel of this very expensive Lebanon adventure was to erode some of the nation's self-assurance. What advantage had been gained? The public were very critical. The P.L.O. had been disloged, but was still active. This had not been a straight combat, and a guerrilla war does not have a decisive end, since the enemy tends to melt into the surroundings.

Continuous War

Israel had been a nation at war continually since its formation. The war had been punctuated by a number of short sharp battles in which the Israeli forces had proved far more successful than the overwhelmingly greater numbers of their opponents. Israel had the disadvantage of having to fight on two or three separate fronts at the same time. It had the problem that its land area was so small that it could not afford to give ground to absorb the enemy's initial attack. Its cities were so near to the enemy's airfields that it could not wait for the enemy to strike first. It was the David and Goliath scenario all over again, but sadly Israel was not putting its trust in the God of Israel. Even so, observers of these dramatic encounters could perceive the hand of God in the preservation of His Land, and its preparation for events yet to come.

The War of Desperation

The Lebanon War was different. The terrain was a difficult and mountainous land. The enemy was elusive, and mixed among people who were not opponents. As a result, mistakes were made which were magnified by a prejudiced world opinion, and Israel finished this operation by exchanging one foe for another. The only winner was the enemy that kept out of it, Syria, whose power in Lebanon was strengthened.

The state of war with Egypt ended with an agreement by which Israel returned Sinai for the third time in exchange for a non-aggression pact. However, normal relations with Egypt were very slow to develop, the principal advantage probably being that Israel could buy Egyptian oil produced from the territory of Sinai that had been given up.

The state of war with Jordan had not been settled, nor that with Syria. The Moslem Arabs living within Israel tended to be uncooperative, even though their living conditions improved considerably. Their animosity was stirred up by broadcasts from Jordan and elsewhere. Israel repeatedly offered to meet Arab leaders at the negotiating table, but there was no response.

The problem was succinctly stated by David ben Gurion years before: "Israel does not have hundreds of years at its disposal". What a pity that he never knew the truth about the God of Israel's plans for Israel, when all the world shall offer allegiance to the King of Israel.

ISRAEL'S WARS AT A GLANCE

EVEN while the State of Israel was being proclaimed on May 14, 1948, it was at war with five neighbouring Arab states, who had vowed to destroy the infant state at birth. Since that day there has been a non-stop war which has flared into ferocious battles from time to time.

1948   **The War of Independence**. Five Arab states combined to "throw the Jews into the sea". There were at least 50 Arabs to every Jewish soldier. A cease-fire was sought, but no peace.

1948-9	**Operation Horeb.** The first battle was over, but war went on. Egyptian Fedayeen sabotaged installations, and terrified people. Israel invaded Sinai, took it, but later withdrew.
1956	**The Suez Crisis.** Nasser's Egypt nationalised the Suez Canal, preventing Israel using it. Britain, France and Israel sought to free it. Israel took Sinai again, but withdrew. Canal was blocked for several years.
1967	**The Six-Day War.** Egypt, Syria and Jordan attacked on three fronts. Israel fought back, took Sinai, Judea, Samaria and Old Jerusalem, and Golan Heights.
1968-70	**The War of Attrition.** The guerrilla warfare of the Fedayeen continued until death of Nasser.
1973	**The 'Yom Kippur' War.** Egypt and Syria attacked on the Jewish Holy Day. Israel appeared to falter. Arab victory seemed sure. Did God confound their counsels? Israel surged forward towards Damascus and Cairo. Arabs sought cease-fire. Israel again withdrew from Sinai in exchange for 'peace' with Egypt.
1982-3	**The Lebanon War.** A war of desperation, intended as a pre-emptive strike against the P.L.O. who occupied South Lebanon and harassed Galilee. The South Lebanon 'Christian' (Phalange) army were sympathetic and helped. The P.L.O. was flushed out but not defeated. Lebanon's Shi'ite Moslems resisted, making Israel's withdrawal difficult. Public opinion was against the operation and world opinion saw Israel as an aggressor.
1986-7	**Guerrilla Warfare.** Sabotage and outrage continued in city and village. Meanwhile Syria strengthened position in Lebanon and Golan.

6

THE INFANT STATE

A LIYAH, 'the going up' to the Land, accelerated immediately the State of Israel had been formed. This was in spite of the background of violence within Israel and of continuous war with her neighbours. Israel welcomed returning Jews from many lands: it is said from 87 countries, but particularly from those of Arab lands, where persecution had become intolerable.

THE JEWISH POPULATION OF PALESTINE/ISRAEL
(approximate)

1827	500
1880	24,000
1914	85,000
1917	55,000
1939	500,000
1948	716,000
1964	2,500,000
1986	3,400,000

During World War I thousands of Jews fled to Egypt. During World War II 90,000 Jews sought refuge in Palestine by legal or illegal routes, but 75,000 were turned away by the British forces, many to certain death.

Feeding, housing, clothing and finding work for over 100,000 immigrants (*olei*) each year was a gigantic task. Some of the newcomers integrated well; others found that the adjustment to a 'western' Jewish way of life was unacceptable. The Yemeni Jews and the Falashas from Ethiopia tended to resist adaptation and, like the earliest refugees, formed little enclaves within Israel so that they could retain their former customs.

145

COMMERCIAL PRODUCTS OF ANCIENT ISRAEL

"Wheat of Minnith, and Pannag, and honey, and oil, and balm"   (Ezekiel 27:17, A.V.)

"Wheat, olives and early figs, honey, oil and balm"
(R.S.V.)

COMMERCIAL PRODUCTS OF MODERN ISRAEL

Agricultural

Citrus Fruits	Cotton
Vegetables	Freshwater Fish
Flowers	Kosher Foods

Chemical

Bromide	Magnesium oxide
Calcium chloride	Potash

Technical

Advisory Services	Finished Diamonds
Aircraft	Medical Products
Electronic Devices	Munitions
Irrigation Systems	Solar Systems

Industry

The first arrivals had all settled on the land, mostly without any agricultural experience. They soon produced subsistence crops and then began exporting. Even under Turkish rule, Palestine had been an exporter of grain to Italy and France. Oranges from Palestine became famous around the world a century ago. Since then a great diversity of fruit and vegetable crops, and out of season flowers, have been exported to many other countries. The agricultural activities of the communal kibbutzim have been supplemented by the development of industrial enterprises to absorb surplus labour. Industrialisation was continuous during the British Mandate period, first of all for local needs. Jews from Amsterdam introduced the diamond finishing industry to Palestine, and now Israel is a major

exporter of finished dia-
monds. With independence
there was a rapid development of engineering works
to produce agricultural
equipment, ships, planes,
engines and munitions.
Chemical works exploited
the natural resources of the
Dead Sea and of the Negev.
The skills of Israeli scientists
led to the manufacture of
medical supplies, electronic
equipment, solar power
systems, irrigation techniques and much more.

Israel must export to live
and, thanks to cooperation
with the U.S.A. and E.E.C.
countries, her products are

*Israeli melons ready for
shipment around the world*

sent out in increasing quantities. New markets are sought for
chemicals and technical systems. Scientific know-how is exported to some of the smaller nations; experts are being sent
out to teach new methods of farming and medical treatment.
Perhaps the most profitable of all Israel's industries is tourism.
Although the country is small, it has a tremendous variety of
attractions. For centuries its shrines have brought in pilgrims of
several faiths. As the land of the Bible, its archaeological sites
and ancient ruins invite others. There is much to offer the lover
of nature, for its wide range of habitats for plants, animals and
birds is unique. To meet the surge of tourism that has been
generated, numerous hotels have been built.

Transport

Access to Israel is mainly by air. Israel is fortunate in having
free air space over the Mediterranean, and not having to seek
permission to use the air space of her enemies. Within the
State, transport is mainly by road. The few railway lines are
used for heavy goods. Bus lines, mainly run by two
cooperatives, cover the whole country effectively.

147

The donkey and the camel, at one time the only means of transporting goods, may still be seen — but as a curiosity to intrigue visitors. Although Israel is at the crossroads of the earth, it no longer fulfils its ancient function of entrepôt, where goods of the east were exchanged for the goods of the west.

Modern coins: 1 agora (barley), 5 agorot (pomegranate), 10 agorot (palm), 25 agorot (ancient lyre)

Water

The divine description of the Promised Land was that it was well watered. In old time, its hills were covered with trees and bushes that retained the rainfall, releasing it during the dry season in the numerous springs and streams. Cities and villages were sited near a source of water. As the hills became denuded and became less efficient catchment areas, a supplementary source of water had to be sought. Storage systems were constructed, usually in underground cisterns cut out of the solid rock, whereby rain water could be retained. These cisterns were often in the shape of a bottle, with narrow neck and bulging interior. Sometimes they had to be plastered to prevent leakage. Jerusalem still has hundreds of cisterns, which, although not normally used, are a reserve in case of need, as during wartime.

Modern Israel uses more water than ever before, both for domestic purposes and for irrigation. All resources are being mobilised, and consumption is restricted. The Sea of Galilee (the Kinnereth) is used as a national reservoir. To this the melt water of the Hermon range descends, and from this the National Water Company (Mekorot) takes the vital supplies to the south via the national water carrier. The water has to be pumped over the hills before it can flow down the long pipe to the Negev. The normal overflow from the Kinnereth into the River Jordan is thus limited to the water not needed for the pipeline. The restricted flow of water down the Jordan is used for irrigation in the sub-tropical Jordan valley, so that the flow arriving at the Dead Sea is even more limited. The level of the Dead Sea is dropping noticeably, and a scheme has been mooted to top it up by a pipeline from the Mediterranean.

The salty waters of the Dead Sea do not sustain any normal forms of life—hence its name. However, its waters have been found to be beneficial for several forms of human ailment and treatment facilities are now provided. At the southern end of the Sea, around Sodom, there are extensive chemical works extracting minerals from the water. Bromide, potash, magnesium and calcium chloride are produced and constitute a major item of export.

Jews are not by tradition maritime fishermen, but the Kinnereth has been the scene of freshwater fishing for many centuries. This still continues, and has now been augmented by extensive fish farming in freshwater ponds, where carp and other varieties are produced, some of which are exported.

Farming and Industry

The first refugees to the land were from Eastern Europe. Their political views were revolutionary and salted with communism. This was a natural reaction from the tyrannical régimes under which they had lived. They formed little agricultural communes known as a *kibbutz*. All members shared everything in common, took no wages, but received from the common purse that which was needful. Later, another type of settlement was formed by independent families who worked for themselves, but shared in bulk buying and selling. These are called a *moshav*.

As industry developed, a comprehensive labour organisation was formed known as the Histadrut (The General Federation of Workers in Israel). It was formed to build up a Jewish labour economy and develop social and industrial institutions for the working class. Its economic activity has become a basis for Jewish society and an essential foundation for the formation of the State. The Histadrut provides health insurance, training schools, leisure activities for the workers; newspapers, and a chain of industrial companies under the aegis of the Histadrut holding company, Koor, besides an international building and construction company, Kolel Boneh. Thus, whichever political party is in power, the Histadrut is virtually a part of the state administration.

Political Parties

As this is being written, there are 26 separate political parties

in Israel, 15 of which have at least one representative in the Knesset. Thus the larger parties can never enjoy absolute power under the present proportional representation system. The wide variety of views held by these many parties present a headache for whoever is in power.

Postage Stamp commemorating the Inauguration of the Knesset Building, 1966

On the left is Rakah, a small communist party, Mapam the Marxist workers party, Achdut

Emblem of Jerusalem

Emblem of the State of Israel: Menorah between Olive Branches

150

19. Jaffa Gate at Night: "You shall call your walls Salvation, and your gates Praise . . . the Lord will be your everlasting light" (Isaiah 60:18,19)

20. Camels and High-rise Flats, Beersheba:
'' . . . things new and old'' (Matthew 13:52)

21. Views from Mount Scopus towards the Jordan Valley and the Hills of Moab: Above—Spring Verdure; Below—Autumn Pasture: "The eyes of the LORD your God are always upon it, from the beginning of the year to the end of the year" (Deuteronomy 11:12)

22. Onion Sowing at a Moshav in the Aravah: "They sow fields, and plant vineyards, and get a fruitful yield" (Psalm 107:37)

ha-Avodah the socialist party, Mapai the labour party, and Ma'arach, an alliance of all the left-wing parties. There is a small Liberal party, and to the right the Likud party (Conservative). Many of the smaller parties are basically religious groups with strong religious views, but with only one representative in the Knesset. As their support is needed by the major parties, their views often get disproportionate attention, so much so that on occasions it could be said that 'the tail wags the dog'.

The Media

The very first printing press in Asia was established in Safed as early as 1563. It was 300 years later before the first Hebrew newspaper was published in Jerusalem. There are now fifteen Hebrew daily papers, six in Arabic and nine in other tongues. Over 650 periodicals appear regularly, mostly on specialised subjects. The radio and television services are independent of the government and are broadcast in several languages.

Israel seeks to influence the Jews of the diaspora by means of a number of publications distributed world-wide. Gentile understanding of Israel's problems is cultivated by a very efficient Public Affairs Service that issues information broadsheets, press releases and answers enquiries.

Religion

While the larger part of Israel's Jews are agnostic or atheistic, approximately one-third are religious enough to acknowledge that they believe there is a God. Perhaps 5% of the total population are Orthodox or Ultra-Orthodox, divided into many small groups holding a variety of views (see chapter 9). Central to all religious Jews is the Torah (the Law through Moses). Besides this written law there has been added the oral law, the Talmud. This is usually regarded as equally binding as the written Law. Those who claim to be governed by these laws are known as Observant Jews (i.e. they observe the law). In practice, the sum total of these laws has been summarised in the 15th century standard code known as the Shulchan Arukh, which is still in use.

It is customary for all Jews, whatever their views, to keep the feasts of Israel in the traditional way. As might be expected,

ISRAEL

מספקת ירקות ופירות
ללא חשש שביעית
במשהרת
בד׳צ ועד הרבנים
של אגודת ישראל ירושלים

THIS STORE
SELLS PRODUCE
IN OBSERVANCE
OF THE
SHMITTAH YEAR

Shemittah Year (the 7th yearly 'Sabbath of the Land'). Notice in Jerusalem's Mahane Yehuda market draws attention to its observance

the agnostics deny that such observances have anything to do with God. None of the Feasts can be kept as originally pre-scribed in the law, since no sacrifices can now be offered. This feature of the divine ordinances ceased with the destruction of the Second Temple in A.D. 70.

The Samaritans, a pseudo-Jewish sect of a few hundred members in the Nablus area, still sacrifice the Paschal lamb each year, as do the Falashas, who have kept up the custom in Ethiopia over the centuries, and continue to do so in private in Israel.

The Synagogue (Greek: 'bringing before') is the meeting place for Jews, and centre of religious activity, but is not a Temple. The Great Synagogue has been completed in Jerusalem in the hope that Messiah will come and meet with them there. Besides the Orthodox synagogues, there are Reform and Conservative synagogues, not recognised by the Orthodox. Each branch of Judaism has its own colleges known as the Yeshiva (plural, Yeshivot).

A recent trend has been the formation of Messianic assemblies of mainly young Jews who have identified their Messiah with Jesus of Nazareth, and eagerly await his return. They deliberately refrain from calling themselves 'Christian' because to a Jew this word has a connotation of centuries of persecution.

RELIGIOUS SECTS IN ISRAEL

JEWISH

Ultra-Orthodox — Divided into a number of small sects who claim to be the only 'true Jews'. Some are anti-Zionist. Some still speak only Yiddish.

Orthodox — Traditional rabbinical Judaism, the official Judaism of Israel based on the Shulchan Arukh, whose rabbis claim they are the only authentic authorities.

Karaites — A few survivors from the Holocaust of a sect that accepts only Holy Scripture and denies the Talmud.

Conservative Judaism — The right-wing of the Reform Movement, but in fact a coalition of many varied views.

Reform Judaism — Originally formed in Germany in 1818, this movement relaxes many orthodox rabbinical traditions.

Liberal Judaism — The left-wing of the Reform Movement, formed in 1902. Not recognised by the Orthodox.

Reconstructionists — A more radical reform movement, mainly in the United States of America.

Messianic Assemblies — Small secret groups who accept Jesus of Nazareth as their Saviour and Messiah.

Humanistic Judaism — A secular movement that keeps elements of Jewish tradition, but denies the existence of God.

Secular Jews — Unattached to any group, yet pro-Zionist, aid charities, join festivals, but shun religion. The majority.

ARAB

Sunni Moslems — The majority of Arabs in Israel, increasing in numbers and building many new mosques.

Christians — Divided between Greek Orthodox, Greek Catholic, Roman Catholic and Protestant denominations.

DRUZE — A separate people, self-styled 'Believers in One God' who live mainly in Galilee and Lebanon.

SAMARITAN — A few hundred descendants of the mixed people left after the Assyrian invasion. Live mainly in Nablus. Religion is a form of Judaism based on the Torah.

OTHERS — Numerous other sects are represented in small numbers in Israel from among the Gentiles.

The unreligious are to some extent organised under the name of Humanistic Judaism. Though they are proud of being Jews, the God of Israel is absent from their thoughts. The Bible is seen as Jewish mythology. The appointed feasts are just a part of traditional Jewish culture.

Israel is a secular state with a religious minority, who hold a confusion of views. Thus the secular state has to tread warily, trying not to antagonise any. Freedom of worship is an essential statute of the land, applying equally to Jew, to Arab or to Gentile of whatever faith. Freedom of religion also means freedom to be irreligious, and this option has been taken by the majority of Israelis.

Zionism

Zionism is not a religion, but was first of all a national movement to establish a Jewish national home, and then an independent Jewish State. There are religious Zionists, but the majority are secular, socialist or revisionist, seeing it as a political movement. There is opposition to Zionism by a few of the small ultra-religious groups, who object to a secular state. They take the view that the formation of a Jewish state ought to await the coming of Messiah, when a truly theocratic state would fulfil their hopes. With the formation of the state, Zionism has become a movement to give financial help to the state and its citizens.

The umbrella organisation that emerged from the first Zionist Congress was the World Zionist Organization with regional groups world-wide. Many other Jewish benevolent societies such as B'nai B'rith ('Sons of the covenant'), founded in 1843, help the movement. The Jewish National Fund (Keren Kayemeth) exists to purchase land for settlement. Jewesses in 50 countries unite in the Women's International Zionist Organisation, said to have half a million members. Temura is a 'pep' group to maintain Zionist ideals. Many other local supporting societies exist to give financial support.

The Hebrew Language

Psalm 119 is divided into 22 paragraphs of eight verses, each paragraph being headed by a letter of the Hebrew alphabet. Each verse within the paragraph begins with the same letter, thus forming an acrostic. Some Bibles use the actual Hebrew letter, and others the anglicised name of the letter. A study of this Psalm could be the beginning of an acquaintance with Hebrew. The form of the letters in use today is virtually that used for the last 2,500 years. Earlier inscriptions use a script similar to that of the Phoenicians.

The language is built on basic three-letter words. By adding various prefixes and suffixes and by using different combinations of vowels, a very wide range of related words has been developed. Thus words with a link in their meaning have an obvious relationship in the way they are written. A problem for users of modern languages is that Hebrew has no tenses of past, present and future. Instead it emphasises the quality of an action as either imperfect, perfect or continuous. Thus the perfect tense, which we would regard as indicating completion, may be used for the future, if that future is certain of fulfilment (as in the case of the divine purpose).

To learn Hebrew in order to become a scholar competent to translate the Holy Scriptures could be a lifetime task. It is not for the amateur. But some of the complexities of the language can be understood with the aid of a good concordance. A feature that will soon reveal itself is the wealth of words in Hebrew, all having a different shade of meaning, that are translated into English by one word. On the other hand, one Hebrew word may be translated into a number of different English words.

To learn modern Hebrew in order to correspond with, or converse with an Israeli, there are teach-yourself books and excellent tapes available from British, American and Israeli sources. Hebrew/English Bibles are obtainable, with Hebrew on one page and the English Authorised Version on the opposite page. As with all books in Hebrew, the pages are numbered backwards, and the Hebrew script is written from right to left.

Modern Hebrew

For centuries the Hebrew language had been virtually dead, only known to scholars. It was used to read the Holy Scriptures to congregations who did not understand it, and to utter prayers that likewise were not intelligible to the hearers. It was thought to be the only language that could be used for sacred matters,

HEBREW ALPHABET

Letter			English Equivalent	Numerical Value
	א		Alef	Silent	1
ב	בּ		Bet,Vet	B,V	2
	ג		Gimel	G	3
	ד		Dalet	D	4
	ה		Hay	H	5
	ו		Vav	V	6
	ז		Zayin	Z	7
	ח		Chet	CH	8
	ט		Tet	T	9
	י		Yud	Y	10
כ	כ	ך	Kaf,Chaf	K,CH	20
	ל		Lamed	L	30
מ		ם	Mem	M	40
נ		ן	Nun	N	50
	ס		Samech	S	60
	ע		Ayin	Silent	70
פ	פ	ף	Pay, Fay	P,F	80
צ		ץ	Tzadi	TZ	90
	ק		Kuf	K	100
	ר		Resh	R	200
שׁ	שׂ		Shin, Sin	SH,S	300
ת	תּ		Tav	T	400

and was not to be degraded by using it for secular affairs. The early immigrants returning to Palestine spoke only the language of the country from which they had come. For well nigh 20 centuries Hebrew had not been the language of the Jewish people, and only at the beginning of the 20th century was it revived.

Today, Hebrew is the spoken and written language of some millions of Israelis. Books, documents, newspapers and magazines are regularly printed in Hebrew, and understood by the readers. Business affairs, shopping, teaching are conducted in Hebrew. Thousands of new words have been added to the Hebrew vocabulary to cope with modern requirements. How has this revolution of the language come about?

Eliezer ben Yehuda

The transformation of the ancient tongue has been mainly the work of one lonely man. A young Jewish boy, born in Lithuania, was educated by a wealthy Jew who adopted him. Eventually going to Paris, he realised that Jews could not have a national identity unless they were united by a common language. He thereupon made it his life's work to revive the Hebrew language in preparation for the time when Jews would have a land of their own. All his life he was plagued with tuberculosis, but nevertheless he went to Palestine in 1881 with a remarkable young Jewess as his wife, set up home in Jerusalem in appalling conditions and began his work.

By means of a newspaper he influenced Jewish thought, and introduced new words in Hebrew, and began work on a modern Hebrew dictionary. Producing the dictionary became his life's ambition. In it were thousands of new words that could be used under modern conditions—words for the workaday world of tools, machines, concepts and materials that were not known to the writers of Biblical Hebrew. Thus Jews were prepared for the eventual colonisation of the land, and for the formation of an independent Jewish state.

The name of this most remarkable man was Eliezer ben Yehuda. He died in 1922, the bulk of his dictionary completed in manuscript, and Hebrew already the spoken language of the returned refugees.

CALENDAR OF ISRAEL'S RESURGENCE

1827 First visit of Moses Montefiore and wife to Palestine

1835 First Jewish Sheriff in London—David Solomon

1837 First Jewish M.P. in Britain—Benjamin Disraeli (nominal Christian)

1837 Mordecai Noah (American Jew) tried to buy Palestine from Turks

1849 *Elpis Israel* published by Christadelphians forecasting British involvement in return of Jews to Palestine

1855 First purchase of land in Palestine for settlement of Jews, by Sir Moses Montefiore and Lord Rothschild

1858 First Jewish M.P. in Britain to be elected as a Jew— Lord Rothschild

1862 Moses Hess wrote *Rome and Jerusalem*, a manifesto of Jewish nationhood

1870 First agricultural school founded at 'Mikveh Israel', Jaffa

1877 First Christadelphian-financed Jewish colony founded at Janna

1877 First visit of a Christadelphian to Palestine

1881 Eliezer ben Yehuda (Hebrew linguist) settled in Jerusalem

1881 *Auto Emancipation* published by Leon Pinsker

1882 BILU movement founded in Russia. First Russian Jewish settlements founded at Rishon le Zion and Petah Tikvah

1882 Hibbat Zion movement founded. Population of Palestine 24,000 Jews

1882– 1905 First Aliyah of Eastern European Jews to Palestine

1894 French Jewish army officer Dreyfus tried as a spy in Paris, trial watched by Theodor Herzl, an Austrian Jew newspaper reporter

1896 Theodor Herzl wrote *Der Judenstaat*, pleading for a Jewish state

1897 Herzl organised first Zionist Congress at Basle

1898 Kaiser Wilhelm of Germany visited Jerusalem

1905– 1914 Second Aliyah of Eastern European Jews to Palestine

1909	Tel Aviv founded as a suburb of Jaffa. Hashomer Jewish defence force formed in Palestine
1914	Jewish population of Palestine 85,000
1914– 1918	World War I. British forces from Egypt drove Turks out
1917	Jerusalem captured from Turks by British troops under General Allenby
1917	Jewish population of Palestine reduced to 55,000
1917	Russian Revolution began. Some Jews became communists
1917	Lord Balfour gave his Declaration of intent to make Palestine a national home for the Jews
1920	The League of Nations gave Britain a Mandate to govern Palestine
1920	Britain appointed Sir Herbert Samuel to be Palestine administrator
1922	Fourth Aliyah began from Eastern Europe
1922	Trans-Jordan separated from Palestine and given to the Arabs
1924	The Technion founded at Haifa
1925	Hebrew University opened on Mount Scopus, Jerusalem
1929	Massacre of Jews by Arabs at Safed and Hebron
1931	Irgun Tzeva'i Le'ummi formed as secret right-wing defence force
1931	Fifth Aliyah began, mainly of German Jews
1933	Adolf Hitler became Chancellor of Germany
1936	Arab strike and revolt. Riots in Jaffa. Jewish population had now risen to 400,000
1936– 1939	Reign of terror in Palestine. British vs. Jew vs. Arab
1939	Ramsay Macdonald's White Paper on Palestine restricting settlement of Jews
1939– 1945	World War II
1940	Aliyah Bet. Rush of refugees to Palestine from Europe
1941	First mass extermination of Jews by Germans at Chelmno
1942	Palmach defence force organised by Palestine Jews

ISRAEL

1945	Half a million Jews in Warsaw ghetto wiped out
1946	British Government offices in King David Hotel, Jerusalem, blown up by frustrated Jews
1947	The 'Exodus' refugee ship turned away from landing in Palestine
1947	British Partition Plan refused by both Jews and Arabs
1948	British administration and forces withdrawn from Palestine
1948	State of Israel declared, and Israel National Council formed as preliminary government
1948	War of Independence. Israel immediately attacked by five neighbouring Arab countries. Arabs seek armistice
1948	Jewish population now 716,000
1949	Israel became 59th member of United Nations Organisation
1949	Israel Knesset formed (elected National Assembly)
1950	Israel government moved to Jerusalem from Tel Aviv
1956	Suez crisis. Israel joined with Britain and France to stop Egyptian aggression
1962	Germany began to give Israel reparation payments
1964	Population of Israel now 2,500,000 Jews
1967	Six-Day War against Egyptian aggression
1968– 1970	War of Attrition against Arab guerrilla tactics
1973	Yom Kippur War against Egyptian aggression
1982– 1984	'Operation Peace for Galilee', and Lebanon War to eliminate P.L.O. bases in South Lebanon
1986	Population of Israel now 3,400,000 Jews

Israel's Flag

7

THE JEWS AND JESUS CHRIST

EVER since Eve was promised a 'seed' who would overcome evil, and Abraham and Sarah had this promise channelled through them, their descendants have been looking for the Promised One who would put all things right. In due course, this Promised One was specified as a prophet (Deuteronomy 18:15) and then as a descendant of King David (2 Samuel 7:12).

Messiah in the Hebrew Scriptures

To David this divinely promised descendant of his became the subject of beautiful and amazing prophecies. It was even revealed to David that his Son would be David's Lord. Normally, a father was reckoned to be greater than his son, but not so this one (Psalm 110:1). The prophet Nathan had told David:

"The LORD declares to you . . . I will establish the throne of his kingdom for ever. I will be his father, and he will be my son" (2 Samuel 7:14).

SEVEN OLD TESTAMENT PROPHECIES OF MESSIAH	
1. His human origin	Genesis 3:15
2. His Hebrew origin	Genesis 22:18
3. His Davidic origin	2 Samuel 7:12
4. His Divine origin	2 Samuel 7:14
5. His place of birth	Micah 5:2
6. His time of birth	Daniel 9:25
7. His birth to a virgin	Isaiah 7:14

Yet, great as his Son would be, David foresaw in his rôle as a prophet that the Promised One would be mocked and despised, his hands and feet would be pierced, and he would be laid in the dust of death (Psalm 22:6,7,15,16). But this tragic Psalm is followed by a message of joy and hope: "Though I walk through the valley of the shadow of death, I fear no evil . . . I shall dwell in the house of the LORD for ever" (Psalm 23). That, in spite of disaster, his royal Son would live to fulfil his mission was known to David, and expressed in Psalm 72:

"Give the king thy justice, O God, and thy righteousness to the royal son . . . In his days may righteousness flourish, and peace abound till the moon be no more! May he have dominion from sea to sea, and from the River to the ends of the earth!" (verses 1,7,8).

Messiah in Isaiah

Messiah's part in God's plan of redemption for sinful mankind was spelt out in Isaiah and other Bible prophets so clearly that when the Messiah came, there were a few faithful Jews ready to welcome him. They were aware that Messiah had a two-fold duty to perform: to redeem both Jews and Gentiles from sin and death, and to be the Lord's Christ, "to perform the mercy promised to our fathers". The salvation that the Messiah was to bring would be both spiritual and eventually literal.

But to the mainstream of Jewry, the need for salvation from sin and death was of far less interest than that of rescue from the Roman oppression. They were looking for a Messiah to lead them to victory over the Gentiles and re-establish the golden age of an independent kingdom of Judah. They were not ready to accept a carpenter's son for their saviour and their king. Jesus did not conform to their preconceived idea of a Messiah. In any case, the Jews in power were doing quite nicely for themselves under Herod's administration, and were not looking for a revolution to improve their lot.

Various Attitudes

The Gospel record in John 7 gives us a good picture of the many various and contradictory attitudes of the Jewish people to Jesus. The Judeans sought to kill him as a rival for power; others thought that he was leading people astray from the teaching of Moses, and yet others that he was merely a good man doing many good works. There was much debating as to whether he could really be the Messiah. Was he, or was he not? The evidence that he was indeed a man endowed with divine power was proved by the many miracles, including even raising the dead. But among the leaders this only caused jealousy and fear of competition for the people's allegiance. This was compounded by the way in which he ridiculed some of their traditions and moral laws, and their inconsistency in observing the law of Moses which they professed to keep.

Even though Jesus allowed the common people to mount him on an ass and cheer him into the city, the Pharisees said, "the world has gone after him" (John 12:19) and their envy was stirred yet further. The materialistic sect of the Sadducees were sceptical of him and utterly refused to accept him, seeing him as a political rival. The ultimate result, all the world knows. Pilate, the Roman governor, before whom Jesus was eventually brought, "knew that it was out of envy that they had delivered him up". He also knew that Jesus was called Christ, and that the Christ (Messiah) was the One for whom the Jews looked for their national salvation.

The Onager, a species of wild ass, likely to be the sort upon which Jesus rode

A Change of Heart

Fifty days later, the group of men and women who had become so dispirited at the death of their beloved Master, were in a very different mood. Their world had changed. They had met him, talked with him, eaten with him, and knew certainly that he was alive and well, and had now been taken visibly to heaven. The miracle of resurrection had taken place and of that they were utterly convinced. They quickly set about trying to convince their fellow Jews that Jesus of Nazareth was the Messiah, the Christ, God's Anointed.

All the first Christians were Jews, although the name 'Christian' was not yet in use. Many thousands embraced the faith, even some of the priests joining them: "There were added that day about three thousand souls" (Acts 2:41). "Many of those that heard the word believed, and the number of the men came to about five thousand" (4:3). "The number of the disciples multiplied greatly in Jerusalem, and a great many of the priests were obedient to the faith" (6:7). "You see, brother, how many thousands there are among the Jews of those who have believed" (21:20).

When the apostles went to the cities of the Roman Empire, their custom was to go first to the Jews in the local synagogue to preach their good news. After that, they gave the message to the Gentiles. Eventually Paul came to Rome, and his first action was to call together the leaders of the local Jews and explain: "It is because of the Hope of Israel that I am bound with this chain" (28:20).

The First Century

Thus it is evident that in the first century A.D. thousands of Jews accepted Jesus as their Messiah. But there were millions who did not. The early Christian church was primarily a Jewish movement; the opposition was at first also entirely from the Jews. Action taken to try to counteract the growing influence of the Christians included an economic boycott against known members, forbidding the reading of Christian literature, and amazingly a cessation of the reading of the Ten Commandments in the synagogues, because the Christians were reading them in their assemblies; and, finally, an addition to the daily prayers for curses to descend on the Nazarenes, as they were called.

In the course of time, pagan opposition to the Christians grew, and often Jews and Christians were coupled in the mind of the authorities as people to be suppressed. When the Romans finally cracked down on the Jewish rebels and destroyed Jerusalem, the few Christians in the city escaped as they had been warned to do by a prophecy of Jesus. The composition of the Christian churches became less Jewish, and

THE JEWS AND JESUS CHRIST

by the end of the first century the prophesied apostasy developed and attitudes hardened. Eventually as the churches became entirely composed of Gentiles, the accusation began to be heard that the Jews had been guilty of 'killing God'. The more corrupt Christendom became, so much the more was the hatred of Jews fostered.

For centuries they were hunted from one country to another, were restricted in their way of life, in their occupations, in their dress and in the places where they could live. Many of them found that they were happier in non-Christian lands. A great gulf grew between Christian and Jew. For a while the effects of the French Revolution ameliorated their plight with liberty, equality and fraternity.

The Christian Creeds
A big factor in widening the gulf between Christian and Jew was the promulgation of the creeds. These declared that Jesus was God, a member of the 'Holy Trinity'. This basic dogma of apostate Christendom made it almost impossible for a Jew even to consider becoming a Christian. The Hebrew Holy Scriptures are quite definite that *"The LORD our God is one LORD"* (Deuteronomy 6:4). This teaching was confirmed by Jesus Christ (Mark 12:29) but was ignored by the propounders of the creeds. Thus the two faiths that both claimed to be based on the Bible became polarised: enmity grew, militant Christendom used violence, torture and death against helpless and non-belligerent Jews. Thus it came to pass that Christendom was the principal agent in fulfilling the many terrible prophecies of God's curses upon the disobedient people as written in Deuteronomy.

To the Jew, with few exceptions, there is no relationship between the Christ portrayed by Christendom and their Jewish Messiah. But is that surprising? For the Christ of Christendom bears but little likeness to the Messiah of the Bible. The Jews of Jesus' time, and most Jews today, see Jesus of Nazareth as just another of the false messiahs who have cropped up throughout history. The Jew will say that the blessings associated with Messiah's coming did not come to pass with Jesus' coming, therefore he was not Messiah.

But the messianic hope is not dead. In spite of the disappoint-

165

ments of two dozen, or more, false messiahs, Orthodox Jewry still looks for the coming of Messiah, and points to signs of his coming. Some hold the view that he will not come until they have removed the Moslem presence from the Temple Mount; others that he is awaiting the building of a Third Temple. There are also small secret groups of mainly young Jews, who believe that Jesus of Nazareth was in fact the true Messiah, and that he is about to return.

Jewish Humanism
The false messiahs served to keep alive the Jewish hope of a saviour who would come and save the nation from their distress. The Jewish concept still seems to be for a saviour of the nation rather than for one who saves from sin and death. It is difficult to assess the extent to which secular Jews have a messianic hope. It has even been said that the nation itself is the looked-for Messiah to save the nations.

According to an opinion poll taken in Israel, about two-thirds of the people are agnostic or atheistic. There is a noticeable swing towards Humanistic Judaism, which seeks to interpret Jewish laws, customs and practices on a Godless basis. The State of Israel was established as a secular state: there is no mention of God in its constitution, although there is an official Rabbinate to advise the government on Jewish religious law. It is understandable that many Jews have taken this stance, for on the one hand their small groups of ultra-Orthodox brethren have made themselves a nuisance, and on the other hand the presence of Christendom in the Holy Land has filled it with shrines and icons that to a Jew are evidence of a form of paganism.

God's Truth for Jews
It is doubtful whether the simple and glorious truth about the nature and mission of Jesus Christ has been made known in recent centuries to any but a very few Jews. The few who are known to have responded to it have been in the diaspora. The message has not yet been taken to modern Jewry in the manner and with the vigour of the Apostles Peter and Paul in the first century. The long ages of persecution have caused the Jews to adopt a ghetto mentality, even if not actually living in a ghetto. They tend to be a closed community in matters of

religious faith. There are even greater difficulties in reaching Israelis in Israel, where it is unlawful to attempt to change a person's faith.

In 1967, after the liberation of Jerusalem, General Dayan broadcast: "We came to Jerusalem, not to possess ourselves of the Holy Places of others, not to interfere with the members of other faiths, but to safeguard the city's integrity, and to live in it with others in unity." The State of Israel has had to adopt a policy of open-mindedness regarding religious faiths. So many religions regard Jerusalem as the Holy City of their faith, and so many have places of pilgrimage, that the government has had to exercise toleration to all.

Thus, much to the disgust of the ultra-Orthodox Jews, the authorities have had to assure all of their right to whatever faith they hold, and to possess and visit their shrines as they wish.

The Temple Mount

Strangely this policy has hurt the Orthodox Jews more than others. The Temple Mount has been the location of the Dome of the Rock since the 7th Century. This, and the mosque of Al Aksa nearby, are regarded by Moslems as their third most holy place. They believe that Mohammed ascended to heaven from here. To avoid confrontation, Israel allows the Moslems to maintain a day and night guard on the area, which they claim is their property, and cannot be sold. Jews are advised to keep out 'lest they defile the Most Holy Place'. Tourists are allowed to admire the Moslem shrines under the strict supervision of the guards. Guide books that assert that the Dome of the Rock stands on the site of the former Temples of Solomon and Ezra, are incorrect. The whole of the Temple Mount was surveyed in detail before the present situation had arisen, by a noted Jewish archaeologist. He eventually identified the site of the Temple as being due west of the Golden Gate, well north of the Dome of the Rock.

In confirmation of his findings, in the appropriate place he found an area of untooled bedrock, under a little cupola known as the Cupola of the Tablets. This, the only unpaved part of the whole vast platform, he was convinced was originally the threshing floor of Araunah the Jebusite, bought by David, and

Jerusalem's City Walls

the very site of the Most Holy Place. Foundation lines of the Temple confirmed his findings.

Christian Activities

There has been a Christian presence in Jerusalem and elsewhere in the land for centuries. Monasteries, churches, chapels and shrines abound. But of recent years certain organisations have been established that have raised the question by religious Jews—"Why are they here?" Elsewhere in the world these people are known to be vigorous proselytizers, and Israel has had to forbid any such activity in order to keep the peace. Yet there are numerous Yeshivot (Jewish religious colleges), where orthodox Judaism is taught and explained, and regular advertisements for Humanistic Judaism may be seen, while the advertising of other faiths is forbidden.

Will the Jewish people accept Messiah when he comes? The prophet Zechariah suggests that, as a nation, they will not. He says that two-thirds of them will be "cut off and perish" because of their unbelief (Zechariah 13:8). But the same prophet speaks of the time when their Saviour King will at last be recognised and accepted (Zechariah 12:10-14).

Thus, the 'olive tree' which represents the spiritual aspect of Israel, has had many of its branches lopped off because of their agnosticism and unbelief, but other branches are being grafted in so that the tree may eventually produce fruit to the honour and glory of the LORD, and the enlightenment of the nations (Romans 11:17). The glorious Messiah, King of Israel restored, will lead a redeemed people, both Jew and Gentile, to receive the covenant blessings that were promised so long ago to faithful Abraham. Thus will the longed-for Kingdom of God on earth be initiated, and all nations be blessed. Abraham's faith will be fully justified, and every aspect of the divine covenant fulfilled.

Jews and the New Testament

In former times the New Testament was a forbidden book to Jews. This century it has been read by many out of curiosity. As a result, attitudes have tended to change. Jesus of Nazareth is seen as a notable prophet and a credit to his Jewishness. They are proud that he has had such a profound influence on so many Gentiles. Even so, they still tend to regard him as a false messiah.

There have been numerous attempts to 'Christianise' the Jews, with but little success. Forcible conversions at the point of the sword, such as happened during the Spanish Inquisition, obtained nominal change of faith. In fact most of the unhappy 'Marranos' still practised their Judaism in secret, while professing to be Christian. The reason must surely be that, as already mentioned, the Christ of Christendom bears very little likeness to the Messiah of the Bible.

For perhaps 1,700 years the average ghetto Jew of Europe may never have heard of Jesus of Nazareth. The spread of refugees into the West has brought them into contact with people who have valued their religious freedom, and from them they have learned that 'Jesus was a perfect Jew'. Such has been the change of attitude that an American rabbi could say: "What does the modern Jew think of Jesus? A prophet? Yes, crowning a great tradition, and who can compute all that Jesus has meant to humanity? The love he has inspired, the solace he has given, the good he has engendered, the hope and joy he has kindled—all that is unequalled in human history" (H. G. Enelow of New York City, 1877-1934).

A Change of Attitude

Rabbi S. S. Wise wrote: "It is no mean joy and ignoble pride in us of the house of Israel to recognise, to honour and to cherish among our brothers, Jesus the Jew" (*The Outlook*, June 7, 1913). In the *Jewish Encyclopaedia*, the editor, Isador Singer wrote: "I regard Jesus of Nazareth as a Jew of Jews, one whom all Jewish people are learning to love. His teachings have been an immense service to the world in bringing Israel's God to the knowledge of hundreds of millions of mankind."

The famous Jewish scientist Albert Einstein was asked:

Q. "To what extent are you influenced by Christianity?"

A. "As a child, I received instruction both in the Bible and in the Talmud. I am a Jew, but am enthralled by the luminous figure of the Nazarene."

Q. "You accept the historical existence of Jesus?"

A. "Unquestionably. No man can read the Gospels without feeling the actual presence of Jesus. His personality pulsates in every word. No myth is filled with such life . . . Theseus and other heroes of his type lack the authentic vitality of Jesus."

Cecil Roth in his *Short History of the Jewish People* (p. 142) wrote: "He presented them (his teachings) in a new fashion untrammelled by the shackles of ceremonial law, and enlivened by continuous parables of haunting beauty."

An interesting comment has been written by another Jewish writer: "The church of Jesus Christ has preserved no portrait of its Lord and Saviour. If Jesus were to come again tomorrow, no Christian would know his face. But it might well be that he who is coming at the end of days, he who is awaited by the synagogue as by the church, is one, with one and the same face" (H. J. Shoeps, "A Religious Bridge between Jew and Christian", in *Commentary*, New York, February 1950).

A Great Teacher

For the mainstream of Jewry in the West, Jesus was a great teacher of morality and an artist in parable, but that is all. They are proud to accept him as a Jew who has made his mark on mankind. But he cannot be, to the Jew, either God or God the Son in the sense conveyed by the doctrine of the trinity. The Jew does not accept that the suffering servant prophecy in

Isaiah 53 relates to their Messiah, but prefers to relate it to the nation, seeing the sufferings of the Jewish people as for the sins of the world.

While the older Jews, who were refugees from persecution in 'Christian' countries, have unhappy memories of the way that 'Christianity' was practised, the 'sabras' (Jews born in the land) have never known that kind of persecution. The Sephardim in Israel have only known of Moslem opposition. Immigrants from western lands have only memories of an apathetic church. The practical help given during the last century by such bodies as the Christadelphians has had an effect in softening the Jewish attitude. The authorities are anxious to let their appreciation of 'righteous Gentiles' be known. The recent apology of the Roman church for the suffering caused by that church in the past may also be having an effect.

Thus, there appear to be a number of factors at work changing the attitude of Jewish people during these last years before the Messiah makes his presence known.

Christian Attitude

Most 'Christians' know little or nothing about the relevance and proper place of Israel in God's glorious plan of salvation. It seems to have been overlooked that the New Testament is the outflow and continuation of the Hebrew Holy Scriptures with its multitude of prophecies that came to pass in the first century, and its vivid pictures of events yet future.

So, although all the first Christians were Jews, with the gradual apostasy of the churches of Christendom the Jews became alienated and there has been little or no Jewish participation in the remnant of true believers. Like the Jews, the remnant of faithful Christians has been persecuted by the dominant powers of an unholy Christendom. The revival of the scriptural 'Hope of Israel' has not yet reached the ears of the scattered people, with very few exceptions. It seems that the good news must wait for the arrival of the Messiah.

8

ISRAEL ARCHAEOLOGY

TODAY's Israelis might be called 'the people of the spade', for digging up the past has become a national pastime. Almost anybody's back-yard might be an archaeological site. Sometimes items of real interest have been found in this casual way. However, professional archaeologists usually choose to dig on a site that offers good prospects of worthwhile discoveries, such as a *tell* (or mound) that indicates the buried ruins of a city.

The Realities of Archaeology

It is impossible to convey to the reader of an account of archaeological discoveries, a realistic impression of what is involved for the archaeologist. The leaders' plans have to be in great detail, yet have to provide for unexpected contingencies. His team have to be prepared for and capable of some really hard work, yet be able to see and concentrate on minute items that may prove to be of significance. Sorting and cleaning potsherds can be a time-consuming and trying occupation. Charting the details of each stratum is an exacting requirement. Yet, the days of unrewarding hard work can be punctuated by

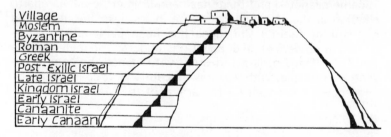

Diagram of a Tell: layers indicate levels (strata) of occupation; 'steps' indicate excavations at each level

the thrills of unexpected discoveries, when the whole team will gather to look excitedly at what has been unearthed.

Digging—Discovering—Dating

In past centuries there was sporadic digging for buried treasure, or for grave robbing, but organised archaeological investigations did not begin until early in the 19th century. Lady Hester Stanhope organised one of the earliest excavations at Ashkelon in 1815. The Palestine Exploration Fund was founded in England in 1865 for "the accurate and systematic investigation of the archaeology, the topography, the geology and physical geography, the manners and customs of the Holy Land, for Biblical illustration". The basis for really scientific archaeology was laid by Sir Flinders Petrie in 1890, when he devised a system of sequence-dating based on the distinctive items that could be found at each level of occupation (see diagram).

The critics, who at one time thought that the Bible was myth and fiction, have been proved to be wrong as a result of archaeological discoveries. For example, the casual way in which the Bible refers to "the gate" of Jericho at the time of Israel's invasion has been shown to be literally true, for the city at that time had only one gate (Joshua 2:5). The "five porches" of the Pool of Bethesda have now been shown to be literally five in number (John 5:2), and not a symbolic number as alleged until 1932. In 1903, the city of Gezer was uncovered. It is mentioned in the Bible as a dowry to King Solomon when he married the daughter of Pharaoh-Shishak (1 Kings 9:16). Thus the archaeologist can often relate his finding to the Scripture record, and confirm the accuracy of that record in detail.

The Purpose of Archaeology

Early excavations were often merely a search for such items as pots and sherds, tools or objects of worship that were suitable for display in a museum. This sort of activity increased during the period of the British Mandate (1918-48). The emergence of the independent State of Israel resulted in archaeology becoming much more organised, with the introduction of new techniques. It became more of a search for the way of life in old time, rather than a quest for artifacts. Soil would be analysed, pollen granules sifted out, middens examined, and a brush used rather than a spade.

Kathleen Kenyon has written: ''All excavation is destruction. The evidence concerning an ancient site is contained in the layers of soil comprising its floors, and those which lie above and beneath them. Once these layers have been disturbed, the evidence is disturbed and has been destroyed altogether unless it has been properly observed, recorded and subsequently made public.''

The Israeli archaeologist Yigael Yadin has said that the proper excavation of a large site such as Hazor could take centuries, if done properly. During this century notable excavations have been conducted at many sites of ancient cities including Lachish, Debir, Beth Shemesh, Jerusalem, Mizpah, Gibeon, Shechem, Tirzah, Samaria, Dothan, Jericho, Bethshan, Hazor, Taanach and Megiddo. From these, and many other 'digs', a lot of information has been gleaned about the ways and habits, the religious practices and trades of the many different peoples who have lived in the land during the past centuries.

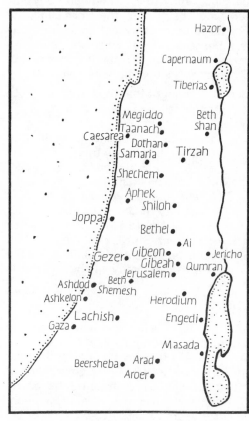

Principal Archaeological Sites in Israel

Archaeologists have tended to work in their own limited sphere of operations, paying scant attention to findings elsewhere. Until 1975 there was no comprehensive survey of the whole archaeological scene in Israel. Then the Oxford University Press issued a four volume *Encyclopaedia of Archaeological Excavation in the Holy Land* edited by Michael Avi-Yonah, which brought together the findings of many workers over the past century. These volumes make one realise something of the organisation, the labour and the sweat that has gone into archaeological excavations in Israel. The fruit of these labours is to confirm the accuracy of the Bible record to the utmost.

Sceptical Archaeologists

There is a tendency among archaeologists to assert that their conclusions are definitive and unassailable. This self-confidence has resulted in doubts being cast upon the Bible record and in particular the chronology of the Bible. It is as well to realise that the findings of archaeologists are often corrected as a result of later and more careful research. If some archaeologists are sceptical of the Bible account, so can the Bible student be of the conclusions of the archaeologist. To the committed student of the Bible, who regards the Bible as the Word of God, archaeological discoveries help the understanding of the Bible, and the Bible helps to an understanding of the archaeologist's discoveries.

Biblical Archaeology

Biblical archaeology is not limited to the Holy Land. Other near-by lands, especially Egypt, Syria and Mesopotamia, have probably provided more direct confirmation of the Bible record than findings in Palestine. This may seem strange at first. But it must be realised that there are comparatively few inscriptions or written records in the Holy Land, while these surrounding countries abound in great collections of written records. The kings of Egypt, Babylon and Assyria kept detailed annals of their doings, and of their exploits in nearby lands. These records have been found on baked clay tablets, inscriptions on monuments, and paintings in tombs, which have survived the centuries intact. Some of these have contributed parallel records of events related in the Bible, even confirming the names of men and of places in considerable detail. Even papyrus records have been preserved in the dry sands of Egypt which have provided indirect evidence of the veracity of the Bible. Massive volumes have been published about these collateral proofs. This chapter is to be restricted to archaeology in Israel's land.

Complications

Archaeology in Israel is complicated by the fact that the land has been occupied by so many different people. Before it was taken by Israel under Joshua's leadership, it had been occupied for centuries by the Canaanites. After the Jews were finally banished at the time of the third dispersion by the Romans, other people came into occupation. Thus many sites of ancient cities form a sort of layer cake of a series of occupation levels formed during many centuries. To discover remains of a Jewish occupation in Old Testament times it may be necessary to remove the occupation levels of later people such as the Romans, the Byzantines, the Crusaders and Moslems, who all did extensive building.

Pottery Lamp decorated with Menorah, Shofar and Incense Shovel

Thus the excavators have the problem of identifying layer upon layer as the ruins are uncovered. To explore a lower layer, the upper ayers have to be destroyed. Any vital evidence will have gone for ever unless a very full record is kept. So, as the digging proceeds, photographs, drawings and plans are made, and together with any artifacts such as pots or sherds, these are all carefully preserved for future study and reference. Only then can a lower layer be opened up. Much of the archaeologists work is now done in a laboratory where all the evidence can be examined in great detail with the aid of scientific equipment.

Dating Problems

In Israel, few inscriptions have been found. The modern habit of laying a foundation stone inscribed with a date was not observed. Even the massive aqueduct from the hills of Hebron to the Temple at Jerusalem cannot be dated, although it is the largest ancient monument in the land. On the other hand, a branch of the main line of this aqueduct to Herodium can be dated to the time of Herod, and a by-pass from near Bethlehem was clearly dated by an inscription placed by its Roman builders. Other massive works of the past, such as the cisterns hewn out of the solid rock beneath Jerusalem, cannot be dated unless some reference can be found to their construction.

At Ramat Rahel, excavators found stones that had been painted red, and this discovery tied up with the record of Jehoiakim's 'vermilion' house mentioned in Jeremiah 22:14. When excavations at Hazor revealed great stables, it was realised that this tallied with the Bible account of Solomon's building activities (1 Kings 9:19). An early scene of excavation was at Lachish. Here an obvious layer of destruction by fire was found, and this could be correlated to the Bible and confirmed by the Assyrian records of King Sennacherib who besieged and destroyed the city. Thus sometimes it is easy to date discoveries, and at other times quite impossible.

Nomads Leave Few Traces

Abraham, Isaac and Jacob and their descendants in the wilderness of Sinai left no ruins of cities for the excavator to unearth. They were nomads, living in tents and causing minimum disturbance to the soil. There may be an exception to this general rule. A row of twelve great stones has been found in Sinai at the foot of a mountain named Har Karkom. It has been suggested that these may be the stones that Moses erected as "twelve pillars, according to the tribes of Israel" (Exodus 24:4). There is no certainty about this, and the site is not at the traditionally accepted place of the giving of the law to Moses. However, it could be that the tradition has got it wrong. Only God knows.

Geographical features are usually easier to identify. Marah, where Israel disliked the water because it was bitter, is today a green and luscious oasis. The area known as Kadesh Barnea, where Israel encamped for a long time, can be easily identified. It is a vast plateau amidst majestic mountains. In this area there is brackish water that comes from a vast underground source which geologists call 'fossil' water. It contains dissolved mineral salts and, like the water at Marah, might be termed 'bitter'. Perhaps Israel had got used to the flavour by this time! Kadesh Barnea yields to the spade traces of a later Iron Age fortress but nothing of the Israelites' earlier settlements; yet its location, name and water supply confirm the Bible records. Its suitability for Israel's long stay is evident. It may be visited on a good military patrol road that is open to tourists—about 45 miles south-west of Beersheba and spelt Qadesh Barnea on the map.

Evidence of Balaam

In the Jordan valley, at a site known as Deir Alla, which was at one time a sizeable town, excavators have come across broken pieces of wall plaster with writing in Aramaic. Eventually some of these pieces were assembled, and to the surprise of the restorers, the writing made several references to "Balaam the son of Beor, the man who was a seer of the gods". It would appear that the writing had been part of a wall panel which had collapsed sometime in the 8th century B.C. It has been suggested that maybe the great earthquake in the time of King Uzziah was responsible for this city's destruction, as there was no evidence of fire, which is usual when raiders destroy a place. Several other sites have shown evidence in their ruins of the havoc wrought by earthquake, possibly this same event. Examples are found at Hazor and Samaria (Amos 1:1).

Israel's Underground

The Palestine Exploration Fund was organised to work at selected sites at the time while the Turks were still in power. The Fund was financed by voluntary contributions, and so tended to be limited in scope. However, the early excavations soon gave evidence that the Bible is a record true to life, true to history and true to geography. Since the foundation of the State of Israel in

1948 the pace of excavation has accelerated. The Ministry of Education has a department devoted to archaeology, and a number of societies specialise in this field of science. The annual meetings of the Israel Exploration Society are attended by the public in their thousands, thus demonstrating the popular appeal of this work. The Israel army includes instruction in archaeology in its training course, for the army often has to dig in, and evidence of the past may be found almost anywhere. The people of Israel have a thirst for a knowledge of their past that is insatiable. Links with their past appear to give them a feeling of closeness to their fathers and their roots, a sentiment they crave. This may be a natural reaction to the long centuries of dispersion during which they have felt rootless.

Jerusalem's Underground

Literally under the feet of the people of Jerusalem is a warren of caves. From some of these the building blocks of the city were quarried. The limestone on which Jerusalem stands is comparatively easy to work in the quarry, but on exposure to air gradually hardens. These great underground workings have never been completely explored. For security reasons access to this subterranean maze has been limited. There are archaeologists who would love to examine them in detail.

Many of the ancient tombs on the hillsides of the city are caves that have been adapted and enlarged. Some of these were used as living quarters until quite recently. When Sir Moses Montefiore first visited Jerusalem in 1827, he was distressed to find many Jewish families living in these cave tombs "like conies in holes in the rock". Also beneath Jerusalem are numerous cisterns for the storage of water. Without these the city could have been forced to surrender to any besieger very quickly, for it has no natural water supply within its walls.

Problems in Jerusalem

To excavate a living city is a very different proposition to the digging of an unoccupied tell. Thus Jerusalem's past has to be uncovered as and when it is possible. New building operations may provide an opportunity. Recently in a suburb, when foundations were being dug for an exhibition hall, the workers found evidence of a Roman camp: this was soon identified as the site occupied by the tenth legion of the Roman army, which was stationed in the city after its destruction in A.D. 70. A more usual way of estimating the date of a level of occupation is by carefully examining the pots and potsherds that are found on almost every site. Differing types of pottery and of decoration reveal the skill of the potter and give some idea of the period when made. Sometimes glassware, metal or ivory objects, even idols and precious stones, reveal something of the people and of their trade relations with other lands.

A unique opportunity arose when it was decided to rebuild the old Jewish quarter of Jerusalem, which had been destroyed during the Arab occupation. This quarter of the city was built on the ruins of houses that had been part of a very prosperous area in first century Jerusalem. Titus' destruction in A.D. 70, and Hadrian's in A.D. 135 had buried a mass of evidence that has only recently been brought to light. The excavators were amazed to find the remains of beautiful tesselated pavements, spacious houses, and objects that revealed a high standard of living of a wealthy people. In that part of the city had been a glass factory. Thousands of little glass kohl sticks for applying eye shadow, and shattered remains of both blown and cast glass vessels were discovered. First century Jerusalem housed many prosperous people, besides the thousands who had but two mites for their next meal.

An Impression of Solomon's Jerusalem

The City of David and Solomon

The city of Jebus that Joab took for King David lay to the south of the present walls. Parts of this hill are still occupied by houses, so that investigations in this area have been limited in scope. Kathleen Kenyon gave much of her attention to this area, but more recent excavations have revealed the foundations of David's citadel and several houses that had been buried in the rubble. This area has been made into an archaeological park, and visitors may see remains of three buildings that were destroyed at the time of the Babylonian conquest, complete with the charred remains of wooden beams and furniture, and bronze and iron arrowheads. In one ruined building many clay bullae, or document seals, were found. One of these bore the name of 'Berekhyahu son of Nehiyahu the Scribe' (Baruch the son of Neriah—Jeremiah 36:4). This is one of the very few inscriptions that have been found in the city.

Baruch's Seal

The King's Head

A certain well known Jew has amassed a great collection of artifacts from his own diggings and from dealers in antiquities. One of these is a limestone bust of a crowned head which came from a site near Amman in Jordan. The new owner of the bust looked at 2 Samuel 12 and found the account of David defeating the Ammonites. He read that "he took their king's crown from off his head, the weight whereof was a talent of gold with the precious stones, and it was set on David's head". The proud owner of the bust imagined he had acquired a bust of King David wearing his captured Ammonite crown!

For several reasons this seems most unlikely to be a bust of David. The Jews were forbidden to make the likeness of any living creature, and David was well aware of this prohibition. It is most unlikely that the Ammonites would want to memorialise David's victory in this way. David was not like a Roman emperor who erected his likeness in every conquered city. It seems much more likely that it is the bust of an Ammonite king, perhaps the very one that David overcame, perhaps even wearing the crown that David wore after his victory. It is this sort of discovery that makes Israel archaeology of perennial interest and a subject for discussion for years to come.

The Site of the Temples

An archaeologist may not need to do any digging. Professor Asher S. Kaufman visited the Temple Mount over 100 times using his eyes and his camera. He sought the site of the Temples. Tradition has it, and guide books declare, that the Moslem Dome of the Rock stands on the holy site. Eventually Professor Kaufman established that both Solomon's and Ezra's Temples stood about 100 metres north-west of that edifice. The closed Golden Gate, that faces the Mount of Olives, is due east of the entrance to Solomon's Temple. Eventually he traced the lines of the foundations of that long lost temple. Perhaps his most interesting find was an area of untooled native bedrock which surely must have been the threshing floor of Araunah the Jebusite king, which David bought (2 Samuel 24:21). This later became

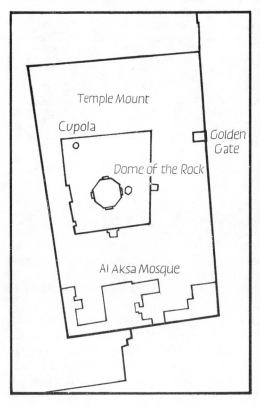

Herod's Temple Mount:
the 'Cupola of the Tablets' is on bedrock
said to be the site of the Holy of Holies

23. Aqueduct at Caesarea:
"To the thirsty bring water" (Isaiah 21:14)

24. Hot Springs at Tiberias: "Like clear heat in sunshine, like
a cloud of dew in the heat of harvest" (Isaiah 18:4)

25. Cliff showing Qumran Caves where the Dead Sea Scrolls were found: "In the roll of the book it is written of me" (Psalm 40:7)

26. View from the Mouth of one of the Qumran Caves.
"They wandered in deserts, and mountains, and in dens
and caves of the earth" (Hebrews 11:38)

27. Archaeologists digging at Bethshan: "Remember the days of old,
consider the years of many generations" (Deuteronomy 32:7)

28. **The walled up Golden Gate, viewed from Gethsemane:** ''I have set watchmen upon thy walls, O Jerusalem . . .'' (Isaiah 62:6)

the floor of the Most Holy Place in Solomon's Temple, and the base on which the Ark of the Covenant stood. It is now covered by a small cupola which is known by the significant name of the 'Dome of the Tablets'. The slabbed surface of the Temple Mount has been made level with this small area of bedrock, which indicates its importance. Beneath the slabs lie hidden 37 great cisterns, capable of holding many millions of gallons of water. These used to be filled from the great aqueduct that brought spring water from the Hebron hills by way of Solomon's Pools and Bethlehem.

At present, the whole of the Temple Mount is forbidden to Jews. This is to avoid a possible clash with the Moslems who have mounted a guard known as the Wakf to protect their Dome of the Rock. Jews are now persuaded to keep clear 'lest they profane the site of the Most Holy Place'. Professor Kaufman was able to make his observations during the period of the British Mandate, when rivalry about access to the Temple Mount was not as keen as it has now become.

'Notice and Warning': this sign in Hebrew and English warns Jews to keep away from the Moslem shrines

Herod's Temple Mount

The vast artificial platform known as the Temple Mount at Jerusalem, covering some 30 acres or more, on which Herod's Temple stood, was one of that king's colossal constructions. It is stated to be the largest religious structure in the world, and was so well designed and built that it has stood the ravages of time, of weather and of war for nearly twenty centuries.

The first Temple at Jerusalem was built by Solomon about 950 B.C. The second Temple was an inferior reconstruction by the repatriated Jews under Ezra's guidance during the fifth century B.C. Both were built on the highest point of Mount Moriah, the actual site being determined by the natural bedrock of Araunah's threshing floor.

By Herod's time, thousands of Jews from all parts of the

Roman Empire came to Jerusalem for the annual holy days. The consequent congestion of the area around the Temple was a cause for concern to the authorities. Herod wished to placate his Jewish subjects, for they had resented his appointment by the Roman Emperor, seeing that he was by descent half Jew, half Edomite. He was fortunate enough to have means to initiate large scale public works. This was not by raising taxes from the people, as Solomon had done, but by the extensive profits of the international trading that had developed during the *Pax Romana* of the Emperor Augustus. This time of peace within the empire had also increased the population, so that Herod the Great had a surplus of labour that could fill the thousands of jobs created by his construction programme. Thus a combination of circumstances gave Herod a unique opportunity to pursue his plans, which included. beside the Temple Mount, a new port at Caesarea, various palaces and fortifications such as at Herodium, Masada and Jericho.

The Temple Mount was intended as a practical solution to a very real problem. Elbow room was vitally needed for the thousands of worshippers at the Jewish festivals. Basically it is a vast platform built to raise the area around the Temple to the level of the Temple floor. This was done by first of all erecting massive walls around the site, the foundations being laid on solid bedrock, even though this meant going down 30 feet in some places. The bedrock was levelled, thus giving the great stones of the wall a really firm foundation. The wall, 16 feet thick, was constructed of great blocks of stone fitted so closely that no mortar or cement was required. If the edges of each stone had not been chamfered, it would be difficult to detect where they joined.

Herod's stonemasons took eight years to prepare the stones, from quarries beneath the city, and take them to the site. When construction began, Josephus records that the work was never halted by bad weather, and that it only rained at night. The great stones, mostly about 3 feet thick, were in various lengths, and varied in weight from 5 tons to 50 tons. Their sheer weight alone accounts for the extraordinary stability of the structure. The movement of the blocks from the quarry to the site was accomplished with the aid of rollers and teams of oxen on earth embankments. Thousands of workers were needed to prepare the earthworks and assist in the placing of the stones.

Technically, this work was, and still is, an outstanding example of skilful engineering. The planning, organisation, supervising and carrying out of the whole operation is a testimony to the abilities of the people of the time. Hidden behind the 'dry stone walling' is another wonder. The space between the mountain slope and the wall was not filled with solid material. Any pressure from the infill was minimised by a system of hollow vaults carefully constructed behind the wall, that took the weight of the platform above, transferring it to the mountainside.

While the size and weight of each block presented problems in quarrying and transporting to the site, it reduced the labour of construction. The alternative of using countless small stones would have required much more labour and copious amounts of cement. The production of a sufficient quantity of cement for such a structure would have involved the burning of hundreds of tons of lime, in turn needing the destruction of a sizeable forest for fuel. Wood was always in short supply, and this may have been one reason for the decision not to use cement.

The Staircase Jesus Trod

In recent years archaeologists have investigated the area around the southern wall of the Mount and found part of the monumental staircase that led up to the two main gateways in Herod's time. The staircase is very broad but is constructed with shallow steps averaging 8 or 9 inches. The tread of the steps alternates between a depth of about 12 inches and 36 inches, then 12 inches and so on. This appears to be a deliberately designed feature of the ascent of some 30 steps in all. It assured an unhurried approach to the holy precinct. These steps are undoubtedly the original Herodian ones, and so would be used by the Lord Jesus and his followers as they approached the Temple.

From this staircase there were two gateways through the wall of the Temple Mount, known as the Hulda Gates. The double gateway which served for both entrance and exit is now blocked by a later building; the triple gateway, probably used by the priests only, is still visible, although it has been filled with stonework.

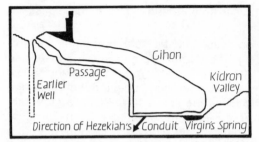

Water supply in
Old Jerusalem before
construction of
Hezekiah's conduit:
Jebusite tunnel and
'Warren's shaft'

To look at the surface of the Temple platform, it is not obvious that beneath its vast surface of paving, there are great rock cisterns. At one time these were probably fed from the great aqueduct that brought water by gravity from the distant Hebron hills and Solomon's Pools beyond Bethlehem. It is unlikely that the rainfall on the platform would be enough to keep them filled.

The labour involved in extracting the water from these cisterns gives enhanced meaning to the labours of those who were condemned to be 'drawers of water'. Vast quantities of water were needed for the ritual washings and baths, besides

Jerusalem's
Ancient
Waterworks,
showing aqueduct
from Hebron hills
and Solomon's
pools, and also
Hezekiah's conduit

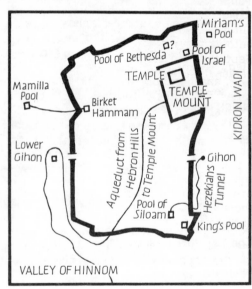

the preparation of the Temple sacrifices. The laver, that great bowl that was elevated on the backs of twelve bronze (or copper) oxen, supplied water for the requirements of the priests, but the filling of it would be a major task for the servants.

Thus Herod's Temple Mount, or Haram esh-Sherif, as the Moslems call it (meaning 'The noble sanctuary' in Arabic) is one of the great monuments of the world, testifying to the skills of those days; but more than that, giving fascinating evidence of the truth of the New Testament records, and the reality of the events in the first century that are so dramatically related by historians such as Josephus. Even after 20 centuries it still remains most impressive. What must it have been when first completed?

Which Tomb?

The tomb of Joseph of Arimathea, in which the body of Jesus was laid, has not been identified. The traditional showpiece tombs are genuine tombs, but date from the period of the kings, around 700 B.C. As Joseph's tomb is stated to have been an unused one, it could not have been a cleaned-up old tomb. The 'Garden Tomb', which was at first called 'Gordon's Tomb' because General Gordon drew attention to it, is useful to illustrate certain features of the rock-cut tombs of the period, but it has every evidence of having been made many centuries before the time of Joseph. The tomb in the Church of the Holy Sepulchre has also been shown to be one made many centuries earlier than the time of Joseph.

It seems likely that the tomb in which Jesus lay, and from which he rose to life, may have been obliterated in one of the many destructions that the city has suffered during the centuries. It is certain that our Lord would not approve of his tomb, or any other place associated with him, becoming a shrine or a place of commercialised religion. When Jerusalem becomes the city of the Great King, as it surely will, it will be the centre of world worship of the Living God, and His Saviour King, and there will be no more superstitious veneration of shrines, icons and idols.

The Pavement

For many years pilgrims have been shown the Pavement where Pilate is said to have sat in judgement upon Jesus (John 19:13), and the Ecce Homo arch where he said "Behold the man" (John 19:5). However, recent archaeological findings are that the Pavement was actually not constructed until after the destruction of the city in A.D. 70.

The evidence comes from Josephus who reported that the Struthion Pool was open to the air at the time of Titus' destruction of the city. Since the Pavement is built upon arches over the said pool, it could not have been there in Pilate's time, and was probably built by Hadrian many years later. The Ecce Homo arch has been dated by noted archaeologists to several years after the trial of Jesus. The nuns who show visitors these shrines no longer claim that they are the actual sites of the sufferings of Jesus. "This is not the place where they really happened", they explain to the thousands of pilgrims who come each year.

Evidence of Crucifixion

No Roman *stauros* (torture stake) has been found. But Roman nails have been found in plenty. At Inchtuthill in Scotland, seven tons of unused Roman nails were found, apparently left behind by Agricola's forces in A.D. 78. Some of these were nine inches long, well made with sharp spikes and heavy heads. Normally they would be used for heavy construction work, but on occasion they could become a horrific instrument of torture.

The only archaeological evidence of crucifixion has been found in an ancient cemetery in Jerusalem. The bones of a crucified man have been found with a nail still penetrating the two ankle bones. The point of the nail had been turned when it struck a knot in the wood and was thus impossible to withdraw when the body was taken down from the stake. The victim had been laid to rest with the nail and some of the wood still attached to him. This serves as a reminder of the task that faced Joseph of Arimathea and Nicodemus when they took down the body of Jesus. The nails had to be withdrawn from the stake and from the bones before they bore the body to the tomb, yet not a bone was broken (John 19:33). These two secret believers did for Jesus what none of the other disciples could have done. It must have been a very unnerving experience for both of them, and one wonders how much they knew of what was to follow.

Evidence of Resurrection

One would not expect to be able to find archaeological evidence that confirms the resurrection of Jesus. However, on a white marble slab found at Nazareth during the last century, but only examined in 1930, is an inscription in Greek of profound significance. It reads (in part): "Ordinance of Caesar. It is my pleasure that graves and tombs remain undisturbed in perpetuity . . . let it be absolutely forbidden for anyone to disturb them. In the case of contravention I desire that the offender be sentenced to capital punishment."

There is reason to think that the Caesar of this inscription was Claudius, who during his reign expelled the Jews from Rome because of rioting "at the instigation of one Chrestos", who was claimed by his followers to have risen from the dead. The Jewish orthodox explanation was then, as now, that "the disciples came and stole away the body" (Matthew 28:13). Hence the emperor sought to control the situation by forbidding the disturbance of graves, and having this inscription erected at Nazareth, the only town in Palestina with which the name of Christ was associated.

Pontius Pilate

Pilate is depicted in the Gospels as a frustrated man who was deliberately and spitefully provoking the Jewish people. Here our knowledge of the past can be augmented by dipping into ancient books, such as the writings of Josephus and Philo. Josephus tells of Pilate introducing into Jerusalem Roman standards that bore the effigy of the Emperor Tiberius. A huge protest by enraged Jews eventually resulted in Pilate giving way. They were withdrawn. But in a further attempt to honour the emperor, Pilate hung shields dedicated to Tiberius in the palace at Jerusalem. Herod's four sons appealed to Caesar, who ordered them to be removed to Caesarea to be hung in the temple of Augustus. Thus was Pilate frustrated as a result of his lack of sensitivity for the religious views of the people he ruled. On another occasion he used part of the Temple treasure to finance the building of an aqueduct. In the resulting uproar many Jews were killed by Pilate's soldiers.

When Jesus was brought before Pilate, although he was well aware of Jesus' innocence, Pilate was in no mood to allow

Inscription containing the name of Pontius Pilate ('. . . VS PILATUS') found at Caesarea

another appeal to be made to Caesar. Hence he allowed the Jewish leaders to have their way. Yet Pilate got his own back, by the provoking inscription that was placed on the cross: "What I have written, I have written" was his scathing reply to the Jews' objections. As Procurator, Pilate had the right to issue coins, so he ordered coins that bore the head of Caesar, as the incident of Jesus and the tribute money reveals (Matthew 22:19). It was difficult for the Jews to protest at this subtle way of honouring the emperor. Pilate also issued some copper coins that bore a design of a pagan priest's staff, which would seem to be a further deliberate provocation by a frustrated man.

The only archaeological discovery for evidence of Pilate's name and office was found on an inscription in the Roman theatre at Caesarea. He was unloved during his life and unmourned at his death by suicide. Even his fellow Roman, the historian Philo, could find no good thing to say of him.

Ivory in Israel

There is no evidence that elephants once roamed in Israel, but Solomon sat on an "ivory throne" and Ahab is said to have lived in "the ivory house that he built" (1 Kings 22:39). Excavations at Samaria have revealed remains of intricately carved ivory work at this location. It appears that the ivory was used as a veneer over wood, and so references to beds of ivory, thrones of ivory and benches of ivory would not appear to mean that the whole structure was made of ivory, but that it was overlaid, or inlaid with ivory. The ruins of Megiddo have yielded nearly 300 items of ivory, possibly dating from the pre-Israelite period. At Safadi, near Beersheba, an ivory workshop complete with workbench, tools and an elephant's tusk were found by a French archaeologist in the 1950s. This also was dated to the period before Israel arrived. Ivory has the advantage that it can be carved with greater finesse than wood, can be polished to an attractive finish, and resists rot. There is no evidence so far that the people of Israel were skilled in working ivory. The luxury items that Solomon and Ahab possessed most likely came from Phoenician sources, and it is likely that they may have reflected the pagan outlook of their makers in the designs.

Hidden in Caves

The numerous scrolls that were eventually found hidden away in scroll jars in the caves near Qumran are a mixed bag. Those of interest to the student of the Bible are the fragments from every book of the Old Testament with the exception of Esther. These scrolls are at least a thousand years older than anything previously known to modern scholars. Chief among these is the amazing complete scroll of the prophet Isaiah, now in safe keeping in a special museum in Jerusalem. To the con-sternation of some Jews, chapter 53 is there in its right place on this scroll. It had been alleged by some rabbis that this chapter had been inserted by Christians! It seems strange that this literary treasure should have been found 'accidentally' by an Arab boy, just at the time when critics were casting doubts upon the authenticity of the Old Testament. Truly, God works in very

The Shrine of the Book in Jerusalem —housing the Dead Sea Scrolls

mysterious ways—ways that few perceive at the time, yet which all work out to His determined end, that He may be glorified by man.

The Roman historian Pliny had written about the Essenes and even described the location of their headquarters. But this clue had been unnoticed for centuries, and so the scrolls remained there tucked away in jars in inaccessible caves until the time when the Lord wanted them to be revealed.

Other Caves

The findings at Qumran sparked off investigations into other caves in the wilderness of Judea. These bare hills contain

Thanksgiving Scroll: one of the non-Biblical Dead Sea Scrolls containing Psalm-like hymns starting "I thank thee, O Lord . . ."

many caves which had never been systematically explored, although no doubt treasure hunters may have looked at them. These enquiries led to the story of Bar Kochba, the false 'messiah of the wilderness'. When the Emperor Hadrian proposed to rebuild Jerusalem as a pagan city to be known as Aelia Capitolina, at the end of the first century A.D., he underestimated the extent of Jewish sentiment for their beloved city. Even though it had been ruined, the Temple destroyed and many of the people sold as slaves, the ruins still remained the focal point of Jewish national hopes and pride. At this time the Jews had not been totally banned from living in the land. Hadrian's proposal united the remaining Jews in fierce and fanatical opposition. A leader emerged, Simon Bar Koziba, later to be known as Bar Kochba ('son of a star'). Under his leadership, control was wrested from the Romans to such an extent that coins were minted for the rebel state of Judea.

An intensive search of the Judean caves revealed that Bar Kochba and his associates had made good use of several of them to hide from the Romans. They had left letters and documents hidden in cracks in the cave walls that have now been recovered. Some of them were actually signed by the rebel leader. An unexpected find was a woman's toilet set, complete with mirror, comb, perfume and powder packed in a goatskin bag together with papyrus documents that identify the date and the conditions of their owner when they were abandoned early in the second century.

Access to one of these caves was only possible by means of a rope suspended from the cliff top above. In this cave were found remnants of fabric which reveal the type of material in use, and the skill of the weaver.

Masada

The great massif of Masada sticks out prominently on the Dead Sea coast. The Israeli archaeologist Yigael Yadin made a thorough search of this site of what was at one time a massive fortress, and a palace of Herod. The storming of Masada by the Romans has been re-enacted for a film epic based on the grim record of Josephus. The excavations of the archaeologists have confirmed Josephus' description. Even the stone balls that were slung at the fortifications by the Roman ballista, still lie around in great piles. The plaster on the walls of some of the ruins still bears the blood stains of the Jews who died by their own hands on that dreadful occasion.

Particularly interesting finds on Masada were a scroll of Genesis and some empty wine jars that are stamped with the name of the Roman consul in the year 19 B.C.—C. Sentius Saturninus—and also marked 'To King Herod of Judea'. Surely these are clear evidence of Herod's dependence on the good-will and support of Rome. The wine was doubtless a gift from the Roman emperor to his vassal king.

Josephus' description of Masada mentioned the great store-houses in which were kept supplies of dates and corn that would remain sound and edible for many years in that dry clean air. Traces of these stocks have been detected in the storehouses, the foundation walls of which are still visible.

Underwater Archaeology

During a recent drought, the level of the Sea of Galilee dropped and revealed in the mud on the shore a well preserved, eight metre long, wooden boat that seems to date from Roman times. Carbon-14 dating at the Weizmann Institute dates it at about 70 B.C. (+ or − 90 years). It was eventually lifted intact and transferred to a bath of chemicals that are intended to preserve the wood. The pickling process could take several years and may prove too expensive to maintain. In the meantime little models of the 'Jesus boat' are being made, so that its shape and style may be studied.

A storm off the Carmel coast resulted in the sands being parted to reveal a great treasure that had been hidden there for many a long century. There is evidence that three ships were wrecked there at widely different times. The ships had disintegrated, but some of their cargoes had been preserved in the sand. A prize find was that of a perfectly preserved sickle-shaped Canaanite sword, complete with its wooden handle. Other items included ingots of lead, of copper and of tin, the oldest to have been found anywhere. The markings on them suggest that they may have been shipped from Cyprus.

Another nearby cargo comprised a huge collection of broken items of bronze, possibly a shipment for melting down. Among these were broken tools such as a jeweller might use, and broken ornaments. A different site contained the largest hoard of coins ever found in the sea, about half a ton of copper coins that had been minted in Syria. While not of great value, these are of great interest.

Caesarea Maritima (Sebastos)

South of Carmel, on the coast, the ruins of the city and harbour of Caesarea are confirmation of the accuracy and truth of the New Testament records. The city was built on a new site by Herod the Great as part of a plan to please his Roman overlord, Caesar Augustus. Before Augustus came to power, Herod had backed his rival, Antony. Hence Herod deemed it prudent to prove his loyalty to the new emperor by ambitious enterprises. This city of Caesarea was designed as the new Roman capital of Judea, and its harbour was intended to rival that of Alexandria.

The City and Mint

The city was walled and had every feature that a Roman capital city should have. It was, in course of time, the headquarters of Pontius Pilate—his name has been found on an inscribed stone (see page 190). Here, Cornelius lived, the first Gentile to be baptized into Christ. Here lived Philip and here Paul was imprisoned and finally embarked for Rome. As capital city, a Roman mint was located here.

The city lasted as a place of some importance until the 13th century when it was destroyed by the Mamelukes from Egypt. The site is so vast that archaeological work on it could last for many years. A notable feature of the city's environs is the nine mile aqueduct that brought water from a spring in the Carmel hills. This was so well built that it operated for several centuries, and much of it still stands.

The Harbour and Trade

Recent underwater exploration of the sunken harbour has been most revealing. The historian Josephus mentioned its construction and commented on the great blocks of limestone used in the construction of its breakwaters. How the builders handled blocks up to 50 feet in length remains a mystery. Josephus did not mention another unusual building material. This was hydraulic cement, based on tuff (fused volcanic ash) which hardens slowly under water. The tuff was probably brought by ship from Italy. Traces of the wooden forms into which the cement was poured, can still be detected. The harbour and its breakwaters were made to a unique design which reduced the accumulation of silt by an ingenious system of sluices, a feature that modern ports on that coast would do well to imitate.

However, Herod and his engineers did not know that their great work was built over a geological fault, and would sink beneath the waves within a few years. It has had to await the inspection of scuba-diving archaeologists 20 centuries later to let the world know of the skills of those Roman engineers and craftsmen. For a time the port was kept busy receiving Roman military supplies and exporting Herod's surpluses of wine, flax and grain grown in Judea, besides silk and spices from overland caravans.

Computerised Archaeology

Israeli archaeologists are using space-age technology for a better understanding of their past. The recording and cataloguing of the immense amount of data produced from a dig is now handled by computer. This enables almost instant reference to be made to a vast amount of information, and facilitates the comparison of new finds with material found previously. Another new aid is being used to classify potsherds, using analysis by gamma rays. Only a mere splinter of each specimen is needed to identify the type of clay from which it was made, and thereby the place of manufacture. Pollen analysis is another technique now being used to determine the prevailing vegetation of the period being investigated. Even ancient middens are analysed to find out what sort of food was being used in old time. Man's curiosity about his past knows no end. It is a pity that he is not more concerned about his future!

Limitations of Archaeology

Archaeologists can only recover from a site those structures and objects that have survived the centuries of burial. Many materials such as wood, fabrics, baskets and skins usually perish with time. It is only in extraordinary circumstances that such items are preserved, a few of which have already been related here. Thus a complete picture of the past is never obtained. Much is left to conjecture and to the archaeologists' interpretation of what he finds. Some archaeologists seem to know what they want to find. They tend to begin with the view that the older their discoveries, the more primitive they will have to be. Hence they may highlight any crude implements that are found, and play down any skills that are evident.

It should not be forgotten that the skill of locating and refining precious metals, and the skill of crafting gold and silver into delicate objects seems to have been acquired at a very early time in man's history. Refined gold and silver in some form was in use to make payments from the very earliest known records. That flints were used as tools from a very early time does not show that such people were primitive, but rather that they were skilled in using what was readily available. In any case flints are still used and that fact does not prove that their users are primitive!

Bible Dates

It is noticeable that conventional archaeologists tend to relate their dating systems to the evolutionary view of the age of man. Even so they find it difficult to take man's history back to more than an estimated 10,000 years. Actually the findings of archaeologists confirm to a remarkable degree the Biblical dating system. While it has become popular to dismiss the early chapters of Genesis as folklore, mere traditions handed down by word of mouth, there are good reasons for students of the Bible to accept the Genesis account as a divinely bestowed record given to Moses by the LORD God whom he worshipped and served, and therefore completely reliable.

The last book of the Bible was dictated to the apostle John word by word (Revelation 1:1) coming to him from the Almighty. There are good reasons for thinking that Genesis was given to Moses in a similar manner. Thus the claim that is made in Revelation by the One who could reveal the future, ''I am the Alpha and the Omega, says the Lord God'' (Revelation 1:8), may have a very literal meaning. The first and last letters of the Greek alphabet may typify the first and last books of God's Word, both being of events that are beyond the ken of man and known only to God. Hence, we should regard Genesis as the yardstick by which archaeology should be measured, and not the other way round as so many seem to think.

THE COINS OF ISRAEL

FOR centuries payments had to be made either in kind, by the exchange of goods, or by weighing out pellets and discs of silver or gold on a pair of scales. It is recorded that Abraham traded in this manner: ''Abraham weighed out for Ephron the silver which he had named in the hearing of the Hittites, four hundred shekels of silver, according to the weights current among the merchants'' (Genesis 23:16). Over a thousand years later, we learn that the prophet Jeremiah ''bought the field at Anathoth from Hanameel my cousin, and weighed out the money to him, seventeen shekels of silver'' (Jeremiah 32:9).

The gold or silver that was used for such payments was usually in the form of small pellets, discs, bars or wedges of irregular size and weight. The shekel at that time was a standard weight, and not yet the name of a coin. The word 'shekel' is derived from the word *shaqal*, Hebrew for 'to weigh'. The first coins were developed from the discs of metal made to standard weights and stamped with a symbol that was intended as a guarantee of its value. At first the symbol was on one side of the coin only, the reverse side being a rough punch mark.

It is thought that the first coins were struck by the Greek king of Lydia in Asia Minor about the time that Israel was taken into Babylonian captivity. These first coins were made of an alloy of gold and silver, called electrum. Soon coins of gold, silver and bronze were being made. The sensible idea of making coins to a standard weight and value soon spread, and the first to be mentioned in the Bible are the Persian darics (Ezra 2:69), which were named after Darius, whose portrait they bore. The Persian treasurer records give the information that 1 part of gold was equal to 13 parts of silver by weight.

Half Copper Shekel
of Simon Maccabeus

Copper Coin
of John Hyrcanus

Coin of
Herod the Great

Shekel of
Simon Bar Kochba

Coins and Archaeology

The discovery of coins in an archaeological dig can be a guide to establishing a date for other items that may be found, besides providing a clue as to the political conditions of the time and place. Often only odd coins are found, presumably lost accidentally. Occasionally a hoard will be found, perhaps buried in fear of an invasion, perhaps as a nest-egg for old age, or maybe the proceeds of a robbery. Several hoards of coins have been found in Israel: at Bethshan, one from the time of Ptolemy Soter of Egypt, another from that of Demetrius I of Syria; at Bethel, a hoard of coins of Alexander the Great; and at Jerusalem, one of Seleucid coins and another of Maccabean coins. A sackful of Phoenician bronze coins came to light recently in the sands off the coast near Carmel. There may be others yet to be discovered by modern metal detectors.

The importance of such finds is that history is established, the Bible record is confirmed and sometimes Bible prophecy is shown to be accurate. The Persian darics (gold) and siglos (silver) were in circulation among the returned Jewish people until the conquests of Alexander the Great. But even before that, it is probable that Greek coins would reach Judea in the course of international trade. In particular the coins minted in Athens were widely used.

The Earliest Jewish Coins

At first, Jewish coins adopted the Athenian designs, but added the inscription 'YDH' in Hebrew, meaning Judah.

After Alexander's death, at first Ptolemy Soter I of Egypt ruled Judea: hence Egyptian coins were used, with Greek inscriptions, since Ptolemy was one of Alexander's Greek generals. It was this Ptolemy who founded the great library at Alexandria, where the Septuagint version of the Old Testament was translated. But by 198 B.C. Antiochus III of Syria had taken control and Seleucid Greek coins circulated in Judea. As the Seleucid power waned, an independent Jewish kingdom was formed in 142 B.C. Shortly after this Simon Maccabeus was given permission to "coin money for thy country with thine own stamp" (I Maccabees 15:6). But it seems unlikely that any Jewish coins were actually made at that time for the reason given in verse 27, seeing that he was leading the Jews to victory over Nicanor.

Later members of the Jewish Hasmonean dynasty (the Maccabees) did mint small bronze coins of very rough finish known as the *prutah* (plural, *prutoth*). One example of these is inscribed in Hebrew, "Jehochanan the High Priest and community of Jews". But even this information does not help in dating the coin, as there was more than one High Priest of the same name. Some 'of this series of *prutoth* bear Hebrew characters on one side and Greek letters on the reverse. Whenever the Jews were able to mint their own coins, portrayal of human or animal forms was avoided in conformity with the second commandment.

First Century Jewish Coins

When Herod the Great was appointed king of Judea under Roman overlordship in 37 B.C., his coins were of bronze with inscriptions in Greek, the international language of the time. Few of his designs had any Jewish significance. When he died, his sons, among whom the land was divided, each minted their own coins, also inscribed in Greek. These coins of the various Ethnarchs and Procurators ceased to be issued after the Jewish revolt of A.D. 66.

Money Changers

From the foregoing it will be realised that in Roman Judea of the first century, there were in circulation a great variety of coins of many different values. These would be mainly of silver and bronze, with perhaps a few gold pieces from nearby countries. Many would have been in circulation a long time. These, with the official Roman coins, made quite a confusion of money. The need for money changers is self-evident (Mark 11:15). With Jews making pilgrimage to Jerusalem from many foreign lands, the obtaining of suitable coins to pay the Temple tax, the half-shekel, was a real need. Coins bearing pagan symbolism were not appropriate. Again, the Roman tribute money was payable in Roman money. When Jesus asked to see the tribute money (Matthew 22:19) he would be shown a silver denarius bearing the head of Caesar. This may have been of the Emperor Augustus, or perhaps of his successor Tiberius. The Roman tax was first levied in A.D. 6 and had to be paid by all males aged between 14 and 65, and all females between 12 and 65. The translation of denarius as 'penny' in the Authorised Version gives a totally wrong impression, for it was a silver coin and the equivalent of a day's wages.

The Last Jewish Coins

Immediately after the revolt of A.D. 66, the Jews began minting both silver and bronze coins inscribed in archaic Hebrew 'Shekel of Israel' and the year of the revolt, 1 to 5. After A.D. 70 and the destruction of Jerusalem, Rome produced coins to celebrate their victory inscribed 'Iudaea Capta' (see page 87). Then, during the final revolt of A.D. 132-5 led by Bar Kochba, the Jews again issued their own silver and bronze coins with several variations. When Hadrian finally crushed the revolt and levelled the Temple, he had a coin struck that depicted the site of Jerusalem being ploughed by oxen. This Roman coin surely proves the truth of the 500 year old prophecy of Micah: "Therefore shall Zion be plowed as a field" (Micah 3:12). Thus ended Jewish coinage until the State of Israel was re-established in 1948.

The Half-Shekel

Under the law as recorded in Exodus 30:13, every male Jew had to pay an annual 'Atonement money' of a half-shekel. When the apostle Peter was asked if Jesus paid this tribute money (Matthew 17:24) the word in the Greek text is *didrachm*, another term for the half-shekel. Therefore the coin that Peter found in the mouth of the fish must have been a shekel, or *tetradrachm*, as it was to pay for both of them. The word *stater* merely describes the coin as a 'standard' coin, which may have been a shekel of Tyre, in wide circulation at the time, and was indeed specified in Jewish law as being suitable for payment of the Temple tribute.

Pieces of Silver

It is recorded that Judas was paid thirty 'pieces of silver' for his betrayal of Jesus. There has been much difficulty in trying to establish precisely which coins these may have been, out of the many silver coins in circulation. At one time the tetradrachm of the Island of Rhodes was thought to be a candidate, because it depicted a head surrounded by lines that were thought to represent the crown of thorns. However, it transpired that it was actually the head of Helios, the sun god, surrounded by rays of light!

Thousands of fake shekels of the first revolt were made in the 16th century for sale to unsuspecting Christians, who took them to be the genuine pieces of silver. However, the coins from which these were copied have now been firmly dated to A.D. 66-70, long after the death of Jesus.

The most likely coins to have been given to Judas would appear to be Tyrian shekels, which were in wide circulation at the time. It is difficult to equate their value to modern coinage, but they would be equal to three or four months wages, so that Judas' reward can be seen as a very tempting reward for a few minutes work.

The Widow's Mite

The Greek for this little coin is *lepton*, meaning 'the thin one'. There was a Greek coin of this name, probably of similar value to the Jewish half-prutah. When Mark adds that "two mites make a farthing", he is saying that two leptons made a *quadrans*, the latter being the smallest Roman coin.

When Jesus instructed his disciples to "provide neither gold, nor silver nor brass in your purses", the word translated 'brass' is *chalkon*, a word used in a similar way to 'coppers' in our day. The word 'brass' in the Authorised Version is due to a misunderstanding by the translators, for this alloy was unknown in Bible times. It should be read as 'bronze', or perhaps 'copper' in some places.

9

THE ATTITUDE OF JEW TO JEW

EVER since nine of Jacob's sons ganged up against their young brother Joseph and sold him into slavery, the people of Israel have been at variance among themselves. Stories of family feuds recur throughout the history of the tribes of Israel. Only when some national disaster loomed over them did they sometimes forget their disagreements and join in a common cause. Of course such a human characteristic is not unique to Jews, but since it is recorded in their unique history, the Bible, it is for all to see and learn the lesson.

United by God

The many years of slavery in Egypt united the people with a desire to get out, and so they were ready to follow Moses en route to the land promised to their fathers by God. It has been said by a very perceptive Jew that "Moses achieved the nearly impossible: he managed to persuade all the Jews to move in the same direction." This was God's doing, and Moses was the divinely prepared instrument for the purpose. His unique training had prepared him for the task of being a leader of men with the humility of a shepherd. The forty years as a prince of Egypt followed by forty years as a shepherd in the wilderness were God's way of producing the character that he required for the Exodus.

The Exodus from Egypt was later seen as 'the birth of a nation' and as the baptism of Israel in the sea and in the cloud that followed them. But no sooner were they free from their Egyptian taskmasters and their true nature came to the surface in incident after incident. Moses' appraisal of the people whom he had led to safety through the 'sea of destruction', aided by a divine miracle, was summed up in his words uttered shortly before he died, "For I know how rebellious and stubborn you are" (Deuteronomy 31:27).

Once again they were united under Joshua as they crossed the Jordan by another divine miracle. In their subsequent history it is noticeable that when under an external threat, if they had a Godly and strong leader, they could unite very effectively. But, again and again, prosperity led to disunity, culminating in the division of the nation after Solomon's death into the two rival kingdoms of Israel (in the north) and Judah (in the south). At times Jews would fight Jews, even hiring other nations to help destroy their brothers.

Sects of the Jews

Even when the majority of the people were dispersed in exile, those who have been privileged to return to the land of their fathers were deeply divided. When Rome took control of Judea the leaders of the nation were split between Pharisees and Sadducees. The division was both political and philosophical.

The Pharisees claimed to be defenders and exponents of the divinely given law, the Torah. Jesus could see their hypocrisy and proceeded to expose it. Their origin was from the Hassidim (the pious ones) of the post-exile period. They had tended to withdraw from public life until, during the reign of the Hasmonean Queen Alexandra Salome, she put the government in their hands. Later, under Herod's rule, they discovered that Jewish salvation could not be attained by political means, and they eventually petitioned for Roman rule. They opposed the Jewish Zealot movement and after A.D. 135, when all Jews were once again dispersed among the nations, their views became those of orthodox Judaism.

The Sadducees were to all appearances a cynical priestly hierarchy who collaborated with the Romans and were ready to buy or sell positions of power and preference. They had no following among the people, but were aloof, censorious and unpopular. Their philosophy, while professedly based on the Torah, denied the judgement and the resurrection, alleging that man's free choice determined his earthly prosperity. Under Herod and the Romans, the Sadducees held the balance of power in the Jewish Sanhedrin. Their materialistic philosophy was exposed by Jesus—hence their antagonism to his teaching. This sect disappeared in A.D. 70.

The Herodians were allied to the Pharisees regarding the paying of tribute to Caesar, but seem to have been a separate party who favoured Herod's rulership. There is nothing known from any other source than the Gospel records (Matthew 22:16; Mark 3:6; 12:13).

The Zealots were described by Josephus as the 'fourth philosophy'. They were founded by Judas the Galilean in A.D. 6 to oppose the Roman census and the payment of tribute to a pagan emperor (Acts 5:37). They maintained their opposition to the Roman occupation of Judea until their last stand at the fortress of Masada, which fell in A.D. 73. Whether the disciple Simon the Zealot had been one of this party is not certain.

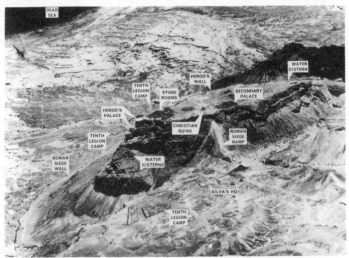

Aerial View of Masada

The Essenes are not named in the New Testament, but are described by the historians Josephus, Philo and Pliny. They were a religious minority who had opted out of the life of mainstream Judea and devoted themselves in isolated groups to study and the simple life. It is thanks to these people that in these last days our confidence in the accuracy of the work of the scribes, who copied the Scriptures, has been confirmed. The Essenes disappeared with the desolation of the land in A.D. 70.

The Remnant: These were not known by this name, except to God. Consisting mostly of common people, some of whom became inspired prophets, there may have always been a remnant, who treasured the promises to the fathers and could see through the rivalry and pretensions of the hypocritical upper classes and priests. The remnant of faithful ones do not have a sectarian name. Of such humble and Godly souls were Joseph and Mary, Zacharias and Elisabeth, Mary, Martha and Lazarus, John the Baptist, the fisher folk of Galilee, the widow who cast two mites, the women who were prepared to 'minister of their substance'. To a superficial observer, these people did not exist, they did not form a cohesive group. It was to these that John and then Jesus called until in less than a decade there were thousands who had sought 'The Way', and who eventually attracted to themselves the name of Christian, given to them in mockery by the pagans of Antioch, probably because it sounded very like the Greek word for 'whitewasher' in reference to the teaching of Jesus that sins can be forgiven.

The Christian faith and way of life was accepted by thousands of Jews in Judea and the diaspora. Orthodox Jews bitterly opposed those who had adopted the new faith, even as they had opposed Jesus. In the First Century A.D. it was the Jews who persecuted the Christians, but as the centuries passed the tables were turned and it was organised Christendom that became the persecutor of the scattered and homeless Jews.

Divided to Fall

In the final years before the destruction of Jerusalem in A.D. 70 there was an even more complex division, which the threat of extermination did not heal. Rival Jewish factions were literally 'daggers drawn' within the city, even while the Roman army was storming it from without. For example, the Sicarii (men of the dagger), the extreme wing of the Zealots, murdered any leading Jews who were regarded as moderates, or were thought to be collaborating with the Romans in any way. They even murdered Jonathan, a High Priest. Another sectarian leader, John of Giscala, with a gang of Idumeans, was also killing wavering Jews. But he was opposed by Simon bar Giora, who came from Masada to join in the confusion. Yet while the besieged city was the scene of Jew slaying Jew, many thousands of rural Jews crowded into the city, thus increasing the chaos and the pressure on the dwindling food supplies.

The Roman dispersion of the nation seemed to soften this attitude, for once again adversity drew them together in a common desire for relief from their sorrows. Yet at the same time, the influence of the nations into which they were dispersed had its effect. This can be seen today in the very different attitudes to life that have developed among the European Jews (the Ashkenazim) and the Oriental Jews (the Sephardim).

History has shown that scattered Jewry only gets the urge to return to the Promised Land when suffering persecution. Thus the main body of those returning to the land before 1948 originated in the lands of Eastern Europe where pogroms and repression had made their life intolerable. After Israel declared her independence in 1948, the Jews in Arab lands found life increasingly difficult and flooded back to the land of their fathers. On the other hand it is very noticeable that those who have been welcomed into friendly countries as refugees have failed to make aliyah. Thus another division has arisen, the yishuv (those who have returned) and the diaspora (the world-wide dispersion).

Liberty of Faith

The State of Israel was established in May 1948 as a secular democracy. Its founding father, David ben Gurion, was a reasonably level-headed elder statesman. He saw the need for the inclusion in the constitution of the new state a provision for liberty of faith and conscience. To try to avoid endless sectarian conflicts the state has forbidden the active propagation of any particular religious views. This provision was essential to prevent the outbreak of religious war between Jew and Moslem, or Jew and Christian, or Moslem and Christian. Like the Turkish authorities of the last century, the secular state claims to protect all forms of religion with an even hand. This has resulted in a most amazing variety of religious views being tolerated by the state, but being intolerant of one another. The least tolerant are probably the ultra-orthodox Jews, such as those who have formed the enclave of Mea Shearim, in Jerusalem, who are said to accost passers-by, if they are not regarded as being properly dressed, and cars that stray into their enclave on a sabbath are liable to be stoned, to show their disapproval.

A minority of the ultra-orthodox religious groups do not even agree that Israel should exist as a political state. They try to ignore the fact of its existence, and refuse to pay taxes or obey laws. Within a month of the formation of the State, while Arab armies were still assailing the nation, there was a clash between the government headed by David ben Gurion and the dissident resistance force known as the Irgun, led by Menachem Begin. This developed into a brief battle in which Jewish lives were lost on both sides. Another extreme political minority seeks to evict all Arabs from the land to make Israel 100% Jewish. Another extreme group aims to destroy the Dome of the Rock and drive out the Moslem presence from Jerusalem.

A History of Division

The long history of Israel has been one of divisions, feuds and factions. Even King David failed to unite all elements of his people. The founder of the new State of Israel, David ben Gurion, had this to say about the Jews:

"On the eve of the establishment of the State, the Jewish inhabitants of this country were quite possibly the most divided and disunited of all the Jewish population groups throughout the world. In no country was it possible to find so variegated and colourful an assembly of communities, cultures, organisations and parties, beliefs and opinions, conflicting international ideologies and orientations, social and economic interests and differences, as in the Yishuv of the land of Israel—itself the child of an ingathering of exiles and centre of all the rifts and rents in Israel. Yet when independence was proclaimed it seemed as though all barriers were destroyed, and the Declaration of Independence was signed by representatives of all parties in Israel, from the Communists . . . to Agudat Israel, which regarded every attempt to bring about the redemption of Israel by natural means as wanton heresy, and an undermining of Jewish faith and custom . . . And not only the parties in Israel, but Jews throughout the world were united that day in their joy and pride at the establishment of the State. Indeed it is hard to judge which of the two was the greater miracle, the miracle of the restoration of independence or the miracle of Jewish unity. However, the two miracles coincided only on that day of marvels. The State was established. But the unity which gleamed so briefly on the day of Proclamation quickly passed, and the internal fissures and divisions have not been any less than those of the pre-state Yishuv. On the contrary, they have grown more numerous and more acute . . ."

David ben Gurion had to point out to the new nation that "Israel does not have hundreds of years at its disposal". He advocated that all parties must be prepared to compromise to avoid a religious civil war. The situation was altered somewhat by the traumatic Six-Day War with their Arab enemies, which seemed to spark off a growing sense of Messianism. The secular socialism of the pioneers is very slowly giving way to a new religious awareness. There are more religious students in the many Yeshivot of Israel today than there were in all world Jewry fifty years ago, and Jerusalem is becoming the centre of a renewed interest in orthodox Judaism.

Mayor Teddy Kollek of Jerusalem has said: "This is a city of strong opinions, and it will be a long time until tolerance is achieved not only between Jews and non-Jews, but between Jews and Jews."

The Ultra-Orthodox Jewish Religious Parties

The Haredim (ultra-orthodox) and the Yerushalmim groups of minority religious parties claim that "We are the real Jews". These groups form not more than 5% of the Jews in Israel, but exert disproportionate influence upon the state. Most of them are of eastern European origin, tend to be fanatically traditional, and base their views on certain scholars of the distant past. They may be said to be fundamentalist and Messianic, but tend to be intolerant of any other views. Many of them have closed themselves off by establishing their own self-sufficient neighbourhoods, almost like voluntary ghettos within Israel. Many express their distinctiveness in their clothing, which in style dates from their sojourn in cold northern lands, and is incongruous for life in Israel. These groups mostly originated by the Jews from one town in Europe keeping together on arrival in Israel and failing to integrate. Their divisiveness has accentuated with time, and has been maintained by keeping their former language and customs.

The most influential of these small groups are listed, but this list is by no means comprehensive:

Agudat Yisrael: Unlike the other groups, these are mainly Jews of Sephardic extraction. Anti-Zionist, they vote but refuse army service, have independent schools that teach both religious and secular subjects.

Ba'alei Teshuva: Secular Jews who have become ultra-orthodox, but are not yet accepted by the Haredim. Growing in numbers and influence.

Belzers: From the town of Belz in Galicia. Anti-Zionist, refuse army service, yet vote and have a representative in the Knesset. They wear black clothes and side whiskers.

Briskers: From the town of Brisk in Lithuania. They have similar views to the Belzers. Centred in Jerusalem.

Eda Haredit: Passively anti-Zionist, do not vote, yet serve in the army. Children given only religious instruction.

Gerrer: From Poland, anti-Zionist, yet vote and have considerable political power. Refuse army. Wear black clothes and side whiskers.

Habad: Pro-Zionist, but refuse army service. Oppose any compromise with Arabs. Some wear black clothes.

Hassidim: Keep strictly separate. Have traditional arranged marriages and independent schools that give only religious instruction.

Hazon Ish: From Lithuania, anti-Zionist, refuse army service, yet vote and have a representative in the Knesset.

Hevron: Anti-Zionist, but have a more 'modern' look. Refuse army, yet vote and have a representative in the Knesset.

Mir: Lithuanian origin, anti-Zionist, refuse army, yet vote and have a representative in the Knesset.

Misnagdim: 'Opponents' of the Hassidim. From Poland and Lithuania. More liberal in their views, yet wear dark clothes, regard work as beneath them, preferring study in a Yeshiva.

Neturei Karta: Actively anti-Zionist, anti-State. Wear black clothes. May use violence against non-conforming intruders to their enclave in Mea Shearim, Jerusalem.

Po'alei Agudat Israel (P.A.I.): The religious workers' Zionist party; refuse army service.

Ponivezh: Small group within Agudat Yisrael, anti-Zionist, but vote and are represented in the Knesset.

Satmar: Hungarian origin. Have centre in New York, have strong financial hold on Haredim. Anti-Zionist, do not vote, but do serve in army. Wear traditional dark clothes.

Vizhnitz: Anti-Zionist, refuse army, yet vote and have a representative in the Knesset. Wear black clothes.

Yerushalmim: Resident in Jerusalem since early 19th century, the 'Old Yishuv'. Came mainly from Poland and Hungary, subdivided into several groups of varying views and customs.

It is noticeable that many of these ultra-orthodox religious parties do not concern themselves with the practical aspects of financing the welfare state that supports them, a few of them being unwilling to pay their taxes. They appear to be totally unconcerned about such matters as foreign affairs, military strategy or commercial markets for Israel's products.

Their version of Judaism has a similarity with Humanistic Judaism in that they fail to see that mankind is in need of salvation from sin and death. While repentance is seen as needful, every man is regarded as his own redeemer by his good works, his culture, his education and his appreciation of the beautiful.

Humanistic Judaism

Orthodox Jewry has tended to become more extreme in recent years. A backlash from this tendency has been the formation of the 'Society for Secular Humanistic Judaism' whose aim is stated to be "to recapture Jewish tradition and Jewish history from the hands of the rabbinical establishment which has sought to petrify it". This movement is seen as a revolt against ritual and ceremony. However, the overall mood is to eliminate the supernatural from Judaism and to rationalise and secularise the nation. This takes the form of reinterpreting the Bible, without God in it!

This tendency is also evident among many American rabbis, who appear to have lost their way and their faith in the God of Israel as He is revealed in the Bible. Humanist views on sin and salvation are being adopted, and the Bible is being regarded scornfully from the viewpoint of the higher critics.

Thus, the Jewish people are being sharply divided between a religious minority who are becoming more Messianic in outlook, and a secular majority who think that they have dispensed with God.

Rabbi working on a Scroll

10

ATTITUDES OF OTHER NATIONS

ATTITUDES to the line of Abraham began to form very early in the life of young Isaac. He had just been weaned when "Sarah saw the son of Hagar the Egyptian, whom she had borne to Abraham, mocking her son Isaac" (Genesis 21:9). The Hebrew word translated 'mock' is the same as used when Potiphar's wife accused Joseph of mocking her, meaning 'to laugh to scorn'. That unhappy beginning to the relationship between the divinely appointed line and other people was to continue for centuries.

As newly liberated Israel emerged from Egypt, they met opposition from the Amalekites, Moabites, Ammonites, Edomites and almost all of the people of the Promised Land. If cooperation was achieved, it was always at a price, usually that of being disloyal to their own God. Probably the most successful cooperation with other people was achieved by King Solomon by means of his series of political marriages with neighbouring princesses. Again, the price was a very high one, the downfall of Solomon's devotion to the God over whose kingdom he ruled.

That remarkable prophecy uttered by Balaam when he blessed Israel, instead of cursing them, included the words, "The people shall dwell alone, and shall not be reckoned among the nations" (Numbers 23:9). This was to prove very true in more ways than one. The attitude of the other nations, the *goyim*, has borne it out over the centuries. Israel have been and still are a separate and distinct people and, try as they may, it has been well-nigh impossible for them to assimilate into the other nations among whom they have lived for so long.

PERIODS OF INTENSE PERSECUTION		
Crusades	. . .	1100 — 1248
England	. . .	1290
Spain	. . .	1492
Russia	. . .	1600 — 1987
Rumania	. . .	1866 — 1914
Bulgaria	. . .	1884 — 1904
Austria	. . .	1897 — 1910
Germany	. . .	1881 — 1946
Morocco	. . .	1903 — 1960

Blessings and Cursings

God's covenant with Abraham (Genesis 12) included the promise, "I will bless him who blesses you, and him who curses you, I will curse". This very comprehensive promise has gone unheeded by the nations all down the centuries. Very few have befriended Israel. Those nations among whom the Jews have been scattered have varied in their attitude from time to time, often at the whim of the ruler. In many countries there have been periods when no Jew was allowed to reside; at other times they were severely restricted. Very few have opened their arms to welcome them, and even so, the policy could change. In spite of general persecution, it is remarkable that Jews have been prepared to fight for their country of residence. During World War I, out of a total world population of 13 million Jews, at least 10 million lived in the European countries at war.

Postage Stamp: Graffiti — 'No to Racism'

Of these, about half a million fought for the Western allies, and a quarter of a million for the Central Powers. It was estimated that at least 60,000 Jews died fighting for their adopted countries.

The Jewish dispersion has been into almost every nation on earth. While it is not prac-

214

ticable to look at every single one, it will be interesting briefly to review the attitudes of those nations who have been involved with the Jews in a big way, such as the Arabs, the British, the French, the Germans, the Dutch, the Italians, the Poles, the Russians, the Spanish, the Turks and the Americans.

The Attitude of Arabs to Israel

Abraham was neither a Jew nor an Arab, yet he is claimed as the father of both these peoples. Ishmael, his son by a slave girl, was not the son of God's promise, nor of the solemn covenant that God had made. Yet, God promised to Ishmael a very substantial blessing. Perhaps this was some compensation for his exclusion from the covenant. The descendants of Ishmael are among the great nations of the Arabs who now have the overlordship of some 14 million square kilometers of Asia and Africa. This includes power over the treasures of oil, which has made the sons of Ishmael among the richest men on earth. God said plainly "I will make Ishmael a great nation, but I will establish my covenant with Isaac" (Genesis 17:20-21).

The first mention in Scripture of Arabia and the Arabians is in the Books of Kings (1 Kings 10:15) and Chronicles (2 Chronicles 17:11), where the relationship between Jew and Arab seems to be amicable. However, this was not always so (2 Chronicles 21:16). When the exiles returned from Babylon and sought to rebuild Jerusalem, one of their opponents was Geshem the Arabian (Nehemiah 2:19). During the following centuries, they both shared the oppression of a succession of great powers—the Greeks, the Romans, the Byzantines, the Saracens and the Ottoman Turks. Under these conditions of their oppression, the relationship improved somewhat. By the first century A.D. it is evident from the record in Acts 2:9-11 that Jews were living far and wide in Arab lands— Mesopotamia, Egypt, Cyrenaica and Arabia are specifically mentioned. Those in the land of the two rivers, Mesopotamia, may have been there six centuries already, ever since the Assyrian captivity. This area was to be the site of the greatest concentration of Jews for several centuries. Famous seats of Jewish scholarship were established, and a measure of authority was exercised by the traditional descendants of the last king of Judah. The Jews became an integral part of the life of Mesopotamia for over 2,000 years. That is not to say that life was always easy. They were despised, sometimes persecuted, and often robbed by their Arab neighbours. With the Roman destruction of Jerusalem in A.D. 70, and the complete banishment of Jews from the land, the surrounding people began to infiltrate. In the seventh century the scene was dramatically changed. Most Arabs adopted the Moslem faith. The Koran instructed them to ''make war upon those who have been given scripture'', an obvious reference to both Jews and Christians. Nevertheless, the attitude of Moslem Arabs was often fairly tolerant, the Jews being regarded as inferior people. In the Arab lands of North Africa, toleration was interspersed with outbreaks of violence, dispersion and even massacre according to the whim of the rulers or the people.

Arab Enlightenment

It is not widely realised that during Europe's Dark Ages, the Arabs led the world in science, medicine and industry. The Jews, dispersed as they were in all lands, became the intermediaries between Arab enlightenment and the benighted lands of the north. For example, it is seldom realised that Arab mathematics form the basis on which modern computer technology has become possible, for Arab numerals were the first to recognise zero. The Arab attitude towards their half-brothers could be cooperative. This was notably so in Spain under their Moorish rulers (A.D. 711-1492) who were Moslems.

For those centuries the Jews enjoyed a golden age of authority, power and learning. There were hundreds of Jewish communities spread across the Iberian peninsula. But at last the long centuries of settled life came to an end with a series of massacres, followed by the expulsion of 60,000 Jews when the Moors were defeated and driven back to Africa. The Spanish Inquisition was Christendom's response to the presence of so many Jews in Spain. Some fled to Africa; very many were given a welcome by the Turks, who knew something of their abilities. The Jews from Spain and from other Arab lands have become known as the Sephardim (Hebrew for Spain). The Spanish Jews had a dialect known as Ladino, a sort of Latinised Hebrew, and their customs derive largely from those centuries of favour under the protection of the Moors.

Arab Hatred

The Jews of the Yemen (in southern Arabia) may have settled there over 2,500 years ago, as a trading outpost. Although they had become the highly skilled craftsmen of the cities, latterly they had been treated worse than dogs, yet were forbidden to leave. When news reached them in 1948 that there was a David 'ruling' in Jerusalem (David ben Gurion), 48,000 of them eventually managed to escape over the mountains to British protection in Aden, and were airlifted to Israel in Operation 'Magic Carpet' in U.S. planes.

Editorial Cartoon against the Jews (from the Jordanian Press)

Almost all of the Jews who lived in Arab lands have now made the journey back to Israel, the majority since 1948. For many the adventure has been very traumatic. They have left the homes they had grown accustomed to over many centuries for the land of their fathers, only to find problems of language, culture, of accommodation, and of absorption. A few of the young Jews from Iraq were led across the desert by an Italian Jew, but later 95% of the Iraqi Jews were flown to Israel, either via Iran or via Cyprus. They had to leave their possessions, businesses and bank balances behind. A similar story, but with many more difficulties, could be told about the thousands of Sephardim who had to leave every thing behind in Morocco, Algeria and Tunis. Confiscation of their property by the Arabs has been a common feature in all their countries. The Ethiopian Jews (commonly called Falashas, meaning 'strangers') were virtually starved out of their homes, and over 10,000 were airlifted in secret in 'Operation Moses'.

Contradictory Arab Attitudes

Early this century, when the return of the Jews had just begun, the Emir Feisal of Syria said, "We Arabs, especially the educated among us, look with deepest sympathy on the Zionist movement.'' It was only when it became evident that Zionist policy was to make Palestine a national home for the Jews, that the Arab resistance began. Individual Arabs had made occasional attacks on refugee settlements from time to time. This was a matter of personal jealousy, and was in spite of the fact that the refugees were paying the Arabs exorbitant prices for their land. However, the energy and enterprise of the Jews soon began to make more jobs for Arab labour, and so an influx began from the surrounding Arab countries.

During World War I, both Jews and Arabs looked to Britain to free them from the Turkish yoke. When the war began, at least 10,000 Palestine Jews were expelled by the Turks, knowing of their leanings towards Britain. The refugees mostly went to Egypt, which was then under British protection. When eventually Britain was given the Palestine Mandate by the League of Nations, the way was open for Jews to return from Egypt and elsewhere. During the period of the Mandate, 1923-48, as the Jewish settlers prospered further Arab enmity developed—despite the improved opportunities for Arab employment. Sporadic raids on Jewish settlements took place, and each kibbutz had to become a fortified colony with a watchtower and armed guards.

Britain appointed a Jew, Sir Herbert Samuel, as High Commissioner for Palestine in 1920. He proceeded to make a most unfortunate choice in appointing as official leader in Jerusalem, Haj Mohammed Amin El Husseini (generally known as the 'Mufti'). He was to cause endless trouble by organising the Arabs against the Jews. In the end he had to be expelled, yet continued to create trouble from a distance. A Mufti's office was supposed to be that of interpreter of Moslem law and practice, but this man used his office to devise and stimulate Arab opposition to Jewish colonisation.

In 1920, the Emir Feisal of Syria sought to set himself up as king of an Arab Empire that was to include all of Mesopotamia, Syria, Lebanon and Palestine, with his capital at Damascus. But the League of Nations had appointed France as the mandatory power over Syria and the Lebanon, while Britain was in control in Mesopotamia and Palestine. The French quickly took action to wreck Feisal's ambitions and ousted him from Damascus. To the observer of the history of that time, this was a reminder that it is God who gives the kingdoms of men to whomsoever He will, and it was not in the divine purpose for Palestine to be ruled by an Arab at that time.

Britain and the Arabs

The Balfour Declaration (see Chapter 4) had envisaged Palestine as consisting of the whole of the British Mandated territory. This originally included the whole of the area later called Trans-jordan, and now Jordan. The Emir Abdullah led his Arabs into Trans-jordan and claimed it as Arab territory. Winston Churchill was British Foreign Secretary, and was asked to clarify the situation. He proceeded to issue a White Paper (1922) that gave four-fifths of the whole mandated territory to Abdullah, who set up his Hashemite Kingdom of Jordan with the aid of a large British subsidy. The area was completely barred to Jewish settlement. Although Abdullah appeared to realise that there must be peace between Jews and Arabs for the area to prosper, he was among those who attacked the new-born State of Israel in 1948. Soon afterwards he was assassinated, probably by Arabs who thought he was too moderate. There followed several massacres of Jews by their Arab neighbours, and Britain sought to restore order by strengthening its peace-keeping forces. The Arabs urged Britain to rescind the Balfour Declaration and allow them to eliminate the Jewish presence altogether. Britain responded by trying to please both parties, speaking with a forked tongue.

Europe was in turmoil during the 1930s. Persecution sent a flood of refugees seeking a new home in Palestine. Britain tried to limit their numbers, but failed to limit the numbers of Arabs who were entering Palestine to take the labouring jobs created by the Jewish enterprise. In 1936 the Arabs staged a general strike. British forces could no longer maintain law and order. Eventually various plans to partition the land between Jews and Arabs were suggested, but neither party agreed. For two years there was a reign of terror. With World War II looming, in 1939 Britain gave way to Arab demands, since their support would be needed in the war. Further restrictions were placed on Jewish immigration and land purchase at the time when the numbers of refugees was increasing. Yet there was still no restriction on the numbers of Arabs infiltrating the land. Whatever Britain did seemed to be resented by both parties, yet the Jews readily aligned themselves with Britain and the Western Allies for the coming world struggle.

The dilemma of the Jews was stated by David ben Gurion who said:

"We will fight the White Paper as if there were no war, and fight the war as if there were no White Paper."

After World War II the British made another Partition Plan, only to have it rejected by both parties. The problem was then handed to the new United Nations Organisation, who made yet another Partition Plan, this also to be rejected.

British Withdrawal

In 1948, Britain completely withdrew and left the Jews and Arabs to settle their problems themselves, thinking that the refugees would soon be overcome. At least 615,000 Arabs who were resident in the land evacuated to Arab countries to leave the way open for Arab armies to invade. They were promised their homes again when the Jews had been swept into the sea. Five Arab nations attacked simultaneously. In spite of a lack of munitions and prepared defences, the beleaguered Jews pushed the invaders back, and established the new State of Israel.

The Arabs who had remained in Israel, and 50,000 who returned after the war, found that the new Jewish government was improving the working and educational conditions for all people alike. The neighbouring Arab states incited resident Arabs to be hostile, hoping that family ties would prove stronger than the benefits that Israel's prosperity had provided. Thus Israel was in the awkward situation of having to assimilate both Jewish and Arab refugees, and yet try to avoid admitting an Arab 'fifth column'. The fact that the Arabs in Israel were better off than those elsewhere seemed to stimulate jealousy and aggravate the situation. Whatever the Jews did was not right in Arab eyes, with the exception of a few thousand who had remained throughout, and were mainly 'Christians'.

*Arabs
in
Old
Jerusalem*

The current Arab attitude has been shot through with double talk. When Hussein's Jordan ruled in Jerusalem he violated the armistice terms of 1949 by refusing to let Jews worship at their holy places. Yet in 1985, when the Jews controlled all of the city, he said: ''I look forward to a time when all the children of Abraham can proceed to their religious sites in the Holy Land in freedom and peace.''

He spoke as if this state of things had not been a reality ever since Israel took control of Jerusalem in 1967. The Arabs have renamed the hill country of Judea and Samaria as the 'West Bank' (i.e. of Jordan) and called this area the 'occupied territory', even though it was an area granted to the Jews in the first place, and snatched from them by Jordanian troops, then retaken by Israel. Arab propaganda tries to make out that this is really Arab land, illegally occupied by Israel. The world's press and public opinion seems to have fallen for this.

The P.L.O.

Arab opposition to Israel since 1948 has been given much publicity through the terrorist activities of the Palestine Liberation Organisation. This group claims to represent those Arabs who fled from Palestine at that time, and those who live in 'occupied territory'. It is claimed that the Jews have no right to be in the land, and that it is all the inalienable homeland of the Palestinians. The fact is that very few Arabs lived in Palestine before the Jews returned, and most of the so-called Palestinians are immigrants from other Arab lands. The P.L.O. has no permanent base. It has offices in several Arab states, has vast financial resources, and a stock of hatred that would be hard to rival. At one time it sought to make a base in Jordan, but King Hussein feared a takeover and told them to leave. Then, using the territory of Lebanon, it created a hell-on-earth for the people living in southern Lebanon, meanwhile harassing Galilee. Israel's Lebanese war succeeded in ousting the P.L.O., which scattered, but eventually returned to Jordan in an endeavour to gain control of the West Bank area. The P.L.O. war of terrorism continues in a different form.

The Arab League states learned from the wars with Israel in 1967 and 1973 that Israel is well able to meet any Arab military threat. The enormous funds that were supplied by Saudi Arabian oil revenues for the waging of those wars are no longer available. The lower price of oil, the financing of the Iraq-Iran war, and the expensive tastes of the Arab princes have drained their finances.

Thus, over the centuries, the relationship between Arab and Jew has varied from co-existence to violent opposition. Much of the time the Jews were treated as inferior relatives, sometimes only tolerated for their usefulness, at other times given a surprising amount of liberty. The relationship is illustrated by the present-day bitter hostility in public announcements and official attitudes and on the other hand by their willingness to take advantage of Jewish technical skills and inventions, provided that they are not labelled 'Made in Israel'.

ARABS v. JEWS

Resentful Arabs have committed isolated acts of violence ever since the first Jewish refugees settled in the Land. After the British Mandate ended, a series of full scale battles commenced:

1948	The War of Independence
1956	The Suez Crisis
1967	The Six-Day War
1968-70	The War of Attrition
1973	The Yom Kippur War
1982	The War in Lebanon (Operation Peace for Galilee)

The British Attitude to Israel

The British attitude has changed from time to time. Probably the first Jews to enter Britain came with William the Conqueror in 1066. It is said that they were his financial backers. The Crusades of 1096 to 1271 fundamentally changed the relationship between Jews and Christians in Europe, and persecution began with the first Jew-hunts in the city of Norwich. In the city of York, the Jews were ordered to leave the city, and rather than do this gathered together in Clifford's Tower in 1190 and committed mass suicide. By 1290, all the remaining Jews in Britain had their property confiscated by King Edward I, and were banished from the land.

It was not until the mid-17th century that the Amsterdam Jew, Manasseh ben Israel, negotiated with Cromwell for the readmission of Jews. This scholarly man took advantage of Puritan attitudes in Britain which, based on their reverence for the Bible, favoured the Jews. At the same time exiled Spanish

Portuguese Synagogue, Amsterdam

and Portuguese Jews were going to Amsterdam, taking their skills with them. It was to Britain's advantage to encourage some of them to settle in London. Eventually a few of these Marranos were quietly established, and allowed to maintain a synagogue. Thus the first synagogue in Britain was for a Sephardic community, soon to be followed by the founding of an Ashkenazi community and their own synagogue.

From these small beginnings, the Jewish presence in Britain slowly grew, mainly from European Jewry. They were not given full rights of citizenship until 1890 when they numbered 30,000-40,000. During the 19th century a number of Jews gained very considerable affluence, with a corresponding influence. Notable among these were Baron Lionel Rothschild

223

of the European banking family, Sir Moses Montefiore, a financial adviser to the Queen, David Solomons, the Sheriff of London, and Benjamin Disraeli who became Prime Minister.

During the first quarter century after emancipation in Britain, the numbers of Jews increased ten-fold. Some arrived by accident, having been told that they were in America by fraudulent shippers. They tended to keep near together in communities (but not ghettoes) for mutual support and for proximity to a synagogue. Thus life in cities was favoured, their main centres being London, Manchester, Leeds, Glasgow, Birmingham, Liverpool, Newcastle, Hull and Edinburgh, in that order. Their main occupations were in city-based trades: retailing, tailoring, cabinet-making, brush-making and some of the professions. Britain's liberal attitude to the Jews coincided with the nation's prosperity until 1948, when a decline set in as soon as Palestine and its Jews were abandoned to their fate.

It would appear that during the 18th and 19th centuries Britain received the blessing of those who favour God's people, but then with their abandonment in 1948 received the curse of Genesis 12:3. It was from this date that the British Empire crumbled. While the Jews of Britain have not been a large part of the population, they have contributed much in skill and experience, in scientific research, in financial wisdom and during wartime, in manpower. Lord Balfour wrote:

"The Jews are among the most gifted races. They have great natural aptitudes, great intellectual talents but only one ideal—to return to Zion. By depriving them of this ideal the world has diminished their virtues and stimulated their defects. If we can help them to attain that ideal, we shall restore their dignity."

Later, Lord Balfour was to produce the Balfour Declaration of Britain's intent to provide Palestine as a national home for the Jews. Britain's part in doing this had been forecast by John Thomas long before there was any sign of such a possibility taking place. The story of how this eventually came about is told in the chapter on Zionism (Chapter 4). Thus Britain has seen a total ban on Jews at one time, has seen them as second-class citizens, and has been a friend in need at another time.

The commercial success of British Jews has raised protests from time to time that the Jews were running the country. In banking, in merchandising and in certain manufacturing skills, British Jews have certainly excelled and have thereby aroused the jealousy of their competitors. Jews in Britain enjoy freedom of worship and the full rights of citizenship. *The Jewish Chronicle* is published in Britain for British Jews and is a well-informed paper that is not without interest to Christadelphians and others who wish to be informed on Jewish matters.

In the 19th century only about 2% of Jews could speak English. By the middle of the 20th century approximately 50% of all Jews in the world could speak English. This dramatic change has come about as a result of the mass migration from Europe to English-speaking countries, and because Britain held the Mandate for Palestine for 30 years, thus introducing English as the language of government, of communications and of science. Even though Hebrew is now the official language of Israel, English is still widely used.

The Chinese Attitude to Jews

Jews migrated to China over 1,000 years ago and founded several communities, of which the only remaining one is Kai Feng. This group now numbers less than 2,000. Their synagogue was destroyed by fire during the 19th century and has not been rebuilt. Like the communities that have disappeared, this one is slowly being assimilated. The reason may be that the two peoples share a very high regard for family life and relationships, and this common bond may have contributed to the loss of identity of the Jews. Intermarriage and lack of persecution has resulted in the people who were at one time separate being absorbed into the majority. There is no Jewish problem in China, but the Chinese problem should provide a lesson for other Jews. *The Jerusalem Post* has said, "As for the Jews of China, they remain something between an exotic memory and a transient whisper". In the 13th century, Marco Polo went to China, and the Jews at that time were sufficiently evident for him to make mention of them.

Modern communist China has welcomed trade with Israel, which mainly consists of armaments. Indeed, during a recent year, Israel supplied China with 100 times more arms than did Britain. There are now Chinese restaurants in Israel, even supplying kosher Chinese food!

In the 19th century a number of rich Jews settled in Hong Kong, under British rule, and prospered. The pogroms and persecution in Eastern Europe at this time sent some thousands of refugees eastwards across Siberia into China. For about a century there were Jewish communities in several of the larger Chinese cities. The total numbers may have been less than 50,000. However, the Japanese invasion of China and then the communist revolution made life in China very difficult and most of the Jews were evacuated, mainly to Israel. Today there are a few hundred in Hong Kong.

The Dutch Attitude to Israel

The people of the Netherlands had been the subjects of other nations until the Spanish Hapsburg rule was thrown off. There did not appear to be a Jewish presence during this period. However, the Republic of the United Provinces, and Amsterdam in particular, soon became a haven for refugees. Now for some four centuries the people of the Netherlands have favoured refugees. In return, the activities of Jewish traders and businessmen built up the great trading empire of their hosts, making Amsterdam a great centre for world trade. Dutch Jews went to the ends of the earth for sugar, spice, diamonds, furs and skins, wines and fruits for Dutch markets. The Jewish diamond trade now carried on in Israel began as a result of their involvement with the Dutch diamond trade.

The Dutch were among the first to emancipate their Jewish citizens, nearly a century before their neighbours did. Jews were never banned; many have risen to high office in the government. The truth of the promise to Abraham, ''I will bless those who bless you'', can be seen at work in this country. The first reverse for Dutch Jews came with the invasion of Holland by the Germans in World War II, when over 100,000 were murdered by the Nazis. The Dutch were pre-eminent among the nations for the lengths to which they were prepared to go to help and protect their Jews. Dutch people hid, smuggled away, fed and cared for Jews as few other people had dared to do, at the risk of their own lives. But, as might be expected, relatively few Dutch Jews have cared to face the hardships and uncertainties of returning to Israel.

The Dutch relationship with the embattled State of Israel has been helpful and practical. It even extended to a boycott on the import of Arabian oil at one time, in spite of this causing great economic hardship to themselves. Since Rotterdam is the world free-market for oil, this ban was a real sacrifice for Holland to make in support of Israel.

The French Attitude to Israel

It is not thought that Jews reached France much before A.D. 800. Those in the Marseilles area were probably traders, others were mainly in the valley of the Seine, while some German refugees were in the Metz area. However, by the 14th century the situation deteriorated: some were murdered and others expelled.

The French Revolution, with its motto of 'Liberty, Equality, Fraternity', changed the attitude of Frenchmen to the Jews, and by Napoleon's time their numbers had grown again. The French were among the first nations to grant Jews full civil rights, in 1790. When French armies invaded Germany, the Jews there were liberated from the ghettoes. Within a few years, Rothschilds were the principal Paris bankers, and a number of French Jewish organisations were formed to help refugees and to establish schools for Jewish children in other lands.

The French attitude of friendship to its Jewish residents and to refugees has had a reaction from the French Jews. When a French financier began to aid refugee settlements in Palestine in the 1880s, Dr. Bertillon asserted:

"The Israelites have doubled in Paris since the last eight years . . . At what are the Israelites aiming? To re-establish the nationality of the Jews. Not a relative, however, of Abraham, Isaac or Jacob in this capital (Paris) exhibits the slightest intention of going to set up housekeeping in Palestine. On the contrary, Rothschild is rebuilding his mansion in the rue Lafitte, and intends having the bayest of bay windows to admit the coming Messiah."

This century, the French attitude to Israel has vacillated. Early in the days of the new state, when Britain had pulled out,

France readily supplied Israel with planes and armaments. However, as American aid to Israel increased, French support waned. The French connection with North African Arab lands has resulted in a big Arab population in Paris. Arab antagonism to the Jews has reared its ugly head from time to time in France. Earlier sympathy for Israel seems to have evaporated.

The German Attitude to Israel

Jews probably entered Germany with the Romans. However, Rome only controlled small parts of the country, mainly the river valleys. There is no record of German attitudes to the Jews before the time of the crusades. With the first crusade, in the 11th century, thousands of Jews were attacked or expelled, and the ghetto system was introduced by order of the Church Council. Some fled to Poland, others to Switzerland or Italy. The Roman Church attempted to make forcible conversions. Yet, in spite of many setbacks, a unique Jewish culture developed in Germany over the centuries, no doubt aided by the German invention of the art of printing, soon used to print Hebrew books. By the 17th century the situation was so ameliorated that Jews were able to hold high office in some of the German principalities. Others were bankers who financed impecunious princes, and were thus able to gain benefits for their brethren. By the mid-19th century Jews were given full civil rights and were in a position to help refugees who were fleeing from the Russian pogroms. It was in Germany that the first stirrings of a movement to return to the Land of Promise became evident.

But the tide turned towards the end of the 19th century. A great surge of anti-semitism seemed to arise out of the Franco-German War (1870-71). Now a few German Jews started to look elsewhere for a life of peace. But when World War I broke upon Europe, out of a German Jewish population of under a million, probably 100,000 served in the German army. It has not been generally known that during this war the Kaiser categorically promised his ally the Pope that his temporal power would be restored and that a Papal State would be created in Palestine. This would be with the sanction of the Sultan of Turkey, who could cede to the Pope the city of Jerusalem, the Holy Places, and a territory including Jaffa as a seaport, "which shall be sufficient to support the dignity of a Cardinal Viceroy." Previous to this the Kaiser had also promised Jerusalem to the Jews! He was unable to fulfil any of these promises. It is noteworthy that in spite of prejudice, a few Jews did reach high office by reason of their abilities. One of these was Rathenau, the Foreign Minister, who was murdered later for his Jewishness.

Anti-Semitic Poster claiming that Jews are 'devouring the peoples of the earth'

A Storm-trooper warning Germans not to buy at Jewish shops, 1933

From about 1930, the German people were poisoned against their Jewish neighbours by Hitler's venom. Intimidation, violence, looting and bloodshed warned the German Jews of their danger, and more than half of them fled. Those who remained suffered even worse things. Their schools were closed, synagogues wee burned down, a yellow star of David had to be worn on their clothing, and then came the concentration camps and finally the gas chambers. Thus was ended nearly 2,000 years of the Jewish presence in Germany.

Even when the world finally realised what had happened, which was not until the end of World War II, it was too late. Many of the tyrants who had carried out the orders of Hitler were eventually brought to trial. But world opinion thought that some

some sort of reparation should be made, and post-war Germany refused to consider it. It was not until the German Chancellor Conrad Adenauer "wished not only to win the trust of the West" but also found the time ripe to force his people to "come to terms with their dark past" that a formal signing of a Reparations Agreement in 1952 was completed. Under this agreement, financial and other forms of aid worth 700 million dollars have been given to the State of Israel in 12 years. While this has been a useful contribution, Israel seems determined not to forget the horrors of the German Holocaust which obliterated one-third of the total Jewish world population. Besides the German Jews, those from Poland and Russia and other countries perished in the Holocaust.

A new generation of Germans is now being told by some that there never was a Holocaust, and that the story is a terrible Jewish slander against the German people. On the other hand there is a feeling among some Germans that reparations should continue in view of Israel's severe financial problems and Germany's relative prosperity. What is remarkable is that in spite of everything, the unique German-Jewish culture that had been developing over the centuries, with its own language—Yiddish, its traditional foods and way of life, is not dead. It lives on in America, in Israel and elsewhere.

EUROPEAN COUNTRIES IN WHICH JEWS HAVE HELD HIGH POLITICAL POSITIONS AT VARIOUS TIMES		
Bavaria	Germany	Rumania
Czechoslovakia	Holland	United Kingdom
Denmark	Hungary	U.S.S.R.
France	Italy	Yugoslavia
	Poland	

The Italian Attitude to Israel

There were Jews in Rome before the beginning of the Christian era. From time to time they were blamed for the ills and setbacks that Rome suffered, and were then persecuted. Many of the first Christians in Rome were from among this Jewish population. Rome's experience of the Jews was of a turbulent,

29. An Iris (Iris Mariae): "Even Solomon in all his glory was not arrayed like one of these" (Matthew 6:29)

30. Border Patrol: ''The sword without, and terror within''
(Deuteronomy 32:25)

**31. Druze Village on the Golan Heights, with
Mount Hermon in the Background:**
''He makes peace in your borders . . . '' (Psalm 147:14)

32. Bazaar viewed from the Damascus Gate, Jerusalem: "He hath made of one blood all nations of men" (Acts 17:26)

fiercely independent people. They constituted a thorn in the side of the Empire for over a century. Yet the Romans appreciated the skills of the Jews and encouraged them to settle in certain cities of the Empire. The Herods, who were Roman stooges, appointed in an attempt to mollify the Jewish temper, failed in their efforts to win them over to Roman overlordship. When the Romans destroyed Jerusalem in A.D. 70, the victory was celebrated by a parade of Jewish captives in Rome, and an arch of triumph which still remains.

But even when Rome had destroyed the city and scattered the people, their third major dispersion, there were still isolated Jewish uprisings until, in A.D. 135, Hadrian issued an edict that forbade any Jew to live in or near Jerusalem.

By the third century, there were extensive Jewish colonies in Italy. They were guaranteed freedom of religion at first. However, as the power of the Church of Rome grew, the Jews were harassed and then persecuted for their part in 'killing God'.

The very first ghetto was probably in Venice, the word being of Italian origin. In the Middle Ages, Italy was divided into several small kingdoms, and the attitude to the Jews varied from one to another. This resulted in considerable movement to the most favourable area. As the Church of Rome gained more power, attempts were made at forcible conversions of Jews. The Fourth Lateran Council of 1215 under Pope Innocent III ordered drastic anti-Jewish regulations for all of Christendom. They were to be concentrated in ghettoes, to wear a badge of shame, and to have easily distinguishable pointed hats. The order of Dominican Friars was founded in 1215 to work specifically against the Jews. However, in spite of all the opposition there was a strong Jewish culture in Italy, and extensive printing of Hebrew books was undertaken later.

By the 19th century Jewish bankers were firmly established, who even made loans to the Papal estates, which were in poor shape at that time. When the World Wars involved Italy, the Italian Jews did not suffer as did those in Germany. Indeed it is known that some religious houses were prepared to hide Jewish children.

The Attitude of the Vatican

Although the Roman Catholic Church was not prepared to recognise the State of Israel when it was formed in 1948, there has been a slow softening of its attitude in recent years. Pope John Paul II has seemed eager to gather all forms of religion into one great papal embrace, with himself as the head. Overtures have been made to the Moslem world, and to the Jewish world. For the Jews this amounts to a complete turn-around from the atrocities of the Spanish Inquisition to a statement that Catholics are to regard Jews as their 'elder brethren'; they are to be respected and asked for their forgiveness for past persecution.

It seems probable that this thawing of relationships could have political, rather than theological, overtones. The Roman Church still sees itself as God's kingdom on earth, and is trying by all possible means to spread its influence world-wide, even among the non-Christians. This doctrine will inevitably lead to opposition to God's appointed King, when he appears.

The Polish Attitude to Israel

The vicissitudes of the Polish Jews over the centuries has been a mirror of the chequered history of the Polish people themselves. This country has suffered agonies, squeezed between two powerful and aggressive neighbours, Germany and Russia. So far as is known, there was no early settlement of Jews in Poland. A few Jewish merchants are known to have traded in the land before A.D. 1000. When the Khazar Empire, a tribe of Turkish origin which had embraced Judaism, was finally crushed, the refugees fled to Poland. Thus there has been a Jewish presence for at least ten centuries. The crusades, when Jews in Europe were persecuted, caused more to seek refuge in Poland, where they were given special privileges by the kings who needed their skills in trading and finance. In the 15th century these were joined by many who fled the Spanish Inquisition, adding a Sephardic element to the resident Ashkenazim majority.

The Polish Jews became a vital and integral part of the country that had given them refuge. They pioneered new industries, built railways, and contributed much to the politics, the literature, the arts and the music of Poland. They numbered several millions, and early in the present century were catered for by 30 daily newspapers and over 130 other periodicals in Yiddish, Polish and Hebrew.

But life was not always easy. When Poland became a province of Russia, together with the Ukraine, the area became the 'Pale of Settlement' within which all Jews were required to live, and to which refugees fled. During the 17th century, the Russian Cossack troops invaded Poland and massacred about 100,000 Jews. An exodus began westwards to Germany and Holland. This persecution was fuelled by government-inspired pogroms from time to time, until whole communities were wiped out.

Postage Stamp: Synagogue in Poland

Golda Meir, in her autobiography, described the horrors of an attack on the village where she lived as a girl. (Eventually, she and her family managed to get to America; later she became Prime Minister of Israel.) Poland, once a place of refuge, became a place of peril. During the Nazi rape of Poland in World War II, Polish Jewry was virtually eliminated. The land which sent some of the first pioneers to Palestine, now has no more Jews to send. *The National Geographic Magazine* (September 1986, page 362) reported that only 5,000 elderly Jews remain in Poland, many in complete isolation, a pitiable left-over from a once vibrant community.

The Russian Attitude to Israel

Probably some of the Jews taken captive by Assyria eventually reached areas now known as Russia. There was a definite influence of Judaism in the Caucasus, Crimea and the steppe lands which at one time flourished in the independent kingdom of the Khazars. These were an Asiatic people who officially embraced Judaism, and for three centuries were a haven for the scattered Jews. But in A.D. 1016 the up and coming Russians destroyed this state, and the Jews were dispersed. Over the centuries Russian expansion brought many more

Jews within Russia's orbit, and for pseudo-religious reasons they were persecuted from time to time. In the 19th century a libellous document was forged and printed in St. Petersburg, called *The Protocols of Zion*. This alleged that the Jews were planning a conspiracy to dominate the world. The intention was to inflame antagonism to the Jews, and it certainly did, not only in Russia but in many other countries.

Russia was last but one of the lands that granted emancipation to the Jews, and this was not very real in practice: it came in 1917, as the result of the Bolshevik Revolution, in which a number of Jews had taken a leading rôle. However, the Russian Soviet established in Siberia what was intended to be an autonomous Soviet Jewish Republic called Biro Bidjan and hoped that all Jews could be isolated there. A few thousand settled in their republic but it did not attract the many.

Before Zionism took shape, there were several organisations in Russia to encourage a return to Palestine. Many of the early settlers were Russian, and some of them took their communist views with them. The kibbutzim established in Israel are based on the communist idea of working for the common good and only receiving in return that which is essential. Leon Trotsky, an early communist leader of the Russian Revolution was in fact Leibe Braunstein, and eventually he was assassinated because of his Jewishness.

The large number of Jews still in Russia have become embarrassing to the Soviet authorities, who hesitate to let them go to Israel, or anywhere else, yet restrict them and persecute them for their Jewish ways. It is true that some who have been allowed to emigrate, ostensibly to Israel, have eventually gone to America, and this has annoyed the Soviets. In 1986 the Jewish population of Russia was estimated to be over two million. The few who have dared to seek permission to leave Russia are investigated by the secret police and marked down for harassment. Those who are not given their emigration papers are styled 'Refusniks' by their friends and relatives in Israel.

Whether Russian policy will change under pressure from other countries remains to be seen. A really large influx of Russian Jews to Israel could cause embarrassment, as their assimilation would not be easy.

The Spanish Attitude to Israel

The story of the Spanish Jews illustrates the extremes of prosperity and degradation that the same country can produce. When Spain was part of the Roman Empire, Jews settled along the Mediterranean coast. The Apostle Paul planned to visit Spain (Romans 15:24), no doubt because there were many Jews there. The Spanish Jews increased in numbers, but suffered under the rising power of Christendom. The Moors (North African Moslems) invaded and ruled over Spain from A.D. 711-1492. They were regarded as liberators by the Jews, and during those centuries persecution was minimal, and Jewry flourished. Hundreds of Jewish communities and synagogues spread across the Iberian peninsula and a very distinctive culture and language developed—Ladino. One of them, Moses Maimonides was a noted physician and philosopher, whose writings are still studied. The influence of Sephardic Jews spread over other Moslem lands where Jews lived.

However, when the Moors were turned out of Spain in the 15th century, the fate of the Jews changed dramatically. Restrictions, massacres and expulsions were the order of the day as 'Christians' took over. Probably 40,000 remained and were forcibly 'converted'. These were known as Marranos or New Christians. They did not always escape persecution, for it was alleged that they practised Judaism in secret. The Spanish Inquisition finally put an end to the long history of the Sephardim, although some of their literature lives on, as does their culture.

In recent years the relationship between Spain and Israel has been anomalous. Spain would not officially recognise the new state, yet had a consulate in Jerusalem. But when, in 1985, Spain joined the European Economic Community, diplomatic relations were soon established. There is a considerable two-way traffic of tourists between the two countries, and commercial ties are improving. Israel's citrus industry has suffered from Spanish competition, and paradoxically Israel's technological help for Spanish agriculture may serve to increase this competition. In 1924 Jews were again allowed to become citizens of Spain, and recently laws on religious toleration have been passed that benefit Jews *and* Protestants.

The Turkish Attitude to Israel

The Turkish Empire at its fullest extent covered a vast area from the Atlantic Coast of Africa to the Persian Gulf, and from the Sudan to mid-Europe. In this area there were many Jews. In some parts they had lived continuously for over 2,000 years. In North Africa, Asia Minor and the Balkans, the Jews were already established in New Testament times, as the travels of the Apostle Paul reveal. The Turks only came on the scene as a great power in the 15th century, and spread their power and their religion, Islam, with the sword. The Turkish attitude to Jews varied according to the mood of the Sultan, or his regional officials. When the Spanish Jews were expelled, they were given a welcome by the Turks.

Isaac Zarfati, a German Jew living in France, wrote to the Jews living in Germany: "I proclaim to you that Turkey is a land wherein nothing is lacking. If ye will, all shall yet be well with you. The way to the Holy Land lies open to you through Turkey. Is it not better for you to live under Moslems than under Christians? Here every man may live at peace under his own vine, and under his own fig tree. In Christendom, on the contrary . . . all your days are days of sorrow."

Palestine was to remain under the Turks for four centuries as an insignificant part of their province of Syria. The area was neglected and the administration lax. Yet it was under such conditions that Jews set up the very first printing press in the Asiatic continent, at Safed in Galilee in 1567.

In 1885, the Governor of Jerusalem, Reouf Pasha, said: "There exists so much rivalry between the different sections of the inhabitants, that as far as we (the Turks) are concerned, we make no distinction between the followers of different creeds: we protect them all alike."

So, although there were problems in registering land ownership with the Turkish administration, returning Jews were usually able to buy land. The Arabs or Turks would gleefully sell a patch of barren land to a Jew at an inflated price, but would look at it with jealousy when the refugee had made it to flourish. The same year, it was reported by Laurence Oliphant that there were thousands of acres of land in Galilee free for the taking. An example of the hopeless inefficiency of the Turkish administration became evident when most European countries had to set up their own postal services to and from Jerusalem. The Austrians were rated most efficient.

Difficulties experienced by Jews settling in Palestine led to a scheme for Mesopotamia to become a home for the Jews. This area had a large Jewish population for over 2,500 years. It had been cleared of Turks by British troops in 1916, was very fertile but under-utilised, and was suggested as a 'real garden of Eden' for the settlement of refugee Jews. About the same time, the ex-Sultan, Abdul Hamid, had said:

"I should like to go down in the pages of history, as doth my ancestor Sultan Selim, as the protector of the Jews. When they were persecuted and expelled from Spain, we threw open the doors of Turkey, and I should equally like to throw open the portals of my empire to those Jews who are persecuted elsewhere."

After World War II, the rise of Turkish nationalism and the almost universal Moslem opposition to the Jews finally led to the 40,000 who lived in nationalist Turkey, to make the one-way journey to Palestine: modern Turkey no longer welcomes refugees, and has very few, if any, Jews living there.

The United States and Israel

The first Jews to be seen in the United States were Dutch Jews who had tried to settle in South America, but who had to flee from Spanish persecution and finally arrived at New Amsterdam (as New York was then called). During the 18th century several settlements were formed and the first synagogue was built. These early Jewish immigrants shared the same hardships as the other pioneers. George Washington gave them a special blessing. Among the early traders were Jews who soon became established, and whose names are still used in many large businesses. It was an American Jew, Mordecai Noah, who sought to buy Palestine from the Turks in 1837, but was rebuffed. Later in that century, a flood of millions from Germany, Poland and Russia arrived to find a big country full of space and opportunity for their skills. The commercial prosperity of the U.S.A. seems to have reflected the open-arms policy to all refugees.

ISRAEL

The heaviest concentrations of Jews in the U.S.A. are in New York State (about two million), Massachusetts, Illinois and California. Their sheer numbers (over 5½ million) have made them into a very powerful political force that has to be taken into account by the politicians. The U.S.A. as a nation has provided far and away the most financial aid to the State of Israel, and the Jews of the U.S.A. are the most generous donors towards the Jewish National Home.

While happy to give their money, they seem to be reluctant to make aliyah, presumably because it would mean changing to a lower standard of living and an uncertain future. There has been extensive cooperation between American and Israeli firms, which has helped Israeli industry to reach very high standards in manufacturing and marketing scientific products. While other nations have refused to give military aid to Israel, the U.S.A. has sent supplies, sometimes under great difficulty. In return, surprisingly, Israel has supplied the U.S. Air Force with some of its very sophisticated 'Kfir' warplanes. As this is being written, the American Sixth Fleet is stationed in the Mediterranean to provide a measure of moral support for Israel, which is seen as an outpost of the Western Alliance.

World Attitude to Israel

This century has seen a dramatic shift in the principal centres of world Jewish population. From a few hundred in Palestine at the beginning of the 19th century to nearly four million in 1986, from several million in Europe to only a few thousands, from some thousands in America to about six million, all this is evidence of a colossal movement of people. The exception is Russia which has a captive population of about 2½ million. These want to move, but are unable to.

Today a large part of the world is closed to Jewish immigration. All Arab lands, India, Malaysia, Turkey, Kenya, Zimbabwe, Mexico, Alaska, Colombia, Peru, Paraguay and Russia are closed. Britain and the U.S.A. have strict quotas. Yet immigration to Israel has been reduced to a mere trickle, its early attraction having been spoilt by the state of continual war, by Arab intimidation, by internal dissent and economic depression. There is a feeling of suppressed anti-semitism the world over, that suffices to keep Jews as a distinct and separate people.

ATTITUDES OF OTHER NATIONS

In their dispersion to many countries, it has been noticed that the Jews have been willing to fight for the country of their adoption. In World War I there were ½ million Jewish soldiers, equally divided between the opposing forces. Probably 60,000 gave their lives. *The Jewish Chronicle* reported an interview with a commanding officer who said: "The Jewish soldier was as alert, active, brave, cool, patient and loyal as any of his comrades. They carried out orders with complete obedience." The world's response has not been so praiseworthy.

```
               THE DIASPORA IN 1983

   Argentina        ...      400,000
   Australia        ...       72,000
   Austria          ...       12,000
   Belgium          ...       40,000
   Brazil           ...      154,000
   Canada           ...      330,000
   Chile            ...       25,000
   Ethiopia         ...       10,000
   France           ...      700,000
   Germany (W.)     ...       28,000
   Great Britain    ...      385,000
   Holland          ...       38,000
   Hungary          ...       85,000
   Iran             ...       28,000
   Italy            ...       35,000
   Mexico           ...       45,000
   Morocco          ...       12,000
   Rumania          ...       31,000
   Russia           ...    2,200,000
   South Africa     ...      110,000
   Spain            ...       12,000
   Switzerland      ...       20,000
   Turkey           ...       23,000
   Uruguay          ...       50,000
   U.S.A.           ...    5,690,000
   Venezuela        ...       24,000
```

Only countries having over 10,000 Jewish residents are listed. There are smaller numbers in 30 other countries. World population of Jews was thought to be about 14 million in 1983.

Anti-Semitism and Anti-Zionism

Anti-semitism is an expression of enmity by non-Jews for Jews. Anti-Zionism may express disapproval of the Zionist secular political movement either by Jews or non-Jews.

Anti-semitism seems to have dogged the race during most of its existence. It is a fulfilment of the divinely expressed curse upon the people of Israel if they failed to remember the LORD their God and keep His commandments. It is not merely the price of being different, as many Jews like to think. Anti-semitism is well-nigh universal in varying degrees and is only explicable in the terms of the divine pronouncement:

"You shall become a horror, a proverb, and a byword among all the peoples where the LORD will lead you away" (Deuteronomy 28:37).

Anti-semitism is not limited to the prejudices of Christendom and the accusation that the Jews had 'killed God'. Moslems and atheists also have the prejudice. It is not just a dislike of Jewish appearance or customs or claims. It sometimes flares into accusations that Jews make human sacrifices, or that they are the cause of plagues. In many lands 'to Jew' anybody means to cheat them.

This writer's experience with a small Jewish community in Britain is that they are naturally wary of being deceived or cheated, but are scrupulously honest themselves. They insist on full value, 'brimming over', but once their confidence is gained, they can become very good loyal friends.

Anti-Zionism is a political opposition to the Zionist aspirations of those Jews who have sought to establish a Jewish political state in the Holy Land. An anti-semite may also be an anti-Zionist, but chiefly Zionism is opposed by certain orthodox Jewish religious groups. Their usual argument is that the founding of a Jewish political presence should be left for Messiah. Some of these small groups refuse to acknowledge the State, even though they live within it, and refuse to serve in the army or to pay their dues.

11

CHRISTADELPHIAN ATTITUDES TO ISRAEL

TO suggest that there were Christadelphians in the first century may sound unlikely. But the name means 'Brothers in Christ' in Greek, and that is how the Apostle Paul addressed the Greek-speaking believers at Colosse, calling them *adelphois en Christo* (Colossians 1:2). They, like the apostle, had embraced "the hope of Israel" (Acts 28:20) which is the basis of the Christadelphian faith today. True brothers in Christ, in whatever century, know the truth about the covenant that God made with Abraham, and that it is only through faith in Jesus Christ that the covenant Hope of Israel will be realised.

All the original brothers in Christ were Jews, thousands of them (Acts 2:41; 6:7). Only after Peter had preached to Cornelius and his family, and under divine guidance had baptized them, were the faith and hope of the believers shared with Gentiles. The Apostle Paul and others spread the good news far and wide in Asia and in Europe, always to the Jews first, afterwards turning to the Gentiles. Friction soon developed between orthodox Jewry and those who had accepted the apostle's teaching. On occasions this flared into out-and-out persecution. For this cause the Apostle Paul suffered much distress: "Of the Jews, five times received I forty stripes save one. Thrice was I beaten with rods, once was I stoned . . . " (2 Corinthians 11:24-25).

The attitude of the apostles was that in spite of the dastardly treatment that the Jews meted out to Jesus and some of his followers, they were to hear the good news of the Gospel first, before the Gentiles heard it. Thus, when Paul arrived at Rome as a prisoner under guard, the first thing that he did was to call together his Jewish compatriots and explain to them why he was there. He said:

"For this reason therefore I have asked to see you and speak with you, since it is because of the hope of Israel that I am bound with this chain" (Acts 28:20).

News of this sect had already reached Rome: "For with regard to this sect we know that everywhere it is spoken against" was their reply. In spite of this evidence of prejudice, Paul went on to give his Gospel exposition concerning Jesus the Christ, and "some were convinced . . . while others disbelieved" (verse 24).

It is almost impossible to assess the relationship, if any, between the true believers and the Jews during the dark ages. In view of the known peaceable way of life of the little groups of Brothers in Christ in Europe, it would be difficult to envisage them joining in the persecution of Jews that characterised the attitude of the Roman Church. As the apostate church strayed further and further from the simple truths of the Hope of Israel, so it became increasingly impossible for a Jew to embrace a faith that began by denying the one and only God of Abraham, and substituted a trinity.

The scanty records of the persecuted Brethren in Christ do not appear to mention any relationship with the equally persecuted Jews. Nevertheless the Abrahamic faith was not quite lost to true believers in Jesus Christ. The threads of the Hope of Israel were picked up by John Thomas and put together in a masterly exposition entitled *Elpis Israel*, around 1848. *Elpis Israel* is the Greek for 'Hope of Israel'; the book was circulated among people who had heard John Thomas speaking on this theme, and within a few years there was a scattering of 'Brothers in Christ' who had embraced the faith of the first century believers, and like Paul, regarded the Hope of Israel as the foundation of their understanding of God's promises. In due course these groups of believers were known as Christadelphians.

Christadelphians and Jews

What was the attitude of Christadelphians to the Jews? In the 19th century there seemed little prospect of a fulfilment of the prophecies of a return to the Promised Land. The Holy Land had been in the hands of the Turkish Empire for centuries and was a neglected and forlorn part of the world. For many years the

Title page of
Elpis Israel
*(The Hope
of Israel), an
exposition
of the
Kingdom
of God
by
John Thomas*

ELPIS ISRAEL;

A BOOK FOR THE TIMES

BEING

AN EXPOSITION

OF THE

KINGDOM OF GOD,

WITH REFERENCE TO

"THE TIME OF THE END,"

AND

"THE AGE TO COME."

BY

JOHN THOMAS, M.D.,
RICHMOND, VIRGINIA, UNITED STATES.

"For the Hope of Israel I am bound with this chain."—*Paul.*

LONDON:
PUBLISHED BY THE AUTHOR;
AND MAY BE OBTAINED AT 3, BRUDENELL PLACE, NEW NORTH ROAD, HOXTON

1849.

Turkish Empire had been shrinking and showing signs of collapse. Christadelphian eyes were set on any events which indicated further Turkish retraction, and on the threat to Middle East stability posed by Russia's expansionist policy. Many pages in *The Christadelphian* magazine in the 1880s were devoted to news of Turkey's ailments and Russia's aggression.

In 1880, there were only a few thousand Jews in Palestine. These lived only in four cities, Safed and Tiberias in the north, and Hebron and Jerusalem in the south. They were not gainfully employed, but claimed to be students of the Torah, and had to be supported by the charity of Jews elsewhere. The fund that maintained them was known as the 'Ḥalukkah'. Yet there were stirrings among the oppressed Jews of Europe, and a few refugees had made the journey and, thanks to aid from several rich European Jews, had set to work to farm patches of the land. Baron Lionel Rothschild and Sir Moses Montefiore were British Jews who were foremost in giving aid and buying land. Beginning in 1874, *The Christadelphian* magazine had a section headed 'The Jews and their Affairs' which reported any signs of movement. The situation did not look very promising, for in 1885 it was reported that there were many homeless families waiting for relief. Rents to Turkish landlords had to be paid a year in advance. A Jewish relief fund organised by the 'Ezrath Nidachim' Society dispensed aid as available. The road from Jaffa to Jerusalem was hardly negotiable. Water for Jerusalem was having to be carried in from a distance, and was expensive.

Beginning of Christadelphian Aid

The Magazine published any development in detail, and reported that Christadelphians in Britain were collecting funds to try to forward the task of settling the refugees. Collections in those days consisted mostly of coppers and sixpences. The words of John Thomas in *Elpis Israel* were an encouragement to take part in the movement that was just beginning. He had written:

"There is, then, a partial and primary restoration of Jews before the manifestation of Christ, which is to serve as the nucleus, or basis, of future operations in the restoration of the rest of the tribes after he has appeared in the Kingdom. The pre-adventual colonisation of Palestine will be on purely political principles; and the Jewish colonists will return in unbelief of the Messiahship of Jesus, and of the truth that is in him. They will emigrate thither as agriculturalists and traders in the hope of ultimately establishing their commonwealth . . . " (page 441).

By 1882 British Christadelphians had collected the sum of £300 for aiding the refugees. Besides this fund, the women had been busy making and collecting a stock of clothing, "made of substantial fabric ... produced at sewing meetings held for the purpose". The remittance and the boxes of clothes were sent to Palestine from "Birmingham and other lovers of Israel", to be administered by Laurence Oliphant who lived on the slopes of Mount Carmel at Haifa. He was asked to select land for purchase, buy tools and oxen, distribute

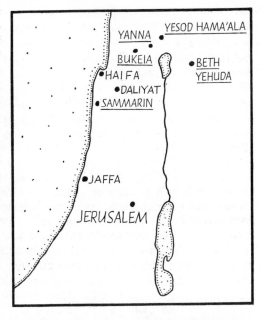

Locations helped by Christadelphian Funds in the 1880s

clothing where needed most, and generally act as agent for Christadelphian interests in Palestine. He was not unknown to the editor of the magazine and others, who were glad to have a trustworthy local representative in the Land, even though he was not a Brother in Christ. He had been a diplomat and foreign journalist, and had espoused the case of Jewish refugees before the Turkish authorities. Mr. Oliphant proved to be a most meticulously careful steward of the funds and goods consigned to him. His reports of how the funds were used, and to whom the clothing was given, were printed in detail in the magazine.

The First Christadelphian-Aided Colony

Laurence Oliphant's negotiations for buying property for the first Christadelphian-aided colony were at Shefr-Amr (Shefaram) about ten miles northwest of Nazareth. This scheme failed, on account of the greed and rivalry of the several owners of the plot of land. A site was found at Yanna, five miles east of Safed (Zefar) where 150 acres were purchased for 100 Napoleons (equivalent of £70). This land was registered in Mr. Oliphant's name, in trust for the Christadelphians. The colony thus formed accommodated 24 Rumanian and four Russian Jewish families, 140 people in all. This colony may still be found, alongside the better known Rosh Pinna kibbutz.

Reports in the Magazine for 1883 mention another settlement that received financial help. This was at Sammarin (Zimmarin), now known as Zichron Ya'acov, 20 miles south of Haifa. In 1885, the fund was used to assist a colony of Polish Jews at Yesod Hamolo near Lake Merom, and the remote village of Bukeia. It was here that the families were all named Cohen and claimed that they had occupied the village ever since Roman times, well hidden in the hills of Galilee. Eventually, on Mr. Oliphant's death, other arrangements had to be made. It is understood that the Rothschild Trust took over the administration of the Yanna colony. The next event was for Christadelphians to make the journey. Interest in Christadelphian circles increased as the slow movement gained momentum. Several of them had plans for practical ways of assisting the movement.

The First Christadelphian Visits

It is thought that the first Christadelphian visitor to Palestine was Viccars Collyer of Leicester (grandfather of the writer). He arranged with Messrs. Thomas Cook and Sons, a Leicester firm that organised tours to foreign parts, to pay a visit to the Holy Land. He had two reasons for wishing to make the journey. As a Christadelphian he wanted to see for himself and report to the ecclesias what was really going on in the land; and he also had a business interest—as a seedsman and horticulturalist, he wished to seek for new seeds and plants that he could introduce to his business. His lengthy report on the journey, and his activities when there, became a serial feature in *The Christadelphian* magazine from August 1887 for several months. Later the magazine reported that he had received an enormous shipment of bulbs.

The next year, a Christadelphian named Campbell of Inverness put forward an ambitious plan for building a railway in

Palestine. As the Holy Land had virtually no roads, apart from the track from Jaffa to Jerusalem which took a horse-drawn carriage nearly a day to cover, this seemed a good idea. But the railway was never built! In 1889, a Christadelphian called Gee, of Crewe, thought that there were good business prospects in the Land. He went out to start up enterprises such as honey farming, perfume production and other activities he thought could be carried on by some of the refugees. He stayed several years, but so far as is known did not succeed in starting anything viable.

Organised Parties

In 1901, Frank Jannaway, his wife, and C. C. Walker (editor of *The Christadelphian*) joined an organised party of over 50 people, to visit the Land. They were shown the traditional holy sites, in which they were not really very interested. The next year the two brethren went back for an independent tour to see the things they wanted to see. This time they went on horseback with camping equipment. This seemed to solve some of their problems, but caused others! The Zionist movement was now drawing attention to the return of Jews to the Land, and beginning in 1907 C. A. Ladson edited a feature in the Magazine entitled 'The Jews and Zionism'. About this time there were numerous schemes to settle refugee Jews in all manner of empty localities: Mesopotamia, Mexico, Kenya, Cyrenaica, Salonica, Australia and other places were suggested. But the Jews wanted Palestine, and nowhere else. The editor of the Magazine remarked in 1909 (page 211) that "The Jewish tide is settling toward the Land of Promise. It is the great sign that God remembers the covenants with the fathers of Israel."

Excited reports in the Magazine speculated whether the then current Persian disorders would give Russia an opening to take control and thus fulfil Ezekiel's prophecy. A British Consulate report on Palestine affairs mentioned a growing French interest in developing the Land. The French did eventually build the Jaffa-Jerusalem railway, and French companies negotiated to extract phosphate and other mining rights.

In November 1909, the Magazine reported on a movement sponsored by Claude G. Montefiore which effectively rejected

*Facsimile
(original size
11½" × 16")
of the
Turkish visa
issued to
C. C. Walker*

the orthodox Jewish faith and laid the 'dry bones' of what was ultimately to develop into 'Judaistic Humanism'. He rejected the authority of the Bible, cast off the bondage of the Law, and discarded the significance attached to the feasts and holy days of the Jews. This Godless philosophy has now become predominant in Israel and the diaspora.

Extended Visits

In 1912, the Jannaways re-visited Palestine. This trip was hindered and nearly prevented by the outbreak of war between Italy and Turkey. Beirut was bombarded by Italian warships and it was feared that the trouble would soon spread. In spite of difficulties, the Jannaways arrived at Jaffa, where the usual uncomfortable transfer of passengers and goods from the steamboat into small rowing boats took place. The train journey of about 54 miles to Jerusalem took four hours. They spent most of the time in and around the city, taking photographs and visiting leaders of local institutions and hospitals. They were particularly interested in the work of the London Jewish Society Hospital, and decided to sponsor a bed in the name of the Christadelphians to be known as the 'Elpis Israel' bed. Australian Christadelphians sponsored another bed to be called the 'Hephzibah' bed. At this time, malaria was almost universal in the city, and tuberculosis was rife, so the beds were continuously in use.

Christadelphian aid for poverty-stricken Jews was dispensed by Mrs. Dickson, wife of the British Consul. A long queue formed to receive this cash aid, and it was not unknown for a recipient to proceed to the rear of the queue, change his appearance, and wait for a second handout!

Frank Jannaway noticed that the Jews were as divided amongst themselves as are the Christians, and seemed to have just as little interest in one another. Conditions were far from settled. The Turkish authorities had been unable to stamp out brigandage, and the mail coaches on the Jaffa road had been attacked and robbed. A strong movement to revive the Hebrew language had begun in an attempt to unify the Jews from their many different origins. While Hebrew had not been a dead language, it had been restricted to religious services and was not in everyday use. This movement was to grow so that eventually Hebrew became the language of the yishuv, having proved to be adaptable to modern requirements.

The Christadelphian quoted *The Times* of September 28, 1912, which deprecated British sympathy with Zionism. It argued that it would be against Britain's interests to offend the Arabs by showing favour to the Jews. This was an early warning of the clashing interests that were to develop. It was not, at that time, because of Arab oil power, but because Britain regarded the Middle East as a bastion against Russian designs on the Suez Canal, Britain's lifeline to her Eastern Empire in India and Australia.

THE JEWS AND ZIONISM.

By Brother C. A. Ladson.

FORTY YEARS HENCE.

Last month a glance was taken at the condition of the Land and the People "Fifty Years Ago," and a glimpse given of their state "Fifty Years After," in the present day. This is simple work, only calling for the wisdom that comes after the event, but who will be bold enough to prophesy to-day concerning these things forty years from now, in 1954 ? Some will say, " Assuredly, by that time the Lord will be here ; there will be a king in Jerusalem." Others, equal in their desire for that blessed fulfilment of the Hope of Israel, but less sanguine, as they review the history of the past, will feel a great hope, but no certainty ; for forty years, though it be half a lifetime, is a small thing in the development of God's purpose. Nevertheless, into it may be crowded events that will shake the world.

Extract from The Christadelphian, August 1914, page 366— one in a regular series which has featured in the magazine ever since

Further Visits

Details of Frank Jannaway's visit were reported in a series of 26 letters in the magazines of 1912-14. This series was followed by another written by C. C. Walker under the title of "Anatolia", which he explained was Greek for 'Eastern Land'. This recorded in great detail his visit with the Jannaways. A comparison of these early visits with current conditions makes fascinating reading.

The editor observed in 1914: "The grasping policy of the King of the North never slackens and the growing prosperity of the Jewish colonies in Palestine acts more and more as a bait in the trap that God is laying for him upon the mountains of Israel" (page 258).

When World War I broke out in 1914, little did the brethren realise that the outcome would be to free Palestine from the Turks, who had neglected it for so long. In 1916, the ecclesias contributed several hundred pounds to the Jewish Colonial

Trust, in the hope that the Land would soon be liberated. But the war raged for over three years before British troops advanced from Egypt under General Allenby and pushed the Turks out. Jerusalem was surrendered without a shot being fired and the General humbly dismounted and walked into the city in 1917. War soon ended, as if God's purpose had now been accomplished. The Land now became available for the people, as the League of Nations gave to Britain the Mandate to govern Palestine.

John Thomas's forecast of over 70 years before was now confirmed. Britain had given the Jews the Balfour Declaration and was now in control. The proclamation of the Gospel received a great boost. Frank Jannaway wrote several books—*Palestine and the Jews, Palestine and the Powers* and *Palestine and the World*—and numerous leaflets were printed and lectures given to show that God's promise to restore the Jews to their Land was a sure sign of the near approach of the return of Jesus Christ, the King of the Jews. The Russian Revolution of 1917 also focused attention on the Bible prophecies that clearly made reference to that power.

Jewish Refugees

In 1939, the editorial feature of the magazine was re-titled 'The Jews and Palestine'. As the threat of war loomed over Europe, an exodus began of Jewish refugees from Germany and Austria. An appeal for funds for their relief was made to the ecclesias.

In July 1939, a specific appeal was made for help with Jewish refugee problems. Christadelphians were asked to take refugee children into their care at home, or to provide a hostel where they could be received. It was reported that, in spite of difficult wartime conditions, a considerable number of refugee girls had already been cared for, and a few boys. A hostel was planned for boys, who were thought to be in the most danger. Then World War II broke out, and there was little news of events until stories of ships loaded with refugees began to be featured.

By December 1939, in cooperation with the Representative Council of Birmingham Jewry, a hostel was arranged for 20 boys, to be furnished for occupation and rent free, while the expenses of maintaining it were to be the responsibility of the Christadelphian community, with Birmingham and Coventry taking the initiative. The next month it was reported that necessary structural alterations to the hostel were proceeding. The hostel appears to have been opened in April 1940, and was named 'Elpis Lodge' ('Hope Lodge'). By July 1940, 16 boys were in residence, with Dr. and Mrs. Hirsch as wardens, to provide an environment of orthodox Judaism. On reaching the age of 16, however, the boys had to be removed to an internment camp as 'enemy aliens'. In spite of the problems, contact was maintained with them.

'Elpis Lodge'

By the end of the war, 48 boys had been trained for employment, had been instructed in English, given a Jewish cultural background and Jewish religious education. The hostel then became the concern of the Refugee Children's Movement. Letters of appreciation were received from the Council of Birminghan Jewry and others.

In August 1940, Christadelphians in Canada, Australia and New Zealand, were moved to offer to take Jewish children into their care. But as passenger liners were among the casualties of the war at sea, this kind offer did not prove practicable.

Post War Attitudes

However, the attitude of Christadelphians was not unanimously in favour of giving material aid to the refugees. Some argued that the Jews were returning in unbelief, and so were not worthy of support. One well-respected Christadelphian was quite vociferous in his condemnation of the Jews and their materialistic projects, in spite of the fact that they were ful-filling Bible prophecy. *The Christadelphian* continued to feature items on 'Signs of the Times', 'The Jews and Zionism', etc., sometimes occupying several pages. The discoveries of the Palestine Exploration Society were favourably reported on from time to time.

Generally speaking there was excitement at the evidence of Zionist enterprise, and this movement was seen as a vehicle for the further preparation of the Land for the events prophesied and the return of the Messiah. Improved transport now made it much easier to visit the Land, and developments were reported at first hand.

In 1939, the editorial feature of the magazine was re-titled 'The Jews and Palestine'. Then World War II broke out, and there was little news of any developments until stories about ships loaded with refugees were fea-tured. The refugee problem was also faced in Britain. Supplies of clothing for refugee children were increased, hundreds of sisters making a range of practical garments. These were distributed by Jewish

'Israel Column' headings in The Christadelphian

relief organisations in Palestine. The war over, the refugee problem was intensified, but the violence of some of the Jews who were fighting for their existence tended to alienate world sympathy.

The Christadelphian Isolation League Sunday School
sponsored the planting of trees in the name of its scholars
at Ma'ale ha-Hamisha in the Judean Hills

The interest of readers of the Magazine was maintained by a feature that was now headed 'Israel and their Land', a result of the name of the new State being made known as 'Israel' by David ben Gurion on May 14, 1948.

Christadelphian Reaction

The fact that Canaan, or Palestine, or Israel, or the Holy Land, is God's Land and that it was promised by Divine covenant to Abraham and his descendants through Isaac for ever, has transcended every-day political intrigue. Britain's exit from Palestine after 30 years as the mandatory power, was a great disappointment and surprise to many Bible students, who had thought that Britain's involvement would continue unbroken until the invasion of the Land by Gog and his hosts. Lengthy expositions had been written to the effect that the power named Tarshish in Ezekiel 38:13 must refer to Britain, and that therefore Britain had to be present in the Land to issue that challenge.

CHRISTADELPHIAN ATTITUDES TO ISRAEL

A Challenge

In 1958, an article in *The Bible Missionary*, another Christadelphian magazine, drew attention to the lack of preaching efforts to the Jews. The example of the Apostle Paul was to offer the Gospel to the Jews first before preaching to the Gentiles. While God's Truth has reached a number of Jews in the diaspora who share the Christadelphian faith, hope and fellowship, little has been done to direct a specific appeal to Jews.

The State of Israel has enacted a law forbidding proselytising, that is, trying to change anybody's religious faith. This law can be understood as a way of trying to avoid confusion in a land where many faiths have 'holy' places, and where feelings run high. The policy of the Turks had been 'to protect them all', and in a similar way Israel tries to enable people of whatever faith to have freedom to worship in their own manner, or to visit their shrines. Thus, in order to keep peace, Israel is bound to say, 'Don't try to change anybody's faith'. In spite of this, there are offices in Israel of such proselytisers as the Jehovah's Witnesses and the Mormons, and an Evangelical Church Embassy.

If the usual ways of preaching in Israel are not open, no doubt other ways can be found. It is known that there are some young Jews who regard Jesus of Nazareth as their Messiah, and are looking for his return. The Orthodox Jews are looking for an unknown Messiah to come and rescue them politically, much as the Jews of Jesus' time wanted a leader against the Romans.

Current Attitudes

Looking at the attitude of the Christadelphian community in the late 1880s, it would seem that the excitement engendered by that first trickle of Jewish refugees a century ago, has been replaced by one of comparative indifference, now that millions of Jews are actually living in the Land. The 'pre-adventual' colonization that John Thomas forecast has taken place, and may be complete. Surely, we should all be thrilled and excited that the Bible prophecies have been so literally fulfilled in our own lifetime. The day of the Lord's return is a century nearer than when the first trickle began. It surely behoves everyone to stay awake and to be keenly aware of what these develop-ments in God's Land portend. There may be some uncertainty about exactly how future developments will take place, but there can be no uncertainty about the salient prophecies, and that the coming of our Lord is nearer than when we first believed—his call may come any day.

Christadelphian Hymns

Every edition of the Christadelphian Hymn Book has contained hymns that express the centrality of the community's interest and concern for the realisation of the Hope of Israel. While only twelve hymns appear under the specific section devoted to Israel, many others reveal the Christadelphian attitude to Israel—past, present and future. For example, "Shine, mighty God, on Zion shine . . .''

The words of a number of such hymns were written by Christadelphians, and appropriate references to Scripture are a common feature. The following words (Hymn 250 in the 1964 edition) contain obvious allusions to a dozen or more Bible passages:

1 Great God of Abram, hear our prayer:
Let Abram's seed Thy mercy share:
Oh may they now at length return,
And look on him they pierc'd, and mourn.

2 Remember Jacob's flock of old;
Bring home the wand'rers to Thy fold;
Remember, too, Thy promis'd word,
"Israel at last shall seek the Lord".

3 Though outcasts still, estrang'd from Thee,
Cut off from their own olive tree,
Let them no longer such remain;
Oh! Thou canst graft them in again.

4 Lord, put Thy law within their hearts,
And write it in their inward parts;
The veil of darkness rend in two
Which hides Messiah from their view.

5 O! Haste the day, foretold so long,
When Jew and Greek (a glorious throng)
One house shall seek, one pray'r shall pour,
And one Redeemer shall adore.

CHRISTADELPHIAN ATTITUDES TO ISRAEL

Christians and Jews

The relationship between Christians and Jews has been surveyed very thoroughly in a book that was reviewed in *The Christadelphian* for January 1986. It has much to say about our contacts with the Jews during the past century. For example:

"From the outset, the Christadelphians were ardent supporters of the idea of the return of the Jews to the Land of Israel, which was essential to fulfilment of the End of Time. Long before the rise of Jewish Zionism as a political movement at the end of the 19th century, the Christadelphians offered practical assistance to Jews who looked to the Land of Israel as a haven of refuge. They supported such pre-Zionist groups as the Hibbat Zion movement in Tsarist Russia. As late as the 1940s when the Nazi destruction of European Jewry was under way, they actively aided attempts to rescue Jews from Europe" (Michael J. Pragai, *Faith and Fulfilment: Christians and the Return to the Promised Land*).

It is very noticeable that the Christadelphian attitude was the complete reverse of the attitude of the largest of the churches of Christendom, who saw the return of the Jews to the Holy Land as a menace to their shrines and 'holy places', and a most undesirable development.

Summary

Christadelphians regard the Jewish people as the recipients of God's revelation of Himself, as the custodians of His Word all down the ages, and as the principal witnesses to the Truth of His Word. Their rise, their fall and their partial return during the past century have all been accurately foretold in Scripture, thus confirming the Divine truth of Bible prophecy. The Apostle Paul wrote:

*"God has not rejected his people whom he foreknew . . .
at the present time there is a remnant, chosen by grace . . .
even the others, if they do not persist in their unbelief, will
be grafted in, for God has the power to graft them in again"*
(Romans 11:2,5,23).

This is the sincere wish of all Christadelphians, who see themselves as "wild olive branches" that have been mercifully grafted into the stock of Israel, and share the "Hope of Israel".

ISRAEL

Christadelphians see themselves as friends of Israel, while by no means approving of all that Jews do, or that the State of Israel does, and deploring the materialistic and atheistic basis of the State. Interest in all things concerning the Land and the people is basically because it is realised that God is working out His purpose in His Land which He covenanted to Abraham, and that God will yet be glorified in the people to whom He gave those great and precious promises.

The Divine pronouncement that "I will bless him that blesseth thee" is regarded as being true for all time, and the Christadelphian community has continued for over a century to try to provide various forms of aid for Jewish refugees. At first it took the form of cash to purchase land, tools and materials, then clothing for working men, later for needy children, then the physical caring for children. This help has been welcomed and appreciated. Significantly the name Christadelphian may be better known to Jews as friends and benefactors, than it is to most Christians. One hopes that such help will continue until the longed-for "king of the Jews" returns to provide his own succour for his people, who will be given a new heart to recognise him and give him the glory and the obedience due to him. May that day soon come.

12

WHAT FUTURE FOR ISRAEL?

UNLIKE the Jews of the dispersion, those living in Israel (the Yishuv) are not seeking personal assimilation into the nations. They are proud of their Jewishness and of their independence. Most of them are in the Land because they are imbued with the spirit of Jewish nationalism. Yet, even so, the State of Israel seeks to be seen as just one of the nations of the world, as a member of the United Nations, as a partner with other nations in world enterprises. As a nation, Israel seeks assimilation with the world's nations.

As Seen by the Yishuv

How amazing it is that after 2,000 years, or more, of dispersion among all nations, the Jewish identity has not been lost. With the establishment of the secular republic, the State of Israel, in 1948, the future of the scattered people seemed assured. At first it was far from secure, but after the remarkable series of military successes over their Arab adversaries, confidence in the security of the State mounted. The viewpoint of the secular majority in Israel is that the State must remain strong enough militarily to hold the position it has achieved. The declared purpose of God for the nation does not appear to be in their thoughts at all. They see their future as being entirely in their own hands.

Ben Gurion's View

The prophetic picture of God's purpose with Israel is not perceived even by those who read the Scriptures and take note of some of the divine prophecies. Thus, David ben Gurion, the charismatic founder of the State who had a weekly Bible Class at his home, saw the fulfilment of prophecy only as the materialistic realisation of his own political ideals. He wrote:

"In the Book of Books, he (the Jew) will find revealed before him the prophecy of the future, the future of his own people and of the human race; the vision of the latter days; the vision of redemption, peace and justice which was uttered in ancient times on the mountains of Jerusalem, and still gleams fresh and heart-stirring as on the day when first it was given, which bears the true tidings of the redemption of Israel and the solution of the two fateful problems of our own days – the problem of capital and labour within society, and peace and war between the nations" (David ben Gurion, *Israel Government Year Book 5714*, page 49).

In typically self-confident mood he viewed the future in these words:

"We have always been a small people numerically and we shall remain a small people . . . But our place is in the history of humanity . . . Few peoples have had so profound an influence upon so large a part of the human race. And there are few countries which have played so central a rôle in world history as the Land of Israel. It must be our aim to achieve a future that can be worthy of our past" (W.Z.O. Pamphlet, 1986).

The View of Religious Jews

Within Israel are a number of small religious groups who do not share the view of the secular majority. Although disunited among themselves, they look for a solution of Israel's problems by the coming of their promised Messiah. They do not regard Jesus of Nazareth as their Messiah, but look for one who is yet to be sent to their aid. Jesus is regarded as one of the many false messiahs.

There is, however, one small group who do look for the personal return of Jesus as Messiah, and for him to take office as the King of Israel. This group seem to have been influenced by current evangelical views, but prefer not to be known as Christians, because that name is closely associated in Jewish minds with the long years of persecution inflicted by Christendom. These 'Messianic Assemblies' appear to have a typical evangelical understanding of prophecy, which raises the question of whether they will actually accept Jesus when he comes, or see him as the 'antichrist', in line with the Jesuit-inspired theory currently in vogue.

Thus both secular and religious Jews see the future of Israel as being firmly based upon their past, and as an essential part of the resolution of the problems of all nations.

As Seen by the Diaspora in the West

The mass migration of millions of European Jews to America has had a very profound effect on the outlook of a large sector of the people. Many have prospered in their new countries and now want to be seen as normal citizens who happen to worship in the Jewish manner. Others do their utmost, often by inter-marriage, to become absorbed into the western way of life, trying to forget their Jewishness by assimilation among the Gentiles. They see their future as Gentiles.

A small number of European Jews have transferred their ultra-orthodox way of life, as lived in the ghettoes of Europe, to the New World, and now live in a ghetto of their own devis-ing. These tend to maintain a rigid barrier between themselves and the secular Jews in the world around them. By contrast, a small number have converted to orthodox Christianity of one sort or another, accepting the church teaching about Jesus.

The future, as seen by these millions of Jews in the West, appears to be as an integral part of the western way of life, and few seem to be aware of the world-shattering events that are about to burst upon them, centred on little Israel.

As Seen by the Diaspora in the East

The millions of Jews who are trapped in the Soviet system include some whose ancestors have lived in Russia for many centuries. These were joined by over a million who fled before the German invasion of Russia in World War II. The cities of the Ukraine, where Jewish culture and tradition were strongest, were wiped out in that war. The Jews fled to areas where there was no synagogue, no Jewish cemetery, no yeshiva (rabbinical school) and nothing to refresh the traditional Jewish veneration for the Holy Scriptures. Thus, a consciousness of Jewishness has been stifled, and has not been encouraged by the secular communist state which aims at assimilating them.

The fact that some of the leaders of Russian communism were, and still are, Jews, has tended to influence the Jews to mix into the cosmopolitan Soviet population and lose their identity as Jews. It would seem that the majority of Soviet Jews see their future as bound up with the future of the communist world.

However, news keeps leaking out that there are Russian Jews who are not integrating and are seeking to escape from communism. Some want to go to the West, and a few want to emigrate to Israel. Those who opt for Israel find that the authorities take a hard line, and that once their desire has been made known they will be harassed and deprived. Nevertheless a few keep getting through. It seems unlikely that Soviet Jews are aware of the great surprise that is in store for them when the King of Israel delivers them (Isaiah 11:12).

Assimilation—A Contrast

The situation was put this way at a conference on Jewish Culture and Identity reported in *The Jerusalem Post* (International Edition) for January 17, 1987, page 13. Attention was drawn to the paradox: in the Soviets, Jewish culture is suppressed, yet in so doing it highlights the Jewish identity; whereas in the West, Jewish culture is not restricted but the Jewish identity is slowly being obscured.

The consciousness of being a part of Israel comes to the fore when appeals are made for financial help for Israel's charities. Indeed, it has become noticeable for a Jew in whatever land he is living to speak of the government of Israel as 'our government'. The words of the divine prophecy uttered by the reluctant prophet Balaam are still to the point: "Lo, a people dwelling alone, and not reckoning itself among the nations" (Numbers 23:9).

Reverse Assimilation

A very different kind of assimilation (if that is the right word) will eventually take place, as foretold by the prophet:

> "*Thus says the LORD of hosts: Peoples shall yet come, even the inhabitants of many cities; the inhabitants of one city shall go to another, saying, 'Let us go at once to entreat the favour of the LORD, and to seek the LORD of*

33. Sailing Boat on Kinnereth: ''His disciples went down
unto the sea, and entered into a ship'' (John 6:16,17)

34. Bethlehem: "But thou, Bethlehem Ephratah, though thou be little among the thousands of Judah, yet out of thee shall he come forth unto me that is to be ruler in Israel" (Micah 5:2)

35. The Garden of Gethsemane: "They came to a place which was named Gethsemane" (Mark 14:32)

36. Huleh, showing Fish Ponds reclaimed from Swamp:
''He turns a desert into pools of water'' (Psalm 107:35)

37. Esdraelon, the Valley of Jezreel: '' . . . a place called
in the Hebrew tongue Armageddon'' (Revelation 16:16)

38. Moroccan Jewish Children at a Moshav:
"In far countries they shall remember me, and with their children they shall live and return" (Zechariah 10:9)

39. Sabra, or Prickly Pear—symbol of the Israeli born in the Land: "This one was born there" (Psalm 87:6)

40. Kibbutz Children: "Lo, children are an heritage of the Lord . . ." (Psalm 127:3)

hosts; I am going'. Many peoples and strong nations shall come to seek the LORD of hosts in Jerusalem, and to entreat the favour of the LORD. Thus says the LORD of hosts: In those days ten men from the nations of every tongue shall take hold of the robe of a Jew, saying, 'Let us go with you, for we have heard that God is with you' " (Zechariah 8:20-23).

This is a prophetic picture of Gentiles seeking assimilation with Jews! It seems inconceivable at present. But is it? The call to disciples of Jesus Christ is to adopt Abraham's faith, to confess the Hope of Israel, and to seek the LORD of hosts while He may be found. These objectives are all possible now, thanks to our Lord Jesus Christ.

"And if you are Christ's, then you are Abraham's off-spring, heirs according to promise" (Galatians 3:29).

This reverse assimilation is enshrined in essence in the covenant with Abraham: "In you shall all families of the earth be blessed." It is elaborated by Isaiah in this beautiful passage:

"And the foreigners who join themselves to the LORD, to minister to him, to love the name of the LORD, and to be his servants, every one who keeps the sabbath, and does not profane it, and holds fast my covenant—these I will bring to my holy mountain, and make them joyful in my house of prayer; their burnt offerings and their sacrifices will be accepted on my altar; for my house shall be called a house of prayer for all peoples. Thus says the Lord GOD, who gathers the outcasts of Israel, I will gather yet others to him besides those already gathered" (Isaiah 56:6-8).

As Seen by Divine Prophecy

The Biblical history of Israel does not end with the return of a part of the nation to their homeland and the establishment of the State of Israel. Divinely inspired prophecy projects the Israel story well into the future. God's covenant with Abraham promised the specific land and the specific people to be his "for ever" (Genesis 17:8). Yet Abraham was one of those who "died in faith, not having received what was promised, but having seen it and greeted it from afar, and having acknow-ledged that they were strangers and exiles on the earth" (Hebrews 11:13).

ISRAEL

God assured the Jews by the prophet Jeremiah in the seventh century B.C. that, in spite of the well deserved punishment to be inflicted by the Babylonians, the nation would never be destroyed (Jeremiah 31:36). Their survival would not be because of their great numbers (Deuteronomy 7:7) but because God had a purpose with the nation in fulfilling His covenant with Abraham (Galatians 3:16-18). King Solomon had a grasp of the great purpose of God with His people—"that all the peoples of the earth may know thy name and fear thee, as do thy people Israel" (1 Kings 8:43).

But Abraham's unshakeable faith that God would eventually, in His own good time, keep His promises, is not shared by many of his descendants. The few who have retained that faith in whatever century, are called by God "the remnant":

"In that day the remnant of Israel and the survivors of the house of Jacob will no more lean upon him that smote them, but will lean upon the LORD, the Holy One of Israel, in truth. A remnant will return, the remnant of Jacob, to the mighty God" (Isaiah 10:20-21).

The Apostle Paul takes up this theme: "Though the number of the sons of Israel be as the sand of the sea, only a remnant of them will be saved" (Romans 9:27).

Adopted Children

Israel's history is dotted with examples of men and women who were adopted into the nation because of their faith. To name a few—Rebekah, Rachel, Leah, Asenath, Caleb, Rahab and Ruth. The faith of Ruth was expressed in her protest to Naomi: "Your people shall be my people, and your God my God" (Ruth 1:16). Such Gentiles who have embraced the Hope of Israel become sharers in the covenant with Abraham. This beautiful truth was confirmed in the first century A.D. by Peter's mission to receive Cornelius (a Roman) into the faith, and by the Lord's instructions to Ananias to go and see Paul of Tarsus: "Go, for he is a chosen instrument of mine to carry my name before the Gentiles and kings and the sons of Israel" (Acts 9:15). The Apostle Paul affirmed that "There is neither Jew nor Greek, there is neither slave nor free, there is neither male nor female; for you are all one in Christ Jesus. And if

264

you are Christ's, then you are Abraham's offspring, heirs according to promise'' (Galatians 3:28-29).

It is an unhappy fact that there are more adopted children of faith looking earnestly for the fulfilment of the Abrahamic covenant than there are of the physical descendants of Abraham. A spirit of agnosticism, even atheism, has swept over the chosen people just as the hand of the LORD is about to be revealed and the covenant fulfilled.

Israel's Change of Heart

The first forty years of Israel's independence as a secular state have been a continual period of war, interspersed with several spectacular battles that have gone in Israel's favour. In spite of the strength of the opposition they have successfully confronted , the new nation has been unable to appreciate that the hand of God has been with them, but have been quick to claim the glory for themselves. Will this balance last? Has this proud self-sufficient nation to learn a lesson?

Several prophecies suggest a change of heart before the coming of the Messiah, so that when he comes he will be welcomed. Jesus said, as he mourned over the fate of Jerusalem, ''For I tell you, you will not see me again, until you say, 'Blessed is he who comes in the name of the Lord' '' (Matthew 23:39). This saying gives the impression that the people will be ready and waiting for the revealing of their Messiah.

The prophet Hosea gives a similar picture. Through this prophet God says:

''I will return again to my place, until they acknowledge their guilt and seek my face, and in their distress they seek me, saying, 'Come, let us return to the LORD; for he has torn, that he may heal us; he has stricken, and he will bind us up'' (Hosea 5:15—6:1).

This is a confirmation of Moses' prophecy of Israel's future:

''But if they confess their iniquity and the iniquity of their fathers . . . if then their uncircumcised heart is humbled and they make amends for their iniquity; then I will remember my covenant with Jacob . . . with Isaac and . . . Abraham, and I will remember the land'' (Leviticus 26:40-42).

What influence can bring such a change of heart? The last verses of the Old Testament may give the answer:

> *"Behold, I will send you Elijah the prophet before the great and terrible day of the LORD comes. And he will turn the hearts of fathers to their children and the hearts of children to their fathers, lest I come and smite the land with a curse"* (Malachi 4:5,6).

Whether the prophet speaks of the prophet Elijah raised from the dead by Jesus to be sent on this mission, or of someone else sent in the spirit and power of Elijah, the effect is dramatic: a change of heart on the part of Israel.

At some stage the atheistic majority of Jews in the land will be eliminated in fulfilment of another prophecy:

> *"In the whole land, says the LORD, two thirds shall be cut off and perish, and one third shall be left alive"* (Zechariah 13:8).

When an opinion poll was taken in Israel asking people about their belief in God, two thirds were revealed as being atheists or agnostics, and only one third had any sort of belief in God, thus confirming this prophecy.

What are the Abominations?

Before the hand of the Lord is revealed, there appears to be a vital work of preparation of the Land for the coming of Messiah. For well nigh eighteen centuries the Land, and in particular the city of Jerusalem, have been the centre for religious pilgrimage for Christians, and for perhaps thirteen centuries for Moslems. To allure and intrigue the pilgrims a profusion of shrines, tombs, monuments and holy places have been either identified or invented. There can be no doubt about the identity of many clearly defined geographical features of the land, such as the Sea of Galilee, the river Jordan, the Mount of Olives, the Kidron valley etc. However, there are very few shrines and holy places that can be definitely identified as genuine. Various religious bodies have staked a claim to certain of these shrines, and reap a rich picking from pilgrims and tourists. Indeed, the situation is such that the government of Israel has had to leave well alone and try to ensure that all faiths can have freedom to control their own holy places and have access to them.

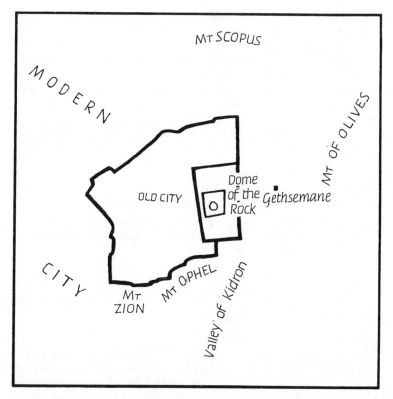

General Map of Modern Jerusalem

The most holy place to Jews is undoubtedly the site of the Temple, even though there has been no temple for nineteen centuries. But the whole Temple Mount area has been under Moslem control for about thirteen centuries, and their great Dome of the Rock, and huge mosque of Al Aksa dominate the holy site. In spite of the objections of Orthodox Jewry, the government of Israel has respected the Moslem claim to it. The nearest that Jews can go is to the Western Wall (or Wailing Wall), which is part of the Temple Mount, but not of the Temple itself. An official edict forbids Jews to go on the Temple Mount 'lest they should defile the Most Holy Place'. The real reason is doubtless lest they provoke a confrontation with the Moslem guards (the Wakf), who suspect that many Jews would destroy the Moslem shrines if they could. Two attempts to do so have already been thwarted. Although a Moslem government no longer rules in Jerusalem, Moslem religious power still obstructs the Jew's most holy shrine.

How long can this state of affairs last? The Jewish authorities know full well that to displace the Moslem presence on the Temple Mount would precipitate a Jihad (holy war) by all Moslem countries, and Israel could not afford to risk such a confrontation. Thus it comes about that all faiths have free access to their shrines except the Jews!

Rival Tombs

The supposed burial place of Jesus is purported by the Catholic Church to be within the Church of the Holy Sepulchre, while the Protestant churches claim the Garden tomb to be the site. They are both interesting early tombs, but archaeologists have pointed out that both are typical of tombs made around 600 years before the time of Jesus, whereas Jesus was laid in a new tomb. It has been reliably established that the 'Ecce Homo' arch, and the 'Pavement' were not actually constructed until some years after Jesus was in Jerusalem. It must be remembered that the Jerusalem that Jesus knew was totally destroyed by the Romans, who later rebuilt it as a Roman city with a heathen temple.

Other false claims for shrines could be mentioned, but as they are profitable to the church authorities who control them, and satisfy the curiosity of pilgrims, it is most unlikely that they will be given up voluntarily. Such places are secretly resented by the Jews, and must surely be abhorred by the Almighty, who must see these places as blots on His city. What is to happen to them? The government of Israel dare not interfere, for to do so would create a furore that they could not control.

The answer to the problem may be found in an obscure verse in Ezekiel:

"Thus says the Lord GOD, I will gather you from the peoples, and assemble you out of the countries where you have been scattered, and I will give you the land of Israel. And when they come there, they will remove from it all its detestable things and all its abominations" (11:17-18).

What are the detestable things and all its abominations in the eyes of the Almighty? Could they be the bogus shrines that are maintained by the apostate churches and the false prophet?

As this is being written, they have not been removed. For secular political reasons, Israel's authorities are anxious to avoid giving offence. The ultra-orthodox Jewish minority is beginning to make its voice heard and protest about sabbath breaking, unbecoming clothes, obscene literature and the worldliness of secular Israel. Will this movement grow in intensity until Ezekiel's prophecy is fulfilled?

Pride Goes Before a Fall

The God of Israel has had very little acknowledgment from His people who have been participants in the miracle of Israel's rebirth as a nation. Is it possible that a change of heart must be brought about the hard way? Must Israel's self-assurance in its military prowess be shaken before the nation is ready to seek the Lord?

Several prophecies suggest that this may be the pattern. For example, Daniel foretells an invasion "at the time of the end" when the invader shall "pitch his palatial tents between the sea and the glorious holy mountain" (Daniel 11:40-45). The Psalmist enumerates a confederacy of Israel's enemies which corresponds remarkably to the present situation. He then foresees Israel appealing to God for His aid, and concluding, "Let them know that thou alone, whose name is the LORD, art the Most High over all the earth" (Psalm 83:18). Such an appeal would not come readily from an atheistic socialist state.

It may be that Ezekiel's prophecy (36:1-7) has reference to a short-lived military success by Edom and the rest of the (Arab) nations, in which Israel is defeated. The little prophecy of Obadiah would seem to have a latter-day significance of similar import.

As in times of old, so again in these days, Israel's national characteristic has been one of confidence in their own power, with but little faith in the God of their fathers. It would appear that this attitude must be finally removed by extreme humiliation of the new nation. Maybe this would be when Elijah appears to lead them to repentance, and eventually to acceptance of the Messiah, whom they have for so long rejected.

Divine Intervention

As the political future of the State of Israel appears to hang in the balance, and its people cannot see the outcome, the words of the Psalmist seem to be appropriate:

"How long, O LORD? Wilt thou be angry for ever? Will thy jealous wrath burn like fire? Pour out thy anger on the nations that do not know thee, and on the kingdoms that do not call on thy name!" (Psalm 79:5,6).

The Psalmist also looks forward:

"Come, behold the works of the LORD, how he has wrought desolations in the earth . . . he breaks the bow, and shatters the spear, he burns the chariots with fire!" (Psalm 46:8,9).

As controller of the elements, the Lord has power to influence the decisions and actions of man. That this power will be used is evident from the vivid description of His intervention when the mountains of Israel are invaded by the colossus from the north:

"On that day, when Gog shall come against the land of Israel, says the Lord GOD, my wrath will be roused. For in my jealousy and in my blazing wrath I declare, On that day there shall be a great shaking in the land of Israel . . . all the men that are upon the face of the earth, shall quake at my presence, and the mountains shall be thrown down, and the cliffs shall fall, and every wall shall tumble to the ground. I will summon every kind of terror against Gog, says the Lord GOD; every man's sword will be against his brother. With pestilence and bloodshed I will enter into judgment with him . . . torrential rains and hailstones, fire and brimstone. So I will show my greatness and my holiness and make myself known in the eyes of many nations. Then they will know that I am the LORD" (Ezekiel 38:18-23).

The Lord's Anger

That very specific prophecy against named nations does not stand alone. The prophet Joel declares God's judgement on those nations that have persecuted God's nation, when the divine control of the elements is again mentioned:

*"Multitudes, multitudes, in the valley of decision! . . .
The sun and the moon are darkened, and the stars
withdraw their shining. And the LORD roars from Zion, and
utters his voice from Jerusalem, and the heavens and the
earth shake. But the LORD is a refuge to his people, a
stronghold to the people of Israel. So you shall know that
I am the LORD your God, who dwell in Zion, my holy mountain. And Jerusalem shall be holy and strangers shall never
again pass through it"* (Joel 3:14-17).

The prophet Isaiah speaks of the same time in similar vein:

*"For behold, the LORD will come in fire, and his chariots
like the stormwind, to render his anger in fury, and his
rebuke with flames of fire. For by fire will the LORD execute
judgment, and by his sword, upon all flesh; and those slain
by the LORD shall be many"* (Isaiah 66:15,16).

Further details of these world-shaking events are revealed in
the prophecy of Zechariah:

*"Then the LORD will go forth and fight against those
nations as when he fights on a day of battle"* (Zechariah
14:3).

How does the Lord fight?

When the Lord Fought for Israel

Israel's history shows how the LORD has fought for His people
in the past. In the days of Joshua's conquest of the land,
"the sun stayed in the midst of heaven, and did not hasten to
go down for about a whole day. There has been no day like it
before or since . . . for the LORD fought for Israel" (Joshua
10:13,14). This unique extension of daylight enabled Joshua's
forces to take "all these kings and their land at one time,
because the LORD God of Israel fought for Israel" (verse 42).
Why did the LORD fight for Israel on this occasion? Because
Joshua was a man of great faith who trusted completely in
God's power to control events.

An example of a king of Judah who also trusted in God so
confidently that he sent a choir of singers before his army to
sing and praise the LORD, is recorded in Chronicles:

"Thus says the LORD to you, 'Fear not, and be not dismayed at this great multitude, for the battle is not yours but God's' " (1 Chronicles 20:15).

The result was that they "all helped to destroy one another". Thus Israel has such precedents as these to give them grounds for faith that God can intervene on their behalf, if they but put their trust in Him.

But is such faith to be found in modern Israel? More than half the nation's national expenditure is for weapons of war. Since 1948, Israel has become a major manufacturer of weapons, even supplying some to the great nations.

The Lord will Fight for Israel

The conflict between the claims and 'rights' of the different peoples in the Middle East has no political solution, and no human solution. The answer can only be in God's hands. The international resistance to Israel's presence in the land that God covenanted to Abraham and his descendants, is resistance to the will of God and His preparations for the divine final solution. For this reason, the power of God will be manifested to a shocked and unbelieving world.

Looking again at Zechariah's prophecy, it is revealed that:

"The Mount of Olives shall be split in two from east to west by a very wide valley; so that one half of the Mount shall withdraw northward, and the other half southward" (Zechariah 14:4).

Then:

"The whole land shall be turned into a plain from Geba to Rimmon south of Jerusalem. But Jerusalem shall remain aloft upon its site . . . " (verse 10).

Such massive movements of the mountains around Jerusalem would require an earthquake that would defy measurement on the scientist's Richter scale. It must be remembered that the Jordan valley is part of the tremendous Rift Valley that stretches from central Africa up to Turkey. Even now, Jerusalem has many minor earth tremors every year, most of which are unnoticed by the population, but are recorded on very sensitive instruments. This fact is a reminder that the area is not geologically stable. Indeed, during the time of the British

Mandate for Palestine, it was found that the Mount of Olives had a geological fault, for which reason the authorities forbade the erection of any more buildings there.

Another event similar to Joshua's 'long day' is spoken of by the prophet Zechariah:

"And there shall be continuous day . . . not day and not night, for at evening time there shall be light" (Zechariah 14:7).

The divine control of the elements is very graphically described in Isaiah's prophecy of the destruction of those that fight against Mount Zion:

"In an instant, suddenly, you will be visited by the LORD of hosts with thunder and with earthquake and great noise, with whirlwind and tempest, and the flame of a devouring fire" (Isaiah 29:6).

The final destruction of the city that is the centre of the apostate Christendom is described in this way by the Apostle John:

" 'It is done!' And there were flashes of lightning, voices, peals of thunder and a great earthquake such as had never been seen since men were on the earth, so great was that earthquake . . . and great hailstones, heavy as a hundredweight, dropped on men from heaven, till men cursed God for the plague of the hail, so fearful was that plague" (Revelation 16:18-21).

Cutting Man Down to Size

It may be asked why such a massive upheaval of the earth and interference with natural events should be required? Is it not stretching the reader's credulity to foretell such calamities in detail? Seeing that similar events have been recorded in the past, these prophecies should be accepted in faith, and taken as a warning. Divine intervention with the normal course of nature in the past, and in the future, is for the same reason: "So shall they know that I am the LORD your God." "So shall I make myself known in the eyes of many nations." This is a very dramatic and unforgettable way of impressing upon sceptical and Godless minds that the Creator God is still in control of nature, and that man is not the master of his own destiny. "The earth is the LORD's" and not man's. Proud and arrogant man, whether Jew or Gentile, must be cut down to size.

The humanist may object that surely such events will cause great loss of life. Yet why should the One who has the power of Creation, and the power to raise from the dead by resurrection, not have the right to take life away?

There may be another good reason for such violent terrestrial activity. The physical shaking of the earth may be the divine way of decontaminating the planet and ridding it at one stroke of the filthy pollution that man has inflicted upon it. There may also be other consequences, such as changing the climate, converting deserts into fruitful land, opening up new watercourses and revealing new features of the planet. Great physical changes would seem to be inevitable for the earth to become paradise restored.

Prophecy and Belief

Whether Israel's humiliation and subsequent dramatic salvation from her foes will be one event or more, is a matter for discussion and deep study. While the prophets are definite concerning the certainty of Israel's change of heart and eventual acceptance of her Messiah, there is uncertainty about the details.

It is as well for the purpose of divine prophecy to be kept in mind. Jesus expressed it this way:

"I have told you before it takes place, so that when it does take place, you may believe" (John 14:29).

Thus, when the disciple of Jesus sees prophecy come to pass, he will glorify God and acknowledge that He knew just how events would come to pass. It is erroneous to think that some event must take place because it was prophesied; rather should it be realised that the prophecy was based upon God's complete foreknowledge of everything that is future. It is His omniscience that should cause us to be amazed and acknowledge Him and believe in all that He says through His servants the prophets in His Word.

God's covenant with Abraham is a far-reaching prophecy that has not yet been fulfilled, but will be in every detail as will now be shown.

The Abrahamic Covenant Renewed

For the people of Israel and of the whole world, the consequences of this dramatic divine intervention will ensure the beginning of the process of humbling the proud human spirit that has defied the Creator for so long. For the people of Israel especially, the promised intervention of the God of Israel should stir memories from their past history. Even in Moses' time, God promised that " . . . neither will I abhor them so as to destroy them utterly and break my covenant with them" (Leviticus 26:44). Then Moses was inspired to prophesy:

"When you are in tribulation and all these things come upon you in the latter days, you will return to the LORD your God and obey his voice, for the LORD your God is a merciful God; he will not fail you or destroy you or forget the covenant with your fathers, which he swore to them" (Deuteronomy 4:30-31).

That Israel's scattering among the nations would not be final was foretold by Isaiah:

"In days to come Jacob shall take root, Israel shall blossom and put forth shoots and fill the whole world with fruit" (Isaiah 27:6).

After pointing out that Israel's iniquities have separated them from their God, the prophet Isaiah speaks of the time when

"they shall fear the name of the LORD from the west, and his glory from the rising of the sun; for he will come like a rushing stream, which the wind of the LORD drives. And he will come to Zion as Redeemer, to those in Jacob who turn from transgression, says the LORD. And as for me, this is my covenant with them, says the LORD: my spirit which is upon you, and my words which I have put in your mouth, shall not depart out of your mouth, or out of the mouth of your children, or out of the mouth of your children's children, says the LORD, from this time forth and for evermore" (Isaiah 59:19-21).

A change of attitude of the people of Israel towards their God is foretold by Jeremiah:

"Return, O faithless children, says the LORD; for I am your master; I will take you, one from a city, and two from

275

a family, and I will bring you to Zion. And I will give you shepherds after my own heart, who will feed you with knowledge and understanding . . . At that time Jerusalem shall be called the throne of the LORD, and all nations shall gather to it, to the presence of the LORD in Jerusalem, and they shall no more stubbornly follow their own evil heart'' (Jeremiah 3:14-17).

A New Covenant

The same prophet goes even further and says:

''Behold, the days are coming, says the LORD, when I will make a new covenant with the house of Israel and the house of Judah, not like the covenant which I made with their fathers when I took them by the hand to bring them out of the land of Egypt, my covenant which they broke . . .'' (Jeremiah 31:31).

(Notice that this was not the Abrahamic covenant, but the Mosaic covenant, the law through Moses.) Then the prophet goes on to say:

''This is the covenant which I will make with the house of Israel after those days, says the LORD: I will put my law within them, and I will write it upon their hearts; and I will be their God, and they shall be my people . . . they shall all know me, from the least of them to the greatest, says the LORD; for I will forgive their iniquity, and I will remember their sin no more'' (Jeremiah 31:33-34; quoted in Hebrews 8:8-12).

The manner in which this transformation will be brought about is hinted at by Jeremiah:

''Behold, the days are coming, says the LORD, when I will fulfil the promise I made to the house of Israel and the house of Judah. In those days and at that time I will cause a righteous Branch to spring forth for David; and he shall execute justice and righteousness in the land. In those days Judah will be saved and Jerusalem will dwell securely . . .'' (Jeremiah 33:14-16).

A New Spirit

The divine intervention in the affairs of Israel as a nation will be parallelled by divine intervention in their personal attitudes:

"And when they come there . . . I will give them one heart, and put a new spirit within them; I will take the stony heart out of their flesh and give them a heart of flesh, that they may walk in my statutes and keep my ordinances and obey them" (Ezekiel 11:18-20).

And again,

"The house of Israel shall know that I am the LORD their God, from that day forward . . . I will not hide my face any more from them, when I pour out my Spirit upon the house of Israel, says the Lord GOD" (Ezekiel 39:22,29).

After a description of God pouring out His indignation on the nations, the prophet Zephaniah says:

"Sing aloud, O daughter of Zion, shout, O Israel! Rejoice and exult with all your heart, O daughter of Jerusalem! The LORD has taken away the judgments against you, he has cast out your enemies. The King of Israel, the LORD, is in your midst; you shall fear evil no more . . . yea, I will make you renowned and praised among all the peoples of the earth, when I restore your fortunes before your eyes, says the LORD" (Zephaniah 3:14,15,20).

Perhaps the most remarkable prophecy to give details of this change of heart on the part of the people of Israel is this one:

"On that day I will seek to destroy all the nations that come against Jerusalem. And I will pour out on the house of David and the inhabitants of Jerusalem a spirit of compassion and supplication, so that, when they look on him whom they have pierced, they shall mourn for him, as one mourns for an only child, and weep bitterly over him, as one weeps over a first-born. On that day the mourning in Jerusalem will be as great as the mourning for Hadad-rimmon in the plain of Megiddo" (Zechariah 12:9-11).

"On that day there shall be a fountain opened for the house of David and the inhabitants of Jerusalem to cleanse them from sin and uncleanness" (Zechariah 13:1).

Israel's Redeemer

"O Jerusalem, Jerusalem, killing the prophets and stoning those who are sent to you! How often would I have gathered your children together as a hen gathers her brood under her

277

wings, and you would not! Behold, your house is forsaken and desolate. For I tell you, you will not see me again, until you say, 'Blessed is he who comes in the name of the Lord' " (Matthew 23:37-39).

These words were spoken by Israel's Messiah, just before he too was killed. He clearly knew that at his second coming in power and glory at the time of Israel's greatest need, he would be received at last as their Redeemer and their King.

The Apostle Paul asks the question, "Has God rejected his people?" and immediately answers:

"By no means! . . . God has not rejected his people whom he foreknew . . . at the present time there is a remnant, chosen by grace" (Romans 11:1-5).

In what way is the 'remnant' different from mainstream Jewry?

"To this day whenever Moses is read a veil lies over their minds; but when a man turns to the Lord the veil is removed" (2 Corinthians 3:15-16).

Not only will the veil be removed from the minds of Israel, but "he will destroy on this mountain the covering that is cast over all peoples, the veil that is spread over all nations" (Isaiah 25:7). Thus, Israel's turning to God will be accompanied by a worldwide acknowledgement of Israel's God, as the word of the LORD goes forth from Jerusalem.

JERUSALEM—JOY OF ALL THE EARTH
Its Rise—its Fall—and Rising again

"Seek the place which the LORD your God will choose"
(Deuteronomy 12:5)

"Jerusalem, the city which the LORD had chosen"
(1 Kings 14:21)

"In Jerusalem shall my name be for ever"
(2 Chronicles 33:4)

"They polluted the house of the LORD which he had hallowed in Jerusalem" (2 Chronicles 36:14)

"I will cast off this city which I have chosen, Jerusalem, and the house of which I said, My name shall be there"
(2 Kings 23:27)

"Is this the city that was called . . . the joy of all the earth?"
(Lamentations 2:15)

"If I forget you, O Jerusalem, let my right hand wither!"
(Psalm 137:5)

"Jerusalem shall still be inhabited in its place, in Jerusalem"
(Zechariah 12:6)

*"For Zion's sake I will not keep silent, and for Jerusalem's sake
I will not rest . . . You shall be a crown of beauty in the hand
of the LORD, and a royal diadem in the hand of your God"*
(Isaiah 62:1,3)

*"Break forth into singing, you waste places of Jerusalem; for
the LORD . . . has redeemed Jerusalem"*   (Isaiah 52:9)

*"I create Jerusalem a rejoicing, and her people a joy. I will
rejoice in Jerusalem, and be glad in my people"*
(Isaiah 65:18,19)

*"This city shall be to me a name of joy, a praise and a glory
before all the nations of the earth . . . In the streets of
Jerusalem that are desolate . . . there shall be heard again . . .
the voices of those who sing . . . for the LORD is good"*
(Jeremiah 33:9-11)

"Mount Zion . . . the city of the great king"   (Psalm 48:2)

"I have set my king on Zion, my holy hill"   (Psalm 2:6)

*"The ransomed of the LORD shall return, and come to Zion with
singing; everlasting joy shall be upon their heads; they shall
obtain joy and gladness, and sorrow and sighing shall flee
away"*   (Isaiah 35:10)

*"Living waters shall flow out from Jerusalem . . . And the
LORD will become king over all the earth"*
(Zechariah 14:8,9)

*"And the name of the city henceforth shall be, The LORD is
there' "*   (Ezekiel 48:35)

The City of Peace

The physical upheaval of the land and the spiritual upheaval of
the people will combine to prepare the way for a completely
new order under the guidance and direction of Messiah. With
Jerusalem as the centre, a magnificent third Temple erected,
"the city of the great King" (Psalm 48:2; Matthew 5:35;

ISRAEL

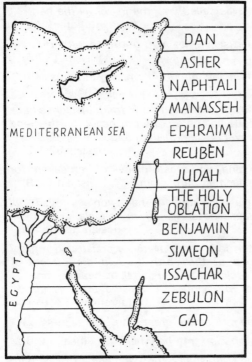

Suggested Future Allocation of the Land based on Ezekiel 48

Psalm 2:6) will dispense judgement and righteousness to all nations. Jerusalem will at last become "the city of peace" for the whole wide world:

> *"Behold, a king will reign in righteousness, and princes will rule in justice . . . And the effect of righteousness will be peace, and the result of righteousness, quietness and trust for ever. My people will abide in a peaceful habitation, in secure dwellings, and in quiet resting places"* (Isaiah 32:1,17,18).

Thus will the kingdom of God on earth be inaugurated, and the many prophetic pictures in the Holy Scriptures become reality at last. Man's real needs will be met as never before: a purpose in life, security, ample food and shelter for all, judgement and justice between man and man, and between nation and nation. Jesus the Christ will be the King of kings and Lord of lords.

His faithful disciples were promised a place of honour:

"Truly, I say to you, in the new world, when the Son of man shall sit on his glorious throne, you who have followed me will also sit on twelve thrones, judging the twelve tribes of Israel" (Matthew 19:28).

Faithful Jews and Gentiles who have become adopted into Abraham's family through baptism into Jesus Christ will inherit the Abrahamic covenant, will receive "power over the nations" (Revelation 2:26) "and they shall reign on earth" (Revelation 5:10). Thus through Abraham's unique offspring, Jesus Christ, and the adopted offspring through faith, all nations will ultimately be blessed in the kingdom of our Lord. This is the objective for which Jesus taught us to pray, "Thy kingdom come, thy will be done in earth, as in heaven."

13

THE ABRAHAMIC COVENANT FULFILLED

THE promise of a land was the first and basic promise to Abraham, the foundation of the covenant. The Psalmist was so conscious of this aspect of God's purpose that he spoke of *eretz* (the land) well over 100 times in his Psalms (*eretz* is sometimes translated 'earth' but refers to God's chosen land):

"Those who wait for the LORD shall possess the land ... The meek shall possess the land ... Those blessed by the LORD shall possess the land" (Psalm 37:9,11,22).

The early Christian understanding of this divine promise was made plain by the martyr Stephen:

"God removed him (Abraham) from there into this land in which you (Jews) are now living; yet he gave him no inheritance in it, not even a foot's length, but promised to give it to him in possession and to his posterity after him, though he had no child" (Acts 7:4,5).

The apostle Paul, when writing of the faith of Abraham said:

"The promise to Abraham and his descendants, that they should inherit the world, did not come through the law but through the righteousness of faith" (Romans 4:13).

Previously Jesus had quoted from Psalm 37 when he said: "Blessed are the meek, for they shall inherit the earth." And the song of the elders in Revelation 5:10 confirms the inheritance of God's saints: "Thou hast made them a kingdom and priests to our God, and they shall reign on earth."

The Promise of a City

Within the scope of the promise of land, God gradually revealed the promise of a city. Abraham visited the city and was on good terms with its king. He knew full well that the city was within the confines of the promised land. But Israel in Egyptian

282

THE ABRAHAMIC COVENANT FULFILLED

bondage knew nothing of it. Moses instructed Israel to "seek the place which the LORD your God will choose" (Deuteronomy 12:5). The record of the kings of Israel confirms that it is:

"Jerusalem, the city which the LORD had chosen out of all the tribes of Israel, to put his name there" (1 Kings 14:21).

The Psalmist foretold that "I have set my king on Zion, my holy hill" (Psalm 2:6) and spoke of "Mount Zion . . . the city of the great King" (Psalm 48:2).

The location of the place which the LORD had chosen is referred to many times by the prophets—for example Psalm 87:3; 122:6; Isaiah 2:3; 24:23; 31:5; 33:5; 52:1,2; Zechariah 14:16 and others. In later times, Jesus, when he had foretold the imminent destruction of the city (which came to pass in A.D. 70), went on to say:

"Jerusalem will be trodden down by the Gentiles, until . . . " (Luke 21:14).

Yet he could see beyond the devastation and call "Jerusalem, the city of the great King", echoing the words of the Psalmist (Psalm 48:2). That "great King" was not king Herod, nor the Roman Emperor!

It was to be Jesus himself when he returns in power and glory to reign and rule from the very city that was about to witness his crucifixion. This city, which has attracted millions of pilgrims all down the ages to its 'holy shrines', will be replaced by a new city built on a divinely prepared site, to a magnificent plan that is revealed by the prophet Ezekiel (chapters 40-48). Its central feature will be a massive temple prepared for all the nations to come and worship the LORD, the God of Israel. Thus the word of the LORD will go forth from Jerusalem for the divine guidance and instruction of all nations on earth (Isaiah 2:3; Zechariah 14:16).

The Personal Promise

But in addition to receiving the promise of a land, Abraham was personally promised that he would be blessed, and be a blessing to others, and that his name would be great in the earth. For all this to become a fact, Abraham would have to be alive to receive his blessing. Jesus plainly stated to the Jewish leaders:

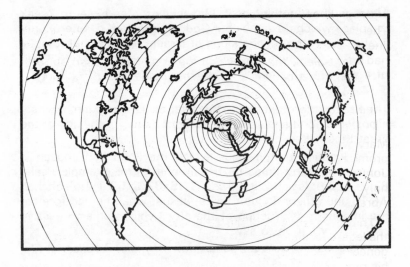

"The Word of the LORD will go forth from Jerusalem"

"Ye shall see Abraham, Isaac and Jacob and all the prophets in the kingdom of God and you yourselves thrust out" (Luke 13:28). For this to be possible, the resurrection of those concerned would have to take place. It may not be realised that Abraham, so long ago, had faith in the resurrection from the dead—otherwise he could not have believed the far-reaching promises God made to him. The restoration to him of Isaac after he had bound him upon the altar and virtually given him in sacrifice to God, was to Abraham a token of resurrection:

"He considered that God was able to raise men even from the dead; hence, figuratively speaking, he did receive him back (from the dead)" (Hebrews 11:19).

The time is now approaching when Abraham's offspring, the one who will implement all the promises, will return to the land to raise the dead and give life to those who share Abraham's faith; for he is also "the Resurrection and the Life". With this event, the personal promise to Abraham will be fulfilled in all aspects.

The Promise of an Offspring

The covenant spoke of a particular offspring of the Abrahamic line who would be a blessing to all nations, including Israel. This had an incipient fulfilment about 2000 years later with the birth of a son to Mary. And Mary said:

"He has helped his servant Israel, in remembrance of his mercy, as he spoke to our fathers, to Abraham and to his posterity for ever" (Luke 1:54,55).

Mary was in no doubt that the child she would bear was the promised offspring of Abraham. Nor was Zechariah (father of John the Baptist) in any doubt that God had remembered "his holy covenant, the oath which he swore to our father Abraham" (Luke 1:72,73).

The very first verse of the New Testament identifies Jesus as the legal descendant of Abraham, through king David; while the genealogy of Luke traces the human descent of Jesus through his mother to Abraham, and Adam. The apostle Paul confirms this conclusion:

"Now the promises were made to Abraham and to his offspring. It does not say, 'And to offsprings', referring to many; but, referring to one, 'And to your offspring', which is Christ" (Galatians 3:16).

This unique offspring of Abraham will be the executor of all aspects of the covenant, from raising Abraham from the dead, leading his people into possession of the land, as Joshua had done so long before (Jesus is the Greek form of the Hebrew name 'Joshua', or more correctly 'Yeshua'). He will gather to Abraham a family of Jews and Gentiles, men and women who have, like Abraham, had implicit trust in God's promises (Galatians 3:27-29). His authority will be at first over his own nation, Israel. Ultimately, all nations upon earth will recognise his authority, so that wars will cease and all mankind worldwide will know the Lord.

The Promise of a Family

When as yet Abraham had no prospect of a family, God told him to look at the stars and number them: "So shall your descendants be" (Genesis 15:5). Then, after Ishmael and

Isaac had been born, Abraham was promised two kinds of descendants:

"I will multiply your descendants as the stars of heaven and as the sand which is on the seashore" (Genesis 22:17).

The promise of a family as the stars of heaven was repeated to Isaac (Genesis 26:4). This same metaphor was used repeatedly of Israel's great numbers: three times by God to Abraham, and four times by Moses. The inference is that Abraham's family would be not only vast but 'heavenly', and this was undoubtedly the divine purpose for the nation of Israel. They were to be a kingdom of priests to lead other nations to a recognition of the Almighty, but they failed miserably in their heavenly calling.

The metaphor of 'sand', used only once to Abraham, would appear to refer to the multitudes of Ishmael's descendants. In later records this metaphor is used repeatedly of Israel's enemies. The inference is that the 'sand' family would be 'earthly' men, while the 'star' family would be 'heavenly'. The theme is taken up by Daniel in his description of the resurrection:

"Those who are wise shall shine like the brightness of the firmament: and those who turn many to righteousness, like the stars for ever and ever" (Daniel 12:3).

Sand Metaphor: Joshua 11:4; Judges 7:12; 1 Samuel 13:5; 2 Samuel 17:11

Star Metaphor: Exodus 32:13; Deuteronomy 1:10; 10:22; 28:62

The Extended Family

All families of the earth were included in the covenant to Abraham. While Israel were indeed the 'chosen people' through whom the covenant would be fulfilled, they were not to be exclusively its beneficiaries. Just as individual men and women of the Gentiles were adopted into Israel in early days, so the prophet Hosea saw others who would accept the God of Israel:

"I will say to Not-my-people, 'You are my people', and he shall say 'Thou art my God' " (Hosea 2:23).

The prophet Joel says that "all who call upon the name of the LORD shall be delivered" (Joel 2:32).

The apostle Paul takes these Scriptures up and explains:

"The scripture says, 'No one who believes in him will be put to shame.' For there is no distinction between Jew and Greek; the same Lord is Lord of all and bestows his riches upon all who call upon him. For, 'every one who calls upon the name of the Lord will be saved'" (Romans 10:11-13).

He spells out the benefits of the extended family of Abraham very clearly:

"In Christ Jesus you are all sons of God, through faith . . . and if you are Christ's, then you are Abraham's offspring, heirs according to promise" (Galatians 3:26-29).

Thus Abraham's unique offspring, Jesus Christ, has extended the scope of Abraham's family to all who, like Abraham, put their faith in Abraham's God.

The International Promise

Beyond the promise of the family and the extended family, is the promised blessing of all nations. As the nations of the world prepare for the world's greatest conflict, the need for this blessing becomes more urgent. How will it come about? Again, Abraham's unique offspring, Jesus the Christ, will be the means by which eventually peace will be established, and war will be no more. The prophets of Israel painted word-pictures of the time of blessing that he alone will bring. King David had been promised a son by God who assured him, "I will establish the throne of his kingdom for ever" (2 Samuel 7:13).

This son of David (and therefore of Abraham) reigning for ever over Israel, will have his authority extended to all nations:

"I have set my king on Zion, my holy hill . . . Ask of me (God), and I will make the nations your heritage, and the ends of the earth your possession" (Psalm 2:6,8).

"Give the king thy justice, O God, and thy righteousness to the royal son! . . . May he have dominion from sea to sea, and from the River to the ends of the earth! . . . May all kings fall down before him, all nations serve him! . . . May men bless themselves by him, all nations call him blessed" (Psalm 72:1,8,11,17).

The New Testament confirms the prophecies of the Hebrew prophets: for example, the apostle Paul explained to the Athenians:

"Now he (God) commands all men everywhere to repent, because he has fixed a day on which he will judge the world in righteousness by a man whom he has appointed, and of this he has given assurance to all men by raising him from the dead" (Acts 17:30-31).

In the last message of Jesus to his servant John we read:

" . . . there were loud voices in heaven, saying, 'The kingdom of the world has become the kingdom of our Lord and of his Christ, and he shall reign for ever and ever' " (Revelation 11:15).

The Everlasting Covenant

The everlasting promise to Abraham lifted the covenant out of the context of an immediate benefit. This in itself was a test of faith. Would God fulfil His promises even though there seemed to be no likelihood, humanly speaking, of any possibility of a fulfilment? At first every element of the covenant was out of sight.

The word 'ever' in English is usually taken to mean 'for all future time'. The Hebrew word *olam* and the Greek word *aion*, which are usually translated 'ever', literally mean 'age lasting' or 'a long time'. The actual duration of the Abrahamic blessings is not revealed until the last book of the Bible, where it is clearly shown to be the 1000 year reign of Jesus the Christ, (Abraham's Messiah) on earth, with power over all nations:

"Blessed and holy is he who shares in the first resurrection! Over such the second death has no power, but they shall be priests of God and of Christ, and they shall reign with him a thousand years" (Revelation 20:6).

After the millennium, Paul explains in simple terms:

"Then comes the end (of the millennium), *when he (Jesus) delivers the kingdom to God the Father after destroying every rule and every authority and power. For he (Jesus) must reign until he has put all his enemies under his feet . . . When all things are subjected to him, then the*

288

Son himself will also be subjected to him who put all things under him, that God may be everything to every one" (1 Corinthians 15:24,28).

Thus Abraham's unique offspring has a great mission to accomplish, which will take an 'age' to complete, the ultimate objective being that all men everywhere will have complete faith in the Creator, whereby he becomes the father of a great multitude who have modelled their relationship to their Creator on faithful Abraham, but have been adopted into that relationship through Jesus, the Christ.

ISRAEL'S SEVEN UNIQUE FEATURES

1. *The Unique Land*	Deuteronomy 8:7; Ezekiel 20:6— *"The most glorious of all lands"*
2. *The Unique City*	Psalm 48.2; Matthew 5:35— *"The city of the great King"*
3. *The Unique People*	Amos 3:2; Malachi 3:12—*"Then all nations will call you blessed"*
4. *The Unique Book*	Deuteronomy 31:24; 2 Timothy 3:16—*"All scripture is inspired by God"*
5. *The Unique Promises*	Genesis 22:16; Romans 8:13— *"By myself I have sworn, says the* LORD *. . . I will indeed bless you"*
6. *The Unique Messiah*	Isaiah 9:6-7; Zechariah 9:9-10; Matthew 16:16—*"You are the Christ* (Messiah), *the Son of the living God"*
7. *The Unique Hope*	Acts 28:20; Romans 15:4; 1 Peter 1:3—*"A living hope through the resurrection of Jesus Christ from the dead"*

14

CONCLUSION

THE purpose of the Creator of life on this planet was, and is, to call to Himself a people who are responsive to His love. The Creator has proved Himself to be a generous, compassionate and merciful Father, and it is His wish to have a family who share His character. Since He is not an automaton (as some philosophers see him), He does not seek a family of robots. Hence He is selecting from the vast mix of peoples upon earth "a people for his name", a people who have developed the sort of character that Jesus displayed. For Jesus "is the image of the invisible God, the first-born of all creation (the new creation) . . . He is the beginning, the first-born from the dead" (Colossians 1:15,18).

So, to try to draw the threads together, Abraham, Jacob (Israel), the people of Israel, the land of Israel, the Hope of Israel, the Anointed (Messiah) of Israel, and the remnant out of all nations who are drawn to worship and believe the God of Israel are all looking forward in faith to the final fulfilment of the covenant with Abraham at the return of Jesus the Christ in power and glory:

"He who conquers, I will grant him to sit with me on my throne, as I myself conquered and sat down with my Father on his throne" (Revelation 3:21).

The angel Gabriel said to Mary:

"The Lord God will give to him the throne of his father David, and he will reign over the house of Jacob for ever; and of his kingdom there will be no end" (Luke 1:32-33).

"Thy kingdom come, thy will be done, on earth, as it is in heaven" is the prayer of all who look in faith to the consummation of God's purpose with this planet and its people.

BIBLIOGRAPHY

Albright, W. F., *Archaeology of Palestine* (Penguin, London).

Ausubel, Nathan, *Pictorial History of the Jewish People* (Crown, New York).

Baly, Denis, *Geography of the Bible* (Lutterworth).

Bein, Alex, *Theodor Herzl* (Jewish Publication Society, Philadelphia).

Ben Gurion, D., *Chaim Weizmann* (Weidenfeld & Nicolson, London).

Ben Gurion, D., *Israel, a Personal History* (Funk & Wagnalls, New York).

Ben Gurion, D., *Rebirth and Destiny of Israel* (Philosophical, New York).

Ben Gurion, D., *Recollections* (Macdonald, London).

Bentwich, Norman, *Israel Resurgent* (Benn, London).

Boulton, W. H., *Palestine* (Sampson Low, London).

Bruce, F. F., *Israel and the Nations* (Paternoster, Exeter).

Cohen, Michael, *Churchill and the Jews* (Frank Cass, London).

Eban, Abba, *My People* (Behrman House, New York).

Encyclopaedia Judaica (Keter, Jerusalem).

Facts about Israel (Ministry of Foreign Affairs, Jerusalem).

Gilbert, Martin, *Exile and Return* (Weidenfeld & Nicolson, London).

Gilbert, Martin, *Jerusalem Illustrated History Atlas* (Board of Deputies of British Jews, London).

Gilbert, Martin, *Jewish History Atlas* (Weidenfeld & Nicolson, London).

Jannaway, F. G., *Palestine and the Jews* (Maranatha, London).

Johnson, Paul, *A History of the Jews* (Weidenfeld & Nicolson, London).

Kollek, Teddy, *Jerusalem* (Weidenfeld & Nicolson, London).

Kops, Bernard, *Neither your Money nor your Sting* (Robson Books, London).

Lambert, Lance, *Uniqueness of Israel* (Kingsway Publications, Eastbourne).

Lossin, Yigal, *Pillar of Fire* (Israel Broadcasting Authority).

Meir, Golda, *My Life* (Weidenfeld & Nicolson, London).

Oxford Bible Atlas (O.U.P., Oxford).

Pearl, Chaim, & Brookes, Reuben, *A Guide to Jewish Knowledge* (Jewish Chronicle Publications, London).

Peters, Joan, *From Time Immemorial* (Michael Joseph, London).

291

ISRAEL

Pragai, Michael J., *Faith and Fulfilment: Christians and the Return to the Promised Land* (Vallentine, Mitchell, London)

Reader's Digest, *Atlas of the Bible* (London).

Roth, Cecil, *Short History of the Jewish People* (Macmillan, London).

Shanks, Hershel, *City of David* (Biblical Archaeology Society, Washington).

Shanks, Hershel, *Recent Archaeology in Israel* (Biblical Archaeological Society, Washington).

Sokolow, Nahum, *History of Zionism, 1600-1918* (Longmans, Green, London).

St. John, Robert, *Tongue of the Prophets* (Wilshere Books, Hollywood).

Teveth, S., *Ben Gurion, the Burning Ground* (Houghton-Mifflin, New York.

Tuchman, Barbara W., *Bible and Sword: How the British came to Palestine* (Macmillan, London).

Vilnay, Zev, *Guide to Israel* (Ahiever, Jerusalem).

Warmbrand & Roth, *Jewish People: 4,000 Years of Survival* (Thames & Hudson, London).

Chaim Weizmann, *Trial and Error* (Schocken, New York).

Whiston, William (translator), *The Complete Works of Flavius Josephus*.

Zion, My Chiefest Joy (Christadelphian Scripture Study Service, Torrens Park, Australia).

GLOSSARY

For lists of special terms relating to the Jewish Religious Literature, the Calendar and Festivals, see pages 48-50, 62-81; defence groups, 122; political parties, 150-151; religious groups, 210-211

Ab (or Av) — 5th month of Bible year (Numbers 33:38) (Jul./Aug.).
Abba — 'father', 'daddy'.
Abib (or Aviv) — 'spring', old name for Nisan (Exodus 12:2).
Adar — 12th month of Bible year (Ezra 6:15) (Feb./Mar.).
Agora — ancient coin, 1/100th of lira (Greek for 'marketplace').
Ahava — 'love' of any kind, specially love of God; a liturgical poem.
Al Fatah — (Arabic) 'victory', terrorist group of P.L.O.
Aliyah (pl. Aliyot) — the 'going up', immigration to the Holy Land; also going up to read the scroll of the Law in synagogue.
Almemar — desk from which scroll is read in synagogue (Aramaic).
Amal — 'labour', Histadrut educational committee and schools.
Amal — the Shi'ite Moslem militia in Lebanon.
Am ha-Aretz — 'people of the land', common or ignorant people.
Amoraim — 'speakers', Jewish sages who wrote the Gemara.
Anglit — the English language.
Aramaic — a Semitic language, Syriac.
Arava (pl. Aravot) — 'willow', one of four species used at Sukkot.
Arba'ah Minim — 'The four species' (Leviticus 23:40) as used at Sukkot: myrtle, willow, palm and etrog.
Aron Hakodesh — Ark in synagogue containing scrolls.
Aseret Hadibrot — 'The ten words', the ten Commandments.
Ashkenazi (pl. Ashkenazim) — 'German', term used for Jews of German and E. European dispersion and culture (Genesis 10:3).

Ba'al — 'Master', 'possessor', 'lord' or 'husband'.
Ba'al Shem — 'Master of the Holy Name', learned hassidic scholar.
Ba'al Teqia — the man who blows the Shofar (ram's horn).
Ba'alei Teshuva — 'repented', secular Jews who become religious.
Bar — 'son' (Aramaic).
Bar Mitzvah — 'son of commandment', boys coming of age at 13.
Bat (or Bath) — 'daughter'.
Batim — 'phylactery', little leather box containing scrolls.
Bat Mitzvah — Jewish girl's coming of age at 12 years and one day.
Be'er — 'well' or 'cistern', usually man-made.
Ben (pl. B'nei or Banim) — 'son'.
Bereshith (or B'rei-sheet) — 'in the beginning', the Book of Genesis.
Beth (or Beit) — 'house' (Beth-lehem = house of bread).
Bet ha-Knesset — 'house of assembly', literal meaning of synagogue.
Bet Tefilah — 'House of Prayer', the Bible name for the Temple.
Bikkurim — 'the first fruits' (Deuteronomy 8:8).

ISRAEL

Bimah (or Bemah)—platform in synagogue
B'nai B'rith—'Sons of the covenant', a Jewish world-wide benevolent order, founded 1843.
Bricha—'escape', European underground refugee organisation
B'rit—'covenant', God's covenant with Israel.
B'rit Mila—covenant of circumcision (Leviticus 12:3).
Bul—old name for month Cheshwan (Marcheswan) (1 Kings 6:38).

Hebrew words never begin with a soft 'ch' (as in cheese), nor with a hard 'Kh' (as in khaki). Anglicised Hebrew words that are often spelt with 'ch' as in 'chalukkah' will be found in this Glossary under 'H' and should be pronounced as an H with a preceding throaty suggestion of a 'c'. A few Yiddish words are exceptions, such as: 'Cholent'— a traditional Sabbath food from E. Europe, and 'Chotchkes'—knick-knacks.

Circassians—a Moslem people exiled from the Caucasus.
Cohen—(see Kohen).
Conservative Judaism—modern religious movement within Jewry.
Conversos—Spanish Jews converted to Christianity.

Darshan—'expounder' of the Law, such as was Ezra.
Dati (pl. datiyim)—pious man.
Dayyan—a rabbinical court judge.
Dhimmis—'the protected people', Arab name for Jews and Christians.
Diaspora—'dispersed' (Greek), the scattered Jews (1 Peter 1:1).
Din—'justice', religious law.
Druze—Arabic speaking sect of Moslem origin in Syria, Lebanon, Galilee. They keep their religious beliefs secret.
Dunam—a unit of land area in Israel (1,000 sq. metres or ¼ acre).

Ein (or En)—a spring of water, usually perennial.
Elul—'gleaning', 6th month of Bible year (Aug./Sept.).
Emek—the valley of Esdraelon.
Emeth—'truth', 'steadfastness'.
Eretz Israel—'The Land of Israel'.
Ethanim—old name for Tishri, the 7th Bible month (Sept./Oct.).
Etrog—citrus fruit used at Sukkot.

Fatah (or Fath)—see Al Fatah.
Fedayeen—'self-sacrificers', Arab terrorists.
Felafel—traditional food made of deep fried chickpeas.
Frum—(Yiddish) 'pious', 'religious'.

Galut — 'exile', Jews living in the diaspora among the nations.

Gaon (or Geon, pl. Geonim) — 'excellencies', Babylonian Jewish scholars of the 6th to 12th centuries, hence the Gaonic period.

Gemara (or Gemora) — commentary on the Midrash by the Amoraim.

Gematria — interpreting Hebrew words by their numerical value.

Genizah — 'hiding', depository for old scrolls in a synagogue, the most famous being that at Alexandria, Egypt.

Gerim — 'proselytes', Gentiles converted to Judaism.

Gesetzt — 'set', 'put'; food put in the oven on Friday to avoid cooking on the Sabbath (German/Yiddish).

Ghetto — part of town to which Jews are restricted. The first was in Venice, hence Italian origin.

Glatt Kosher — ultra-orthodox kosher.

Goel — 'kinsman', 'redeemer'. Example: Boaz for Ruth.

Gola — the diaspora, Jews living scattered among the nations.

Goy (pl. Goyim) — 'people', used to describe Gentiles.

Gush Emunim — a religious movement encouraging the settlement of the acquired territories by Jews.

Hadas (pl. Hadassim) — 'myrtle', one of the four species used at Sukkot.

Hadassah — Esther, Women Zionists of America, and a Hospital.

Haftarah (or Haphtarah) — 'conclusion', the sabbath reading from the prophets as read by Jesus (Luke 4:16-20).

Haganah — 'defence', illegal Jewish defence force 1920-48, resistance arm of the Jewish Agency for Palestine.

Haggadah — 'narration', the whole of the non-legal matter in rabbinical literature, ritual reading for Seder.

Hagiographa — see Kethuvim.

Hahag — 'festival', one of the appointed holy days.

Hakhal — Jewish name for the Temple at Jerusalem.

Halakha — 'the way', traditional oral law of the Midrash.

Hallel — 'praise', prayer of thanksgiving, specially Psalms 113-118.

Hamantashen — Purim pastry in shape of Haman's ears.

Har — 'a mountain'.

Hashem — 'The Name', orthodox pronunciation of YHWH.

Hasmonean — Maccabean priestly dynasty, 2nd and 1st century B.C.

Ha-Tikvah — 'The Hope', National Anthem.

Histadrut — General Federation of Workers.

Holocaust — the mass murder of Jews in Europe, 1933-45.

Hora — a traditional Jewish dance.

Hosha'na (or Hosanna) — 'Save, I pray'.

Hummus — a traditional food paste made of chickpeas and spices.

ISRAEL

'H' indicates a pronunciation similar to the Scottish 'ch' in 'loch' which is often rendered 'Ch' in Anglicised Hebrew. Pronounced as an 'H' with a suggestion of a hard 'c' before it.

Halitza—law concerning brother's widow (Deuteronomy 25:5).
Halukkah—'distribution', a fund that maintained Jews in the four holy cities of Jerusalem, Hebron, Tiberias and Safed.
Halutzim—'pioneers', hard workers, the early colonists.
Halva—sweetmeat of ground sesame seeds and honey.
Hametz—leaven (sour dough) or yeast.
Hamsin (or Hamseen)—a hot, dusty, desert wind.
Hanukkah (or Channukah)—'dedication', the eight day Festival of Lights celebrating the re-dedication of the Temple in 164 B.C.
Haredim—'trembling ones', ultra-orthodox religious Jews.
Harosett (or Charoseth)—a Passover confection made of nuts, fruit and wine, symbol of clay used to make bricks in Egypt.
Hassidim (or Chassidim)—'the pious ones', a sect of Polish Jews.
Hatan (or Chatan)—the bridegroom (see also Kallah).
Hazzan (or Chazan)—a cantor or synagogue official.
Herem—excommunication from the synagogue.
Herut—'liberty', right-wing nationalist political party.
Heshwan (or Marchesvan)—8th month of Bible year (Oct./Nov.).
Hodesh (or Chodesh)—'month', beginning of each month.
Humash (or Chumash)—the Pentateuch, the five books of Moses.
Huppa (or Chuppah)—canopy over wedding ceremony
Hutzpa—insolence, impudence, sauciness.

I.D.F.—Israel Defence Forces, formed 1948.
Ima—'mother', 'mummy'
Irgun Tzeva'i Le'ummi—military arm of right-wing extremists, 1931-48.
I.S.—Israel shekel, modern coin.
Israel (or Yisrael)—'Ruling with God', or 'He who fights with God'.
Ivrit—the Hebrew language.
Iyyar (or Iyar)—2nd month; Biblical name Ziw or Zif (Apr./May).

J: *The letter J is not used in Hebrew: see entries under Y*
Jeshimon—'desolation', the Judean wilderness.
Jew—developed from 'Judean', member of the Hebrew race.
Jihad—(Arabic) Moslem holy war against 'infidels'.
J.N.F.—Jewish National Fund (Keren Kayemeth le Israel).
Judea—area of the Holy Land between Samaria and the Negev.

Kabbalah—'reception', mystic interpretation of Holy Scripture by some rabbis in the Middle Ages.
Kaddish—'sanctification', prayer to sanctify the Almighty.
Kadesh (or Kodesh)—'holiness'; also a place name.

296

Kafr—(Arabic) 'village' (also Kefr, Kfar).

Kahal—a Jewish congregation.

Kalla—the Bride (see also Hatan).

Kapote—long black coat worn by E. European Jews.

Karaites—'champions of Scripture'. Jewish sect who reject the oral laws of the rabbis and the Talmud (8th century to present).

Karpas—parsley dipped in salt water as used for Passover service.

Kasher (or Kosher)—'permitted', food, vessels and objects that are suitable for use according to Jewish law.

Kashrut—'fitness', the Kasher food laws.

Keren Kayemet—Jewish National Fund to buy land for settlement.

Keriah—rending, tearing of garments as sign of deep grief.

Kethuvim (or Ketubim)—'the writings', the third portion of the Hebrew Holy Scriptures, Psalms to Chronicles.

Kevutsa—a small collective farm settlement.

Kfir—'young lion', name of famous Israeli built war-plane.

Khazars—Turkish tribe in Crimea who adopted Judaism in 8th-10th century.

Kibbutz (pl. Kibbutzim)—communal village for agriculture or industry; about 250 now established.

Kibbutznik—a member of a kibbutz.

Kiddush—'sanctification', prayer said at sabbaths and festivals.

Kinnereth—'the harp', the Sea of Galilee.

Kippa (pl. Kippot)—skullcap worn by Jews to distinguish from the shaven heads of sun worshippers.

Kislev (or Chislev)—9th month of Bible year (Nov./Dec.).

Kitsch Kittel—a long white garment for special occasions.

Klal Yisrael—the world-wide community of the people of Israel.

Knesset—'assembly', the Israel parliament.

Knesset Hagdola—the assembly founded by Ezra which arranged the canon of the Hebrew Holy Scriptures.

Kohen (or Cohen)—'to be right', descendants of the priestly families (other surnames in use—Kagan, Kane, Kaplan, Katz, Rappaport etc.).

Kokh (or Kukh)—burial niches in rock tombs to receive urns.

Kosher—see Kasher.

Kotel (or Kotel Ma'aravi)—Western Wall (wrongly called 'Wailing Wall'), nearest point to Temple site.

Kuppa—the poor box for contributions for general relief. Term used in similar way to current use of 'charity'.

Ladino—dialect of Spanish Jews, still spoken in Turkey, Greece and parts of Yugoslavia.

Lag be-Omer—the 33rd day of the counting of the Omer.

Lashon ha-Kodesh—'The Holy Tongue', the Hebrew language.

Latkes—potato pancakes, traditionally eaten at Hanukkah.

Lavi—'bold lion', name of an Israeli war-plane.
Lehayim—'here's to life', traditional Jewish toast to a friend.
Lehem—bread.
Levirate marriage—marriage of childless widow to husband's brother (Deuteronomy 25:5).
Likud—major right-wing conservative political alliance.
Lulav—branch of palm (or by extension all the four species) used at Sukkot (Leviticus 23:40).
LXX—Abbreviation for the Septuagint Greek version of the Hebrew Holy Scriptures, translated during 2nd century B.C.

Ma'apilim—illegal immigrants during period of British Mandate.
Maccabees—followers and successors of Judas Maccabeus.
Magen David—Shield of David emblem, only since 17th century.
Maimonides—Famous Jewish philosopher, physician and sage in 12th century, real name Rabbi Moshe ben Maimon.
Makom—'place', a term sometimes used for 'God'.
Malot—'circumcision' performed by a Mohel.
Mamzer—an illegitimate child (Deuteronomy 23:2).
Mapai—Party of Workers in the land of Israel.
Mapam—The United Workers Party (Marxist and Zionist).
Marchesvan (or Cheswan)—8th month of Bible year. Bible name Bul' (1 Kings 6:38) (Oct./Nov.).
Maror—'bitter', horseradish used as 'bitter herb' at Passover; the Talmud suggests lettuce as a bitter herb.
Marrano—'swine', Spanish name for Jews forcibly converted during Spanish Inquisition, but secretly practising Judaism.
Mashiah—'anointed', Messiah.
Masora—'tradition', notes on Scriptures compiled by the Masoretes of Tiberias, 5th-8th centuries.
Masoretic Text—the Hebrew Holy Scriptures as compiled and edited by the Masoretes, the basis of modern translations.
Matza (or Matzo)—'unleavened' Passover bread.
Matza Shemura—'guarded', special Matzo for ultra-orthodox.
Me'a Shearim—'the hundred gates', early refugee settlement in Jerusalem, now the ultra-orthodox area of the city.
Medina Yisrael—The State of Israel.
Megilla—'scroll'; Megillot—'small scrolls', such as Ruth and Esther.
Menahem—'comforter', old name for month of Ab (Jul./Aug.).
Menora (or Menorah)—'place of light' name of seven-branched lampstand (Exodus 33:17) now national symbol of Israel.
Mezuzah—'doorpost', the small scroll quoting Deuteronomy 6:4 placed on the upper right hand of doorposts.
Midrash—commentary of the Torah, detailing matters not explicit in the Talmud: Halachic (legal) and Haggadic (story).

Mikveh (pl. Mikvot)—ritual bath for purification by immersion.
Millo—David's acropolis built between Ophel and Temple Mount.
Minyan—'number', quorum of ten adult males required for public worship.
Mishkan—'dwelling', God's dwelling, the Tabernacle, the Temple.
Mishnah—'repetition', traditional oral law codified A.D. 200.
Mishneh Torah—'repetition of the law' codified by Maimonides.
Mitzpa—'lookout', a pioneer border settlement.
Mitzvah (or Mitzwa)—precept or good deed.
Mizrah—'rising of the sun', 'East', symbol of the Holy Land.
Moed—'appointed assemblies', divinely ordained holy days.
Mohel—'circumciser', an office for any competent person.
Moshav (pl. Moshavim)—farm settlement on J.N.F. land whose farmers cooperate in buying and selling, otherwise private.
Moshava (pl. Moshavot)—farm settlements of all private property.
Mossad—Israel's secret service world-wide, first formed to aid illegal entry of refugees.
Mufti—official expounder of Moslem law, a Moslem leader.
Mumar—'changed', an apostate from Judaism (also Meshummad).

Nabi (or Navi) (pl. Nevi'im)—'prophet'.
Nagid—'leader', 'ruler' (Governor of the Bank of Israel).
Nahal—wadi, a seasonal river bed.
Nassi—'prince'. Title of President of the Sanhedrin.
Negev (or Negeb)—'South', the southern area of Israel.
Neve—'oasis'.
Nevi'im—the books of the prophets in Holy Scripture.
N.I.S.—New Israel Shekel since 1985.
Nisan—1st month of Bible year, formerly known as Abib (Esther 3:7) (Mar./Apr.).

Ohel—'the tent', the covering of the Tabernacle.
Olam ha-Ba—'the age to come', the next world.
Olam ha-Zeh—'the present age'.
Oleh (pl. Olim)—'One who goes up', an immigrant who makes aliyah.
Olim Hadashim—New immigrants to Israel.
Omer—Hebrew measure of capacity. Also name of first sheaf of barley offered on 2nd day of Passover (Leviticus 23:10).
Orthodox Judaism—strictly traditional sector of Jewish religion.

Pale (The)—area in Russia to which Jews restricted from 1772.
Palmach—'the striking force' of the Haganah 1941-1948.
Parasha—'portion', the weekly reading from the Torah.
Parve—food containing neither meat nor milk.

Payot (or Peot or Pyot)—side curls as worn by some Haredim (Leviticus 19:27).

Peace Now—a movement for peaceful co-existence between Jews and Arabs.

Pentateuch—(Greek) The Five Books of Moses.

Pentecost—Feast of Weeks, 50 days after Passover, celebrating the wheat harvest. Later, traditional date of giving of Torah.

Perushim—'separatists', Hebrew word for Pharisees.

Pessach—'Passover', celebrating release from Egyptian bondage.

Phylactery—see Tephillin.

P.L.O.—(Arab) Palestine Liberation Organisation.

Pogrom—(Russian) 'violent', used of attacks on Jews.

Proselyte—'one who has come to', a convert to Judaism.

Purim—'lots', the Feast of Esther (Hadassah) celebrating defeat of Haman's plot, Adar 14,15 (Esther 9:24).

'Q' see K

Rabbanites—a Rabbinic sect of Jews who opposed the Karaites.

Rabbi—'master' derived from *rabah* = 'great'. A Jewish teacher, ordained after study at a Yeshiva. Not a priest.

Ramadan—(Arabic) Moslem month of fasting from sunrise to sunset.

Rambam—name used for Maimonides, the Jewish sage.

Ramban—name used for Nahmonides, 12th century Spanish Jew.

Rashi—Rabbi Solomon ben Israel, noted French Jewish commentator, A.D. 1040-1105.

Rav—(Chaldean) 'great', title of Abba Arikha of Babylon.

Reb, Rebbe—(Yiddish) rabbi, scholar, pious man.

Reform Judaism—modified Judaism in line with modern ideas.

Refusnik—Russian Jew refused exit from Russia.

Rishon le-Zion—'First in Zion', one of earliest refugee colonies.

Rosh—'head', 'chief'.

Rosh Chodesh—the first day of each month, the new moon.

Rosh Hashanah—'head of the years', first day of the Jewish civil New Year and Feast of Trumpets. Tishri 1.

Rosh Hashana le Ilanot—'New Year of the Trees'. Shebat 15.

Sabbatai Zevi—a famous false messiah of 17th century Europe.

Saboraim (or Savoraim)—'expositors', scholars of the Babylonian Jewish academies in 6th and 7th centuries A.D.

Sabra—Jew born in Israel. Name of a cactus fruit that is prickly outside but soft within, said to be typical of an Israeli.

Sanhedrin—Supreme Council of Jewish nation until A.D. 425.

Schlemiel—(Yiddish) an unlucky or uncomplaining person.

Schmaltz—(Yiddish) chicken or goose fat; overdone humour.

Schmittah (see Shemittah).

Scroll—roll of parchment from the skin of a clean animal.
Seder—'order', ceremony of the first two nights of the Passover.
Sefer Torah—'the scroll of the law' for public reading.
Sephardi (pl. Sephardim)—'Spanish', Jews of the Spanish and Arabic tradition.
Sepharim—'scrolls', 'books', Hebrew Biblical literature.
Shabbat—'Sabbath', the 7th day of the week (Exodus 20:8). From dusk on Friday to darkness on Saturday.
Shalom—'peace', traditional greeting and well-wishing.
Shammash—'servant', centre lamp of a Menorah from which other lamps lit; also caretaker or beadle of a synagogue.
Shannas—'willow', one of the four species used at Sukkot.
Shavuot—the Feast of Weeks, Pentecost, fifty days after Passover.
Shebat (or Shevat)—11th month of Bible year (Jan./Feb.).
Shechina (or Shekhina)—'Holiness', The Divine presence, God's omnipresence.
Shephelah (or Shefela)—foothills of Judea.
Shekel (or Sheqel)—Unit of weight and money.
Shekalim—the Sabbath of the Shekels, sabbath before Adar 1.
Shema—the Jewish creed confessing the Unity of God.
Shemittah—Sabbatical Year, seventh year when land had to be fallow and debts were remitted (Leviticus 25:1-22).
Shemura Matza—especially pure Passover bread.
Sheol—grave, underworld.
Shia (pl. Shi'ites)—extreme Moslem sect, mainly in Iran.
Shin Bet—The General Security Service of Israel.
Sho'ah—the Holocaust, when six million Jews died.
Shofar (or Shophar)—ritual ram's horn sounded on special occasions.
Shomer—'watchman', supervisor of Kasher food.
Shtetl—(Yiddish) small Jewish village in E. Europe.
Shul—'school', or synagogue.
Shulchan Arukh—'prepared table', a 15th century code of Jewish law and practice by Joseph Caro, still in use.
Shushan Purim—Adar 15, day after Purim (Esther 9:13).
Siddur—a prayer book.
Simchat Torah—'rejoicing of the Torah', last day of Feast of Sukkot.
Sivan (or Siwan)—3rd month of Bible year (Esther 8:9) (May/Jun.).
Sopher (or Sofer, pl. Sopherim)—a scribe, a literate man.
Stern Group—a dissident resistance group prior to 1948.
Succa (or Sukkah)—a booth, as used at Sukkot (Feast of Tabernacles.
Sukkot—Feast of Booths, or Tabernacles.

Sunni—moderate Moslem sect, mainly among Arabs.
Synagogue—'a place of meeting'. Hebrew 'Bet ha-Knesset' (House of Assembly).

Tallit—a prayer shawl with tassels at each corner.
Tallit Katan—small tallit worn at all times by strict Jews.
Talmud—'teaching', comprising the Mishna and Gemara.
Tammuz—4th month of the Bible year (Ezekiel 8:14) (Jun./Jul.).
Tanakh—acronym for 'Torah, Nevi'im, Kethuvim', the three sections of the Hebrew Holy Scriptures.
Tanna (pl. Tannaim)—'expounder', sages who prepared the Mishna.
Targum—'translation', Aramaic transliteration of Holy Scriptures.
Tashlikh—'Thou shalt cast', a religious ceremony at Rosh Hashanah casting sins into the sea, or a river (Micah 7:19).
Tebet (or Tevet)—'winter', 10th month of Bible year (Esther 2:16) (Dec./Jan.).
Tel (or Tell)—'mound', heap of ruins of an ancient city.
Tephilla (Tefilla)—'prayer'.
Tephillin—'Phylacteries', small leather boxes containing tiny scroll worn on arm and forehead while at prayer, the 'frontlets' of Deuteronomy 6:8. Scroll quotes Deuteronomy 6:4-9; 11:13-20; Exodus 13:1-16.
Terephah (or Treifa)—'forbidden', food that is not kasher.
Tetragrammaton—'four letters' (Greek), the Holy Name YHWH.
Tevila—ritual bathing in a Mikveh, also baptism in general.
Tikvah Israel—'The Hope of Israel'.
Tisha be-Ab—The fast of Ab 9 in memory of destruction of Temple by Babylonians and Romans.
Tishri—7th month of·Bible year (Sept./Oct.).
Torah—'the teaching', the Law, five books of Moses.
Tu bi-shebat—'Festival of Trees' held Shebat 15, also called 'New Year of Trees'.
Tzahal—acronym for Tseva Hagana le-Israel (I.D.F.).
Tzedukim—'Sadducees', political religious party of higher priestly families before A.D. 70.
Tzitzit (or Tsitsit)—'fringes' as on old garments and on Tallit prayer shawls (Numbers 15:38).

Ulpan—school for intensive study, especially of Hebrew language.
Unahidin—'unitarian', the name the Druze give themselves.

Vatikim (or Watiqim)—'established members', veterans.
Ve-Adar (or Adar 2)—extra month inserted between Adar and Nisan on leap years to adjust calendar to solar time.
Vort—(Yiddish) engagement to marry (German 'Wort' = word).

Wakf—Moslem 'Religious Endowments Foundation' guarding the Moslem shrines in Israel.

Yad—'hand', pointer used by readers of a scroll.
Yad le-Achim—'hand to the brothers', ultra-orthodox movement to counter Christian missionary activities.
Yad Vashem—The Holocaust Memorial in Jerusalem.
Yahrzeit (Jahrzeit)—(Yiddish) Commemoration of the dead by fasting and lighting a candle (Proverbs 20:27).
Yarmulka—(Yiddish) the Kippa or skull-cap (see Kippa).
Yehudim Meshichim—Messianic Jews who believe in Jesus.
Yerida—'going down', deserting Israel, opposite of aliya.
Yerushalayim—official spelling of Jerusalem in English.
Yerushalmin—Old Yishuv, resident in city since early 19th century.
Yeshiva (pl. Yeshivot)—Academy of higher rabbinical studies. Israel has about 370 Yeshivot with 60,000 students.
Yeshua ha-Mashiach—'Jesus the Messiah'.
Yiddish—(from German Jüdisch) European Jewish polyglot language combining Hebrew, German and Slav words, written in Hebrew.
Yigdal—the 13 principles of the Jewish faith (in prayer book).
Yishuv—the Jewish community in pre-state Palestine. Old Yishuv pre-1880; New Yishuv 1880-1948.
Yisrael—Israel.
Yom—'day', sunset to sunset, also used figuratively.
Yom ha-Atzma'ut—Israel Independence Day, Iyyar 5.
Yom ha-Sho'ah—'Day of destruction', Holocaust Memorial, Nisan 27.
Yom Kippur—'Day of coverings', 'Day of Atonement', Tishri 10.
Yom Tov—'a good day', a day of festival.
Yordim—Jews who leave Israel.
Yoreh—'the shot', first rain of the rainy season in October.

Zedek (or Tsedek)—'righteousness'.
Zemirot—'songs', hymns and psalms sung at the Sabbath meal.
Z.F.—The Zionist Federation.
Zif (or Ziv, Ziw)—old name for month Iyyar.
Zion—'fortress', name of one of the hills of Jerusalem.
Zionism—Jewish secular movement to return to the Promised Land. Name coined by Nathan Birnbaum in 1890.

INDEX

305

ISRAEL